# Leadership and Management in China

MW01202140

With the rise of China in the global economy, it has never been more important for business leaders to understand Chinese leadership philosophies and practices. This is the first book to explain how ancient Chinese thinking and Western thought have shaped the development of leadership styles in China. Leadership theories associated with Confucianism, Daoism, Legalism, the *Art of War*, and the writings of Mao and Deng are analyzed by both Chinese and Western experts. To set this in a modern business context, the book includes interviews with top executives, who reflect on how their business values are affected by ancient Chinese philosophers, modern Chinese leaders, and Western management writers and thinkers. The book also includes research on paternalistic leadership as practiced by business leaders in Taiwan, Hong Kong, and mainland China.

*Leadership and Management in China* provides a significant step forward in understanding the complex and varied nature of leadership styles in modern Chinese business.

CHAO-CHUAN CHEN is Professor of Management and Global Business at Rutgers Business School, Rutgers, The State University of New Jersey.

YUEH-TING LEE is Professor of Psychology and Dean of the College of Arts and Sciences at the University of Toledo.

# Leadership and Management in China

Philosophies, Theories, and Practices

Edited by

CHAO-CHUAN CHEN AND YUEH-TING LEE

CAMBRIDGE
UNIVERSITY PRESS

CAMBRIDGE UNIVERSITY PRESS
Cambridge, New York, Melbourne, Madrid, Cape Town, Singapore, São Paulo, Delhi

Cambridge University Press
The Edinburgh Building, Cambridge CB2 8RU, UK

Published in the United States of America by Cambridge University Press, New York

www.cambridge.org
Information on this title: www.cambridge.org/9780521705431

First published 2008

Printed in the United Kingdom at the University Press, Cambridge

*A catalogue record for this publication is available from the British Library*

*Library of Congress Cataloging-in-Publication Data*

Leadership and management in China: philosophies, theories, and practices / edited by Chao-chuan Chen and Yueh-ting Lee.
    p.   cm.
Includes index.
    ISBN 978-0-521-87961-3 (hbk.) – ISBN 978-0-521-70543-1 (pbk.)
1. Management–China. 2. Leadership–China. I. Chen, Chao chuan. II. Lee, Yueh-ting III. Title.

    HD70.C5L43 2008
    658.4'0920951–dc22
                                                        2008000809

ISBN 978-0-521-87961-3 hardback
ISBN 978-0-521-70543-1 paperback

*To the memory of Jim Meindl: great teacher, collaborator, and friend*

*To our beloved wives: Wen-hua Ren and Fong Wei*

# Contents

| List of figures | page ix |
| List of tables | x |
| List of contributors | xi |
| Preface | xv |
| Acknowledgments | xvii |

Introduction: The diversity and dynamism of Chinese
philosophies on leadership                                         1
*Chao-chuan Chen and Yueh-ting Lee*

**Part I   The Confucian foundations**

1   The Confucian and Mencian philosophy of benevolent
    leadership                                                     31
    *Xin-hui Yang, Yan-qin Peng, and Yueh-ting Lee*

2   Bridging Confucianism and Legalism: Xunzi's philosophy
    of sage-kingship                                               51
    *Yan-qin Peng, Chao-chuan Chen, and Xin-hui Yang*

**Part II   Alternative traditional Chinese leadership
            philosophies**

3   Daoist leadership: theory and application                      83
    *Yueh-ting Lee, Ai-guo Han, Tammy K. Byron, and
    Hong-xia Fan*

4   Leadership theory of Legalism and its function in
    Confucian society                                              108
    *Kwang-kuo Hwang*

5   Strategic leadership of Sunzi in the *Art of war*              143
    *Hai-fa Sun, Chao-chuan Chen, and Shi-he Zhang*

**Part III   Modern Chinese leadership theories and practices**

6   Paternalistic leadership in Chinese organizations:
    research progress and future research directions                      171
    *Jiing-lih Farh, Jian Liang, Li-fang Chou, and*
    *Bor-shiuan Cheng*

7   The leadership theories and practices of Mao Zedong and
    Deng Xiaoping                                                         206
    *Xin-an Lu and Jie Lu*

8   Chinese traditions and Western theories: influences on
    business leaders in China                                            239
    *Zhi-xue Zhang, Chao-chuan Chen, Leigh Anne Liu, and*
    *Xue-feng Liu*

9   Linking Chinese leadership theory and practice to
    the world: leadership secrets of the Middle Kingdom                  272
    *George Bear Graen*

*Index*                                                                  298

# Figures

I.1 Chinese and Western philosophical influences on
    modern Chinese leadership                              *page* 16
1.1 Confucian model of benevolent leadership                    38
2.1 Xunzi's philosophy of human nature                          56
3.1 The Daoist model of wateristic personality
    (Daoist Big Five)                                           94
4.1 The Confucian ethical system of benevolence–
    righteousness–propriety for ordinary people               124
5.1 Sunzi's model of strategic situationalism                 158
6.1 Farh and Cheng's model of paternalistic leadership        175
6.2 A multilevel model of paternalistic leadership            198
8.1 A summary model of Chinese business leaders'
    management philosophies                                    260
9.1 A leadership network                                        290

# Tables

I.1  Major schools of philosophy in Ancient China          *page* 2
4.1  A comparison between five major aspects of
     Confucianism and Legalism                                  128
5.1  Thematic contents of the *Art of war*                      147
5.2  Frequency of keywords in the *Art of war*                  152
5.3  Examples of the humanist foundation of
     strategic leadership                                       154
6.1  Distributions of ideal leader choices and actual
     leaders across the eight types of paternalistic leader     188
6.2  Means of trust in supervisor and satisfaction with
     supervision across paternalistic leader types              190
6.3  Revised construct domain of paternalistic leadership
     dimensions                                                 194
8.1  Frequencies of management philosophical notions
     mentioned by the thirty-five interviewed business leaders  244
9.1  Chronology of competing social structures in China         277
9.2  Leadership in mainland China                               281
9.3  Ten limiting characteristics of a traditional SOE          283
9.4  Third-culture management issues in
     Sino-Western ventures                                      294

# Contributors

TAMMY K. BYRON
*PhD candidate and Lecturer in History*
*University of Arkansas*

CHAO-CHUAN CHEN
*Professor of Organization Management*
*Rutgers University*

BOR-SHIUAN CHENG
*Professor of Psychology*
*National Taiwan University*

LI-FANG CHOU
*Assistant Professor of Management*
*Yuan Ze University, Taiwan*

HONG-XIA FAN
*PhD candidate and Lecturer in Management*
*Chinese Academy of Sciences and University of Illinois*

JIING-LIH FARH
*Professor of Management*
*The Hong Kong University of Science and Technology*

GEORGE BEAR GRAEN
*Emeritus Professor of Organizational Psychology,*
*University of Illinois at Urbana-Champaign*

AI-GUO HAN
*Professor of Linguistics*
*Rowan University*

*List of contributors*

KWANG-KUO HWANG
*Professor of Psychology*
*National Taiwan University*

YUEH-TING LEE
*Professor of Psychology*
*University of Toledo*

JIAN LIANG
*Assistant Professor of Management*
*The Hong Kong University of Science and Technology*

LEIGH ANNE LIU
*Assistant Professor of International Business*
*Georgia State University*

XUE-FENG LIU
*Assistant Professor of Organization Management*
*Shanghai University of Finance and Economics*

JIE LU
*Professor of Public Administration*
*China Academy of Management Science*

XIN-AN LU
*Associate Professor of Human Communication Studies*
*Shippensburg University*

YAN-QIN PENG
*Professor of Psychology*
*Suzhou University*

HAI-FA SUN
*Professor of Management*
*Sun Yat-Sen University*

XIN-HUI YANG
*Professor of Psychology*
*Nanjing Normal University*

SHI-HE ZHANG
*Professor of Administration*
*Chong Qin College of Administration*

ZHI-XUE ZHANG
*Associate Professor of Organization Management*
*Peking University*

# Preface

This is the first book to our knowledge that introduces, explains, and theorizes on Chinese leadership philosophies and practices. The contributors include well-established mainland and overseas Chinese leadership and management scholars such as Larry Farh from the Hong Kong University of Science and Technology and Kwang-kuo Hwang from the National Taiwan University. The Chinese authors were joined by Western scholars including George Graen, renowned for his Leader–Member Exchange Theory and his cross-cultural leadership research and consulting.

At a time when China is becoming more central in a globalizing world economy, business managers as well as scholars from outside China increasingly feel the importance of understanding the thoughts and views of Chinese leadership and management. As one of the oldest civilizations in the world, and with the largest population, China has produced internationally known statesmen, philosophers, thinkers, and leaders; yet, among the vast volume of literature on leadership within and outside China, we see so little on Chinese leadership, and by Chinese scholars. This book represents a significant step toward filling a serious gap in the teaching, research, and practice of leadership and management.

The book has three parts. It begins with Confucian philosophical foundations of leadership theory and practice in Ancient China (Part I). Part II presents alternative ancient philosophical approaches to leadership, such as Daoism, Legalism, and the *Art of war.* Part III consists of modern and contemporary Chinese leadership theories and practices such as paternalistic leadership, Mao's revolutionary theory and practice, and Deng's theory and practice of economic reform. An interview study led by Zhi-xue Zhang, specially designed for this book, is featured in Chapter 8, and it reports how top business executives in mainland China draw philosophical insights on leadership and management from both Chinese and Western sources. In the final chapter

George Graen comments on the significance of Chinese leadership theories for the wider world.

The contributors were drawn to this project by a common mission to present to the world something that researchers, students, consultants, and practitioners can turn to for a better understanding of Chinese leadership perspectives. This book, we believe, has a lot to offer to those who do business with the Chinese in China, Asia, or anywhere in the world, to those who are or aspire to be multinational business leaders, and to those scholars who are seeking leadership universals or peculiarities.

# Acknowledgments

The idea of a book on Chinese leadership philosophies came about six years ago in 2002 when Jim Meindl and I met at the Academy of Management Meetings (chatting with Jim was always one of the highlights at the Academy and I miss it so much now that he is gone). We continued to talk about this idea on the phone and finally decided to do it in 2003. I started to make contacts with scholars from Chinese universities, who, we believed, would bring more indigenous perspectives to the topics. After many phone conversations and email exchanges I planned to go to SUNY at Buffalo in early July 2004 to meet with Jim and talk about the book and other research interests. He had invited me several times to go back to visit my *alma mater* and I was looking forward to it. Little did I know that my trip would be to attend his funeral. Jim died unexpectedly of a heart attack. I was so shocked and saddened that I could not bear the thought of doing the book as it would be such a painful reminder of his tragic departure. The book project was shelved for a year as I was grieving for the loss of a great teacher, collaborator, and a close friend.

Time did not heal (contrary to what people usually say of personal tragic losses) because it still hurts every time I realize Jim is gone. But time did channel my sadness, regret, and helplessness into motivation to complete the unfinished work, about which Jim was passionate. I felt I owed it to him and to readers of Chinese leadership and management to carry out the book project. In the year 2006, recovered and reenergized, I picked up everything and started in earnest to work on it. During this time, Yueh-ting Lee, a friend and one of the contributors to the book, came to my aid as a coeditor. His knowledge of classic Chinese literature was reassuring to me. George Graen, a scholar of Japanese and Chinese cultures, graciously agreed to write a chapter connecting the Chinese theories to the international world, and to do that he read each and every chapter of the book and provided timely and valuable feedback. To them I am deeply grateful.

Thanks are also due to Larry Farh, Kwang-kuo Hwang, and Zhi-xue Zhang for contributing their chapters and for their thoughtful comments on an earlier draft of the Introduction. Beside them, I wish to thank other contributors such as Jie Lu, Xin-an Lu, Yan-qin Peng, Hai-fa Sun, Xin-hui Yang, and Shi-he Zhang for their understanding, patience, and cooperativeness when the book was delayed.

I am grateful to Mary Child, a good friend and a true professional, from whom I received so much general advice about book editorship. I truly appreciate the help of Shan Haarsager, Yueh-ting Lee's administrative assistant, who gave me quick turnarounds when proofreading parts of the typescript at short notice. Thanks are also due to Caroline Murray and Paula Parish at Cambridge University Press and to Chris Doubleday, the copy-editor, for their professional assistance.

As is quite typical of my research, this book is a collaborative family effort. My wife, Wen-hua Ren, shared her time helping me search and obtain relevant literature, let me bounce thoughts and ideas off her, and shared my joy and worry. My niece, Amy Hui Wang, volunteered her precious vacation time to help me put the individual chapters into a single file for submission. I fully utilized my son, Ken Chen's, superb skill in drawing figures. All the help from colleagues, friends, and family made my first experience of book-editing so much less daunting and more fun. To all of them I extend my deepest appreciation and gratitude.

Chao-chuan Chen

# Introduction: The diversity and dynamism of Chinese philosophies on leadership

CHAO-CHUAN CHEN AND YUEH-TING LEE

O VER 8000 years ago, the fundamental religious belief in China was a form of shamanism (Lee and Wang, 2007; Xu, 1991; Yuan, 1988). Shamanism is the spiritual belief or practice of a shaman who can connect the inner world with the outer world, the body with the soul, and the living with the dead. As time went on, Confucianism and Daoism developed out of shamanism as two of the fundamental Chinese belief systems and these have affected Chinese behavior and thinking almost on a daily basis for thousands of years (see Hsu, 1981). When the formerly subordinate states of the Zhou dynasty (841–256 BCE) began to break away to create competing states, chaotic political and social changes ravaged China. Accompanying these social and political changes were many schools of thoughts, including Confucianism (Chapters 1 and 2), Daoism (Chapter 3), Legalism (Chapter 4), and the school of military arts philosophy (Chapter 5), known in history as the "100 Schools of Thought" (see Table I.1). Each school (*jia*) was headed by its own master or masters (*zi*), and had academics and disciples to study, teach, and propagate their respective philosophical and ideological perspectives and views. These masters contested to offer advice, primarily to rulers, on expanding powers and restoring peace and order to society. It was common for rulers or leaders to receive scholars or advisors from different schools and hear their debates on ways of governing. The ancient leadership philosophies featured in this book come from the major philosophical schools of thought during the historical period.

Despite this, when Western scholars think of Chinese leadership or Chinese culture in general there is often a serious lack of appreciation of the diversity and dynamism in Chinese philosophies and ideologies: Confucianism is for many the shorthand for Chinese culture. In this book, Chinese cultural diversity and dynamism and, by extension, the diversity and dynamism of Chinese leadership thinking, strike us most

1

Table I.1. *Major schools of philosophy in Ancient China.*

| Schools | Pioneers or representatives | Basic focus/meaning | Examples |
|---|---|---|---|
| Daoism (*Dao Jia*) | Laozi, Zhuangzi, Lie zi and the hermits | Naturalistic, or the way it is | *Dao* (the Way), *de* (morality), *zi ran* (nature), *shui* (water), *wei wu-wei* (active non-action) |
| Confucianism (*Ru Jia*) | Confucius (Kongzi), Mencius (Menzi), and the literati | Social order or hierarchy | *ren* (humanity), *yi* (righteousness), *li* (ritual), *zhi* (knowledge), *xin* (trust), and *xiao* (filial piety) |
| School of *Yin–Yang* (*Yin–Yang Jia*) | Fu Xi, King Wen and the practitioners of occult arts and astronomy | *Yin–yang* opposites | The Book of Change as well as the five elements (i.e., metal, wood, water, fire, and soil) |
| School of Name (*Ming Jia*) | Hui Shi, Kong Sun Long and the debaters | Relativity and universals | "A white horse is not a horse" |
| Legalism (*Fa Jia*) | Hanfei and the men of methods | Man-made laws and rules | Clear-cut rewards and punishments |
| Mohism (*Mo Jia*) | Mozi and the knights | A close-knit organization and discipline; no war | All-embracing love and technology to prevent war |
| School of the Art of War (*Bing Jia*) | Sunzi, Sun Bing, and the war strategists | War is necessary for peace | The best way to win a war is to defeat enemies without actual fighting or killing |

*Sources*: Based on the work of Fung (1948: 30–37) and Lee (2000: 1066).

forcefully and convincingly. From the beginning, there was not just one Chinese thought or just one Chinese philosophy. The first part of this book features three major philosophies as related to statesmanship and leadership: Confucianism, Daoism, and Legalism. While each school of philosophy is analyzed in its own chapter, we will here discuss their differences and similarities on some fundamental issues concerning human nature and social systems, and will also discuss Sunzi's *Art of war* as it relates to these three philosophies (see also Chapter 5). We then discuss how modern Chinese leadership theories and practices have been affected by traditional Chinese and Western thoughts on leadership and management. These modern Chinese leadership theories and practices include the revolutionary theory of Mao and the economic reform theory of Deng (Chapter 7), paternalistic leadership (Chapter 6), and philosophical thoughts by current business executives on organization, leadership, and management (Chapter 8), and conclude with a commentary (Chapter 9) by a Western student of modern Chinese leadership. Clearly, the twenty-first-century leadership in China is not well understood by the outside world. Such lack of understanding contributes to the tensions between leaders and managers inside and outside of the Middle Kingdom. That such a situation has existed for the last century and more is expected given the recent depression of China's economy and struggles with foes both inside and outside of China. At the dawn of the twenty-first century this ignorance of leadership in China is unforgivable. This book is an attempt by Chinese scholars to begin the process of examining Chinese philosophies and theories of leadership from indigenous perspectives. Due diligence requires a deeper understanding of the new, the emerging, and the traditional lessons of leadership.

## Traditional philosophical perspectives on leadership

### Human goodness vs. badness and the rule of virtue vs. law

Confucius and Mencius, the two founding fathers of Confucianism, believed in human goodness; that is, humans are born with natural kindheartedness. As evidence, Mencius pointed to human beings' natural, instinctive compassion shown to others suffering, their shame over evil deeds, and their ability to know right from wrong. Human beings therefore have a natural inclination to think and act in ways that follow the moral and social norms and benefit society. Bad behaviors like disregard of others, disobedience, and violence are unnatural distortions of human goodness caused by social conditions and by lack of moral education.

Based on the human goodness assumption, Confucius and Mencius advocated that the ideal kingship and government are benevolence toward the common people and stressed that leaders should rely on education to reinforce, extend, and further develop human goodness. The assumption of human goodness was contested and even despised by other schools of thought such as the Legalists, who pointed to human selfish desires and feelings and criminal acts of theft, robbery, and murder as evidence of human badness. On the basis of human badness, the Legalists contended that morality is hypocritical and useless and advocated relying on the iron fist to maintain social order.

This strong challenge to human goodness might therefore undermine the viability of the tenets of Confucian philosophy of benevolence and the rule of virtue. Xunzi, a Confucianist who nevertheless bridged Confucianism and Legalism, proposed a coherent philosophy that decoupled human goodness from benevolent government. While upholding the general philosophy of benevolent sagehood, Xunzi argued vehemently against Mencius' thesis of human goodness and proposed an explicit antithesis of human badness. Xunzi pointed to human hedonistic desires and emotions, such as wanting food when hungry and warmth when cold, as natural instincts. Because desires are many and resources are few, natural instincts, if left uninhibited, are bound to lead to aggression and violence, and hence to social disorder and disintegration. Xunzi conceded that humans, despite their basic hedonistic motives, are equipped with the capacity for consideration, which allows them to develop goodness, conceived as the acquired human nature. Human goodness therefore is learned, developed, and cultivated through concerted efforts at the individual and institutional levels. By acknowledging or even insisting on the badness of human nature, Xunzi elevated even more the necessity for education, morality, and ritual and conduct propriety, upholding the rule of virtue and morality as advocated by Confucius and Mencius. Furthermore, Xunzi emphasized the supplementary function of rules, regulations, and even punishment.

Paradoxically, Xunzi's theory of human badness serves to legitimize human self-interest as an important factor in leadership. According to Xunzi's theory of human badness, peasants and sage-kings are all born alike with basic egoistic and hedonistic desires and interests. What distinguishes the sage and the noble from the common or the petty is first and foremost the degree of goodness, namely, learned virtues that result from self-cultivation. Xunzi never claimed that acquired good nature could and should eliminate or replace the basic born nature. In places, his philosophy smacked of an instrumental view of morality, in suggesting that the cultivated person has not only a more benevolent but also a more effective way of satisfying basic needs.

Xunzi's arguments of human badness, his recognition of self-interest, and his emphasis on rule-based propriety serve as a bridge between Confucianism and Legalism, the major proponent of which is Hanfei, Xunzi's student. Hanfei, a standard-bearer of the Legalist school of thought, preferred strict and effective enforcement of laws over the exhortation of Confucian moral values. His Legalist philosophy of leadership and government was based on the assumption of human self-interest, especially its competitive and subversive side. Unlike classic Confucianists, who based a philosophy of benevolence on moral virtues and ritual propriety, Hanfei had no confidence in morality and did not care for rituals. Instead he believed in power, laws, and manipulation as major means of government and leadership. The Legalist philosophy shared the vision of creating stable, peaceful, and prosperous states, though by a different means, namely, the rule of law under the sovereignty of the emperor. Hanfei believed in the separation of public and private self-interest and proposed fair and effective ways of exercising power and laws. For example, laws and regulations must be objective and universally enforced so as to be fair and laws should be practical, enforceable, and well publicized so as to be effective.

Where does Daoism stand regarding human goodness and badness? It was not a central concept in Daoism but we may infer a Daoist position on this issue from writings by Laozi and Zhuangzi on the relationship between humans and the natural universe. The Daoists assumed a unified and coherent universe and believed that nature is guided by immanent patterns and forces, known as the *Dao* (the Way), rather than by any omnipotent external creator. Human beings are constituent members of the natural universe, not its masters or members with privileges. The natural way of the universe, the *Dao*, should also be the way of human existence and human relations.

On one hand, this position seems to suggest that human nature is beyond moral judgment because being natural is the way it should be. Being one with nature is the ideal state of human existence. In this sense, true human nature is good. However, Daoists also viewed human self-interested desires as major blocks standing in the way of humans being in harmony not only with nature but also with other humans. Only sages who have the capacity to understand and know the Way can rise above selfish desires and possessions to achieve peace and harmony with nature. Sages, of course, are not born: one becomes a sage through learning. Paradoxically then, following the natural way requires being unnatural in the sense of being enlightened. It seems that in the Daoist value system, while the supreme state of affairs is the original natural state, which is free of desire and self-interest, human beings are actually not natural enough, and the way to become natural is to emulate the way of nature.

## Individualism, relationalism, and collectivism

Chinese culture has been characterized as collectivistic by social psychological and organizational research (Hofstede, 1980; Markus and Kitiyama, 1991; Triandis, 1995). Furthermore, Chinese culture has been shown to emphasize the importance of social affinity and obligation to personalized collectivities over either individuals' self-interest or the collective interest of large and impersonal collectivities (Brewer and Chen, 2007; King, 1991). However, such characterizations, while useful for contrasting Chinese with non-Chinese, and Eastern with Western cultures, obscure important ideological and philosophical diversity within Chinese culture. We contend that while the culture may be dominated by a certain ideological perspective at a certain historical stage, for a certain domain of life, and in a certain situation, the Chinese are no strangers to alternative divergent ideologies including those taking the individualist, the relationalist, and the collectivist perspectives. The *individualist* perspective views people as primarily independent individuals rather than members of communities, places priority on individual rights and interests, and promotes social exchanges with other individuals and communities for the fulfillment and satisfaction of individuals' rights and interests. The *relationalist* perspective views people as social and relational beings, that is, as members of social communities rather than independent individuals, places priority on duties and obligations to other individuals and communities to which an individual is affiliated, and engages in maintaining and enhancing the common welfare of the community. The *collectivist* perspective views people as either individuals or as members of communities or both, but it places priority on the interest and welfare of superordinate communities over either individual or subordinate communities and engages in activities that promote the common welfare of superordinate communities (Brewer and Chen, 2007).

The classic Confucianism is probably the most typical form of relationalism (Hwang, 2000; King, 1985). Although Mencius and Xunzi differed in their assumptions concerning human goodness and badness, there was no difference between them in their emphasis on the importance of cultivating virtuous human characters that maintain and extend affinity and love for fellow human beings. Furthermore, Confucianists believed that virtue started at home with members each fulfilling their role responsibility and held the familial model as a template for the community and the state. Confucius, however, also believed that the supreme goal of government was to build a universal world of peace and harmony and the mechanism for developing this universal community of all human beings was to build upon and extend family-based relationalism to larger and more superordinate communities. In theory, Confucianists seemed to advocate collectivism rather than relationalism. However, Confucian philosophy saw more commonality and complementarity between small communities and their more encompassing communities. And because of the Confucian position on the moral supremacy of family and friendship, especially for the common people (he held higher standards for scholars and officials), the collectivist perspective recedes to a secondary (if not subordinate) position relative to the relational one (Hwang, 1987; King, 1991). This can be seen in the oft-cited story in which Confucius would advise violating law rather than reporting the wrongdoings of one's parents. In reality, therefore, Confucianism clearly puts relationalism first, collectivism second, and individualism last. However, even in Confucianism there exist individualist beliefs such as the importance of introspection (*nei xing*), the non-subjugatability of the individual will, and the importance of self-development and self-enhancement (Munro, 1985).

The Legalist perspective contrasts sharply with Confucianism (see also Chapter 4). As discussed above, Hanfei argued that individuals, including rulers, were driven by self-interested motives. However, he did not believe self-interested motives were bad or evil as did his Confucianist teacher, Xunzi. The belief about human self-interested motives by itself may not mean that Legalists believed in the legitimacy of individual rights, but in rejecting Confucian morality it certainly did not put priority on individuals' social and moral obligations. More enlightening is that Legalists proposed the separation of public and private interests, which in effect affirms the legality and morality of individual self-interest. Hanfei also proposed objectivity and universality of laws to ensure effectiveness and fairness and to use objective and rational principles to select talents, evaluate performance, and administer the state. Finally, Hanfei believed that rule by law was more effective in running the state and more instrumental in promoting the stability and prosperity of society. Hanfei's Legalism seems to be most consistent with individualism in its recognition of the legitimacy of self-interests and motives, but in the end it is much more amenable to collectivism than to relationalism.

The Daoist position as proposed by Laozi and Zhuangzi is more complex. On one hand, Daoism proposed the most holistic perspective on human existence in that human beings are an intrinsic part of the universe. The way of nature is the supreme way of the universe, hence of the society and of the individual. The ultimate purpose of human existence is to be one with the Way, with all things, in harmony and union. Individuals should therefore embrace and adapt to their environment just like water to the various contours of the land. In this sense, the Daoist philosophy is collectivist with regard to the large community of the universe; it is neither relationist nor individualist because Daoism questioned attachment or obligations to one's self or self-interest as well as to social institutions such as the family or the state. On the other hand, of all Chinese traditional philosophies, Daoism, by Laozi and Zhuangzi, stands out as the champion of the individual and individualism (Berling, 1985). First, in the submerging of self to the *Dao* of nature, a person becomes truly his or her natural self; individuality, indeed sagehood, is achieved through wholeness. Second, Laozi and Zhuangzi valued individual solitude above all else (Whitman, 1985). Withdrawal from the public was not viewed as aberrant or abnormal but rather a legitimate and wise means of survival and a lofty means of turning away from the conventional world for union with the *Dao*. Lastly, Laozi and Zhuangzi advocated tolerance and non-interference by the government as a means of achieving peace and stability. Daoism, while viewing total submergence of self with the *Dao* as the ultimate objective, also contained individualist seeds of the self, the right of individuality, and freedom from social control. In summarizing the above discussion of the *Dao* and the relationship between the individual, social institutions, and the universe, it is reasonable to see Daoism as putting individualism before relationalism and holding collectivism in its most general and broad sense, that of the universe.

## Social hierarchy and social equality

The extensive hierarchy in Chinese society in general and the leader–member relationship in particular have been unquestioned. In fact, they have been taken for granted in almost all philosophies and theories featured in this book except for Mao's theory of communist and socialist revolution. In Chapter 2 on Xunzi, the concept of social distinction (*fen*), which reflects the Confucian view of social systems, is discussed in more detail. Here it suffices to say that hierarchy in the Confucian leadership philosophy bears a symbiotic relationship to authority, unity, order and stability, morality, and productivity as opposed to rebellion, anarchy, disorder, moral deterioration, and economic poverty. Xunzi argued that society or community formation was what distinguished humans from animals and hierarchy was natural in human society because of the inherent individual differences in human biology, skills, and needs and because of limitations on resources. He also defended the need for hierarchical distinctions on social, moral, and economic grounds. Lastly, Xunzi held that social distinctions were fair and functional if they were based on superiority of moral character, ability, and performance and the basic human needs were met for all members of the society. Overall, Confucianism legitimized and advocated a clear social hierarchy more forcefully and coherently than hierarchy in economic and material possessions. Indeed, reducing the economic and material benefits of the elite might be one way of gaining legitimacy for its social distinctiveness. Furthermore, in granting social distinctions, Confucianists gave more weight to moral character than to ability or task performance.

Daoism was not built on the premise of social distinctions, neither did it envision a society of hierarchical order or encourage individual motives and behaviors to seek social or material distinctions. Nevertheless, Daoism did not promote social equality either, at least not in any sense of socio-political activism. First, there was a hierarchy in the Daoist ontology of the universe: the *Dao* of One gives rise to the dual of *yin* and *yang*, which in turn give rise to the trio of heaven, earth, and humanity, which in turn give rise to all other things. Second, one major theme of Daoist being was to be able to move up and down in the hierarchy of social status, just like water following the contour of the terrain. Note that the hierarchy was not to be abolished or reduced but to be followed and adapted to, and those who were best at practicing active non-action (*wu wei*) deserved to be leaders. So, while the Confucian primary criterion of granting social distinction was benevolent morality, the Daoist one was active non-action. Nevertheless, the Daoist views of non-action and of focusing on "being" rather than achieving provided a non-assertive, if not skeptical, counter-perspective to social hierarchy, and their views of human existence tended to have a flattening effect on the social hierarchy.

Hanfei's Legalism did not challenge the social hierarchy beliefs of Confucianism although the individualist assumption of individual self-interests could provide a philosophical foundation to do it. Instead, Legalists designed different means of maintaining social hierarchy and order, namely through laws and regulations and through power manipulation and control, not unlike those of Machiavellianism. Accordingly, instead of Confucian morality, the primary basis of social hierarchy was one's abilities, possibly more political rather than task-oriented, that contributed to performance. Sunzi, in the *Art of war*, took for granted hierarchy, obedience to orders, and the unity of the chain of command as the given structure of the army, which sounds reasonable considering the military nature of the organization and the context of warfare. It was the qualifications insisted on by Sunzi for the hierarchy that were quite unusual for his times and even for today. Sunzi insisted that once out in the field the general should have autonomy to conduct warfare based on the *Dao* of war and the sovereign should not interfere. In the field, the general is obligated to abide by the *Dao* of war (*zhang dao*) rather than by the order of the king (*jun ming*). Additionally, Sunzi seemed to hold different criteria for judging the legitimacy of social hierarchy, that is, morality for the supreme leader but ability, especially wisdom, for high-ranking but non-supreme leaders.

While all of the traditional philosophies by and large accepted hierarchy of power and status there was also a consensus that hierarchy and distinction should be based on some kind of merit, be it morality, ability, or actual performance, and merit was achieved by individuals rather than ascribed to them through inheritance, such as birth, class, or other social categories (Parsons and Shils, 1951). In general, modern Chinese leadership philosophies and theories to be discussed later (Chapters 6–8) are less hierarchical than the traditional ones. The paternalistic leadership theory (Chapter 6), even though it was originally based on authoritarianism, is currently undergoing revision in order to address negative responses to overemphasis on hierarchy. The theories of Mao and Deng (Chapter 7) emerged during periods when Chinese intellectuals, writers, and reformists were most critical of the long history of Chinese authoritarianism and when they were exposed to Western philosophies of social, political, and economic modernism (Lee, 1985). Although Maoist theory and practice after the founding of the People's Republic of China have been labeled by Western scholars as neo-traditionalism (e.g. Walder, 1986), it represents the most explicit and radical departure from traditional Chinese social hierarchy toward social equality.

## *Individual, dyadic, institutional, and active non-action leadership*

Western leadership research in organization and management has been categorized into trait, behavioral, transactional, and transformational approaches (Yukl, 1998). Another way to differentiate leadership approaches is based on the locus or the unit where leadership is enacted. The individual level of leadership refers to how leaders conduct themselves and serve as the model of character and behavior for their followers. Dyadic leadership is concerned with how leaders relate to and interact with their subordinates. Institutional leadership refers to leading by creating organizational systems. While these levels of leadership are correlated with each other, different leadership philosophies may emphasize different levels. The distinction between action and non-action leadership contrasts the Daoist approach with other approaches.

The Confucianist approach to leadership seems to focus first and foremost on the individual leader. Self-cultivation (its level of comprehensiveness and perfection) is not only the qualifying attribute of a leader but also the primary means of exercising leadership in that the leader person is the source of inspiration and the model for the followers. In addition, leadership involves the cultivation of character in the followers and such efforts unfold largely in the highly personalized role relationship between superiors and subordinates. Dyadic and hierarchical relationship-building and the fulfillment of role requirements are therefore a primary mechanism of leadership. In this sense Confucianist thoughts on leadership focus on the individual and the dyadic level. This does not mean Confucius and Mencius neglected institutional-level leadership. Indeed, character cultivation was believed to be most effective in a virtuous culture of benevolence and ritual propriety and Confucianists stressed the importance of building moral and educational institutions. Nevertheless, the individual and the dyadic are still the primary means of socialization and enculturation in the Confucian leadership philosophy.

Sunzi's strategic leadership philosophy could be viewed as an integration and synthesis of ideas from Confucianism, Legalism, and Daoism. Sunzi believed that for a war to be justified, not only must it serve a high purpose of benevolence, but it must be victoriously waged, humanely and benevolently, by minimizing the actual and potential destruction of the enemy. In running military organizations, Sunzi incorporated more Legalist institutional measures of reward and punishment rather than the Confucian moralistic measures. He proposed such systematic measures of organization and management that one wonders if Henri Fayol, one of modern management's founding fathers, was inspired by Sunzi when he described the classic managerial functions of planning, organizing, coordinating, commanding, and controlling. Of course, the strategic and psychological manipulations and tactics of Sunzi also recall Hanfei's concepts of power (*shi*) and tactics (*shu*). Sunzi also incorporated the Daoist philosophy of non-action by stressing the importance of understanding larger political, social, and geographical forces outside the control of the commanders, of not forcing unprepared battles, and of not acting upon desires and emotions including even lofty ones such as honor, bravery, and heroism.

In contrast to the Confucianist approach, the Legalist approach was primarily at the institutional level. According to Legalism, effective leadership lay in setting up a clear power structure and in devising and enforcing objective, consistent, and enforceable rules and regulations.

Hanfei did not rule out the importance of individual or dyadic levels of leadership, as he proposed sophisticated manipulation tactics in enhancing one's power bases and dealing with dyadic relations. These individual- and dyadic-level tactics serve to supplement and enhance the effectiveness of legal institutions.

Although both Confucianists and Legalists upheld active leadership, while differing in their focus, Daoists advocated non-action at the individual, dyadic, and institutional levels. At the individual level, leaders served as models of non-action, which meant viewing themselves as an integral part of the universe, accepting larger forces at work, following the natural course of things, and cooperating with the natural rhythms of life. At the interpersonal level, it meant loving fellow human beings, and being cooperative and altruistic in dealing with others. At the institutional level, non-action meant non-interference, allowing self-rule and autonomy of the subunits and individual members of the organization. Of the three levels of non-action, Daoism focused on the individual level of the leader as much as Confucianism did on self-cultivation; but instead of viewing the sage-ruler as the model of virtue, Daoism viewed the sage-ruler as the model of non-action.

## Modern Chinese leadership theories and practices

### Paternalism, socialism, and capitalism

The last few chapters of this book present major theories of leadership and management that are very much alive in the thoughts and actions of contemporary Chinese managers. Paternalistic leadership (Chapter 6) is a theoretical model originating from research on owners of overseas Chinese family businesses and has also been found to be part of the leadership behavior of Chinese managers in mainland China. Much of paternalism is rooted primarily in Confucianism in terms of the emphasis on respect for hierarchy, benevolence, and the rule of morality. Paternalism is a good illustration at the behavioral level of how the familial model of the father–son relationship is extended to superior–subordinate relationships in the modern workplace.

While the paternalistic philosophy is an exemplar of classic Confucianism, the socialist ideology as represented by Mao and Deng appears to be anti-Confucian. First, a proclaimed mission of the Chinese revolution led by the Communist Party was to eliminate inequality, namely, the gap between the workers and the peasants, the city and the countryside, and mental and manual labor. In addition, Mao's comment that "women hold half of the sky" became the rally call for women's equal status with men. Gender equality became a prominent goal during the Cultural Revolution, which witnessed nationwide "affirmative action" that required representation of women in Revolutionary Committees at all levels of administration. Second, following the Marxist-Leninist doctrine of the proletarian dictatorship, the traditional Confucian hierarchical pyramid was inverted so that the ruling class of the rich and the intellectuals was pushed to the bottom of the social strata while the former ruled class of the poor and the manual laborers was lauded as the master of a socialist society. The status of the working class reached its peak during the Cultural Revolution, when representatives of workers and peasants sat on Revolutionary Committees of government, educational, and industrial organizations. Third, Mao's class-based and ideological philosophy of leadership and organization was in direct conflict with the Confucian philosophy of familial and relational loyalty and commitment. It was no coincidence that Mao waged an ideological campaign during the Cultural Revolution to denounce Confucianists (ancient or modern-day) as the staunch champions of the old order.

Despite the above obvious conflicts, there are some common elements between Confucianism and socialism. First and foremost, Mao and the Confucianists shared the Confucian rule-of-virtue approach to government, the assumption of the goodness of the common people, and the belief in the efficacy of moral education and enculturation. Second, we see an interesting parallel between Xunzi's stance toward classic Confucianism proposed by Confucius and Mencius and Deng's stance toward orthodox socialism as proposed by Mao. While Deng endorsed the fundamental tenets of Mao's ideology just as Xunzi endorsed these of Confucianism, both were more pragmatic and realistic about the nature of human beings, and about the balance between self-interest and public duty, moral education and material rewards, and ideological integrity and economic development. In so doing, Xunzi led the transition from Confucianism to Legalism and Deng led the transition from orthodox socialism to market-oriented socialism.

While some Confucian beliefs and values are compatible with the socialist doctrine, others are consistent with capitalist beliefs and values. Weber conceptualized modern capitalism in terms of the belief in, and the pursuit of, economic rationality (Poggi, 1983), which includes casting away superstitions, the production of goods for the market, the pursuit of material wealth, and the commitment to efficiency and productivity. Weber contended that Protestant religion contributed to the success of capitalism in the West and he identified Protestant ethics as consisting of diligence, asceticism, and a non-wasteful use of time. The question is: do Chinese traditional philosophies, especially the dominant one of Confucianism, contain the seeds of modern capitalism or is modern capitalism unique to the West? We find plenty of evidence of modern capitalism in the earliest traditional schools of thoughts in China. To start with, even though known for their emphasis on elaborate rituals and ceremonies worshiping the heaven, the earth, and the ancestors, Confucianists, especially Xunzi, explicitly restricted them to symbolic, socio-cultural, and expressive functions and rejected superstitious beliefs that these rituals would bring material benefits. Second, part of the Confucian philosophy of benevolence is the provision of livelihood to the common people. Materialism, while discouraged for the intelligentsia, was not just allowed but encouraged for the common people. Third, organizational efficiency in terms of division of labor, coordination, and accomplishment of results are systematically dealt with by Xunzi regarding the administration of government and by Sunzi regarding the administration of military organizations. Lastly, following Weber's definition of capitalism, Redding (1993) identified the "Chinese spirit of capitalism" as consisting of three sets of Chinese core values: (1) familism, (2) work ethics, and (3) money, frugality, and pragmatism. It seems reasonable to assert that Chinese traditional culture contains both socialist and capitalist values.

## Western influences on modern Chinese leadership theories and practices

The above discussion of the influence of traditional Chinese philosophies does not mean that all of the Chinese contemporary leadership theories and practices are totally home-grown or that Western philosophies and practices have little impact on Chinese business leaders. Chapter 8, which directly addresses the sources of influence through interviews with thirty-five Chinese CEOs, shows that current Chinese business leaders draw inspirations and guidance not only from traditional Chinese philosophies and Chinese role models but also from Western

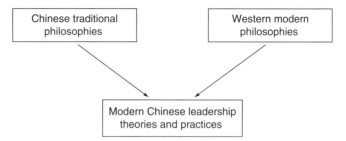

**Figure I.1.** Chinese and Western philosophical influences on modern Chinese leadership.

management philosophies and Western business role models. With increasing business globalization, the advancement of information and communication technologies, and the international expansion of Western business education, more and more Chinese business leaders have access to Western academic as well as practitioner-oriented writings and direct personal interactions with Western management academics and business leaders. There is evidence that Western business practices and their underlying leadership and management philosophies have been affecting the thinking and action of Chinese business executives. It should also be pointed out that Western philosophies that were introduced to China through translations in the late nineteenth and early twentieth centuries had a serious influence on modern Chinese thinkers (Elvin, 1985; Lee, 1985; Munro, 1985) and on revolutionaries, including some of the intellectual pioneers of the Chinese Communist Party; Mao and Deng's writings on socialist revolution and construction are no exception. Most modern Chinese revolutionary thinkers appealed to Western concepts of liberty, freedom, and equality to advocate social, political, and cultural reform in China although much of the Western individualist orientation of these concepts was ultimately coopted into a utopia of socialistic and communistic equality of all individuals, groups, and nations (Elvin, 1985). Modern Chinese leadership theories and practices, be they paternalism, socialism, or capitalism, seem to be eclectically constructed with threads from various traditional Chinese and modern Western philosophies. Such Chinese–Western stranding is evident in the catchy, politically correct guiding principle of "socialism with Chinese characteristics" or, more appropriately, "capitalism with Chinese characteristics." Figure I.1 depicts sources of influence from Chinese and Western philosophies.

## Theoretical and practical implications

We characterize the current Chinese culture in general and Chinese business leadership and management in particular as the coexistence of multiple philosophies, perspectives, and approaches, some of which are very different or even conflicting while others are similar and complementary. In the following we summarize some general themes that the Chinese leadership philosophies and perspectives can bring to the world. We then stress the utility of eclectic and holistic approaches to leadership challenges in China.

### *Some common themes of Chinese leadership philosophies*

**Chinese humanism**

The first theme of Chinese philosophies is Chinese "humanism" or "humaneness," namely, benevolence. Western humanism or the human relations' philosophy of management puts greater emphasis on the autonomy, agency, and rights of the individual employees. Chinese humanist philosophy stresses kindheartedness in one's relationship with other fellow-beings in the social and natural world. In leadership, its straightforward application is being sensitive and attentive to the basic needs of the followers. More importantly, it means a commitment to building and maintaining a humane organization in which members' livelihood is provided and their social-psychological well-being is taken care of. Clearly there is a paternalistic tone to Chinese humanism. Such paternalism could very well be both an impetus and an impedance to the accomplishment of other organizational objectives such as efficiency and profit. In general, to the extent an organization or a leader is believed to be humane, that is, putting priority on serving the long-term interest of the employees, there is greater legitimacy of authority and greater employee commitment and loyalty to the organization. In contrast, benevolence or humaneness does not seem to be a central concept in the vocabulary of American business leadership even though it was found to be a universally endorsed leadership attribute (House *et al.*, 2004). It does not seem to mesh very well with the Western leadership concepts of vision, charisma, strategy, intelligence, or effectiveness. Western business leaders have no problem professing to serve the best interest of the shareholders through tough leadership with their workforces; they could even be great philanthropists to external communities and causes, but charity is not expected to start internally with business employees. In any case, benevolence to employees does not seem to be as morally compelling in Western as it is in Chinese thoughts of leadership. In fact, paternalism has a more pejorative than positive connotation in corporate America.

### Culture-building

The second remarkable point is the importance of culture-building in the incipient Confucianism some two thousand years ago, especially in Xunzi's view of culture-building as part of the fundamental task of community-building. Culture is what makes an organization or a community rather than a mere tool created for accomplishing organizational business objectives (Tsui *et al.*, 2006). Culture is therefore the essential part of community identity. Furthermore, Xunzi placed culture-building squarely on the shoulders of organization leaders. Indeed, it is not only a major part of the job responsibility but also the moral duty of the leader to create a community culture for the organization. While culture can be conceived in abstract guiding principles and virtues, Xunzi elaborated proper behavioral norms and social and symbolic rituals in shaping and maintaining organizational culture. The Chinese therefore seem to have a rich tradition of ritualistic and symbolic culture to induce organizational identity, and organizations are expected to be cultured in ways that go beyond achieving task efficiency and productivity.

### Moral character of the leader

The third theme, which is related to the first, is the great importance of the moral character of the leader, which runs across all of the leadership theories discussed in this book except for Legalism. The high tolerance for leader authority and leader discretion in relation to subordinates and to the established rules and regulations is matched and balanced by the high moral standards expected of leaders. Confucianism held explicit "double" moral standards: higher for leaders than followers, and higher for high- than for low-position leaders. Western transformational leadership theories emphasize the leader's ability to transform followers' self-interest to the collective interest of the organization, but the Chinese leadership philosophies put self-transformation of the leader as the prerequisite and the foundation of the followers' and the organizational transformation. The concept of moral integrity is multifaceted but focuses primarily on selfless motives and intentions and on priority for social and relational obligations over concerns for material benefits. Autocratic leadership therefore goes hand in hand with the leader's moral integrity in China. Democratizing Confucian leadership, however, does not relax the moral standard expected of the leader. Leaders who practice participative management may be more effective if they continue to uphold a higher standard of propriety for themselves than for their subordinates.

### Dialecticism and holism
Besides humaneness, dialecticism or the *yin–yang* way of thinking is probably the other most commonly shared perspective among all the Chinese philosophies and theories. *Yin* and *yang* stand for paired opposites of any sort: heaven and earth, good and bad, leader and follower, up and down, with the opposites being both independent elements yet interdependent with each other in the larger unit, which itself is a subunit of an even larger unit. The holistic way of cognition attends to and assigns causality to the complete field, especially to the background and the contextual factors rather than to the object or the actor (e.g. Morris and Peng, 1994; Nisbett *et al.*, 2001; Peng and Nisbett, 1999). While the holistic and dialectic beliefs of the Chinese can be attributed to the complex social relations and systems of Confucian societies (Nisbett *et al.*, 2001), they were also direct testaments to the influence of Daoism (see Chapter 3). Daoist *yin–yang* thinking has left its marks on Chinese philosophies, martial arts, medicine, science, literature, politics, and daily life (e.g. Black, 1992; Lee, 2003; Lee and Hu, 1993; Peng and Nisbett, 1999). Dialectic and holistic reasoning can be said to have influenced all of the schools of thought featured in this book, especially Sunzi's strategic leadership and Mao's theory of contradiction.

Although there is a striking contrast between the holistic views of the Chinese and the analytic views of the West, the Daoist *yin–yang* reasoning is similar to the Hegelian expression that everything involves its own negation, as in the Hegelian dialectic of thesis–antithesis–synthesis (Fung, 1948). Nevertheless, relative to the Western logic of reasoning, the Daoist *yin–yang* reasoning prefers an ideal state of the middle and the harmonious coexistence of opposites. When the development of anything brings it to one extreme, a process of reversal to the other extreme takes place (i.e. *wu ji bi fan*). Accepting opposites but taking no extreme stands, staying in the middle or moving toward the mean, is therefore the mainstay of *yin–yang* dialecticism. The Confucian doctrine of the mean and the value of harmony, as reflected in the interview study of Chinese executives (Chapter 8), are consistent with this dialectic way of thinking. Having said that, the more dynamic view of dialecticism also posits that opposing forces are in constant change and their relative positions may evolve or even reverse when leaders seize or create the right conditions. Such dynamic views of contradiction and change may underlie much of Sunzi's theory of strategy in war (Chapter 5) and Mao's military success with the revolutionary army, as well as his disastrous class struggle campaigns after the founding of the People's Republic of China.

### Control mechanisms

The fifth theme that runs through the various leadership philosophies concerns mechanisms of control for achieving cooperation. A great variety of control mechanisms have been proposed, including personal trust through dyadic relationship-building, impersonal bureaucratic controls of rules and regulations, cultural controls of rituals and values, and legal controls of punishment, etc. While all of these mechanisms are familiar and practiced to various degrees, Chinese business leadership seems to be more adept at informal relational and cultural controls than at formal bureaucratic system-wide controls despite a long history of dynastic bureaucracy. Rule by law or through rules and regulations in China tends to be more prohibitive and punitive than promotive and supportive. However, the proliferation of Western style MBA education and the practices of multinational companies in China seem to be popularizing and improving formal and market-oriented control systems in Chinese business organizations.

### Leadership agency

A final theme that has important theoretical and practical implications is concerned with the leader being the agent of action and change. Research in social psychology and cross-cultural psychology (e.g. Markus and Kitayama, 1991; Morris and Peng, 1994; Nisbett and Peng, 2001) suggests that the Chinese conception of the individual self is oriented more toward interdependence than independence, that Chinese cognition is more holistic than analytic in that it is more oriented toward the situation and the field than toward the person and the actor, and that the locus of action lies in the group rather than in the individual. All these might suggest a rather passive or constrained model of Chinese leadership. However, analyses of Chinese leadership philosophies have found more complexity regarding this issue. First, there are diverse conceptions of individual selves and human nature in Chinese philosophies. That the Chinese emphasize the extension or even the merging of the self with fellow human beings, to communities, and to nature does not mean that they do not have an independent and complete sense of self. Indeed, all three types of self-conception, the individualist, relational, and collectivist selves (Brewer and Chen, 2007), exist in Chinese individuals. Second, the holistic world outlook of the Chinese does not necessarily lead to a reduced sense of individual agency especially from the point of view of the leader. Sunzi's strategic leadership demonstrates a very realistic and holistic approach to war and meticulous and systematic attention to geographical, meteorological, and socio-political fields of a particular battle or war, yet that does not prevent him from placing a very strong agency in the general and his commanders relative to the soldiers or the contingent situations. Xunzi holds it to be the duty and responsibility of the leader to cultivate community through creating and developing culture. Indeed, Lee (1985) entertained the possibility of a romantic and heroic Chinese leader that emerged out of the collective and holistic self with the vision of an ideal world, a conviction that the self is on the side of history, and a determination to personally translate that vision into reality. Lastly, even the philosophy of non-action does not prevent individual proactiveness. One variant of active non-action is no big action (*wu da wei*) but proactive small actions, which requires holistic insights or foresights into the hidden, underlying forces of the situation and taking small actions that make subsequent drastic actions unnecessary. In summary, research is needed to explore further the complexity of the Chinese people's conceptions of self and of leadership agency, and their cognition of self–situation relationships.

## *Eclectic and holistic perspectives of Chinese leadership*

While Confucianism has been dominant in history for a long time, Chinese managers have also been exposed to, and are familiar with, ancient and modern schools of thought including Legalism,

Daoism, socialism, and some Western management theories. Such diversity of thoughts and perspectives, while a source of conflict, is also tremendous intellectual capital for Chinese leaders, who only a few decades ago were thrust into a new and changing world that was drastically different from that to which they were accustomed. This world is more global, diverse, uncertain, and competitive, which exposes both China's strengths and its vulnerabilities. To effectively lead and manage in this new environment, the divergent Chinese philosophies of leadership provide both challenges and opportunities for organization and management scholars and practitioners. The major challenge is how, in the midst of diversity, change, and global competition, to create a relatively coherent and unifying philosophical vision for the organization and for the majority of its members (Tsui *et al.*, 2006). Leaders of business organizations operating in China, for example, face the growing divergence of beliefs and values between the more traditional workforce of the rural areas, the inland regions, and the older generation and the more modern workforce of the metropolitan areas, the coastal regions, and the younger generation; the culture of money, wealth, and materialism versus that of relationship, tradition, and spirituality; the need for efficiency and productivity through discipline and control versus the need for innovation and flexibility; the paternalistic and socialist model of treating employees as family and community versus treating them as resources and commodities exchangeable on the market; the growing legitimacy of pursuing corporate profit versus corporate social responsibility to the employees, the government, and the natural environment; sensitivity and responsiveness to the domestic and global economic and market forces versus the social and political constraints associated with the one-party state system of China. To be sure, conflicting forces exist in all societies and organizations, but their magnitude and velocity may be greater because of the Chinese economy's size and speed of development.

These challenges call for the multiple and divergent perspectives and approaches that are revealed in this book. To take advantage of the rich and diverse set of Chinese leadership philosophies, researchers and practitioners of leadership must develop sufficient familiarity and understanding of the different philosophies and take eclectic and holistic approaches to their application. Without attempting to build specific leadership models we propose a general approach of eclecticism and holism to the study and practice of leadership in China.

An eclectic approach recognizes the legitimacy and validity of competing perspectives. It does not stick to one perspective all the time and on all issues; rather it draws on elements from multiple perspectives to tackle complex issues at hand. It is particularly useful when there is a need to legitimize and promote reform and change because eclecticism is more pragmatic but remains principled to the followers, as it justifies change by appealing eclectically to existing philosophies that resonate with followers. The diversity of Chinese philosophies provides plenty of room for the eclectic approach. For instance, there is a variety of leadership styles in Chinese firms (Tsui *et al.*, 2004). Although relationalism and leader–member relationships continue to be important in Chinese leadership and management (Hui and Graen, 1997; Wang *et al.*, 2005), counter elements such as the importance of the rule of law, procedural justice, and merit and equity-based rewards have also been appealed to by reformist leaders and accepted by organizational members (e.g. Chen, Chen, and Xin, 2004; He, Chen, and Zhang, 2004). The same can be said about respect for hierarchy and participative leadership. Although unequal relationship and respect for hierarchy is a persistent Confucian tradition, concepts of equality, democracy, and participation from Daoism, Maoism, and imported Western management practices are quite salient and there is evidence that delegation and power-sharing have positive effects on the attitudes and behaviors of Chinese subordinates (Chen and Aryee, 2007; Zhang, Chen, and Wang, 2007).

Further examples of eclecticism can be found in the political leadership of the Chinese Communist Party. Mao appealed to Legalism and Marxism against Confucianism and capitalism for his ideological and cultural revolution; Deng appealed to the Chinese traditional values of collectivism, familism, and modern scientific management to instill accountability, competition, and economic development (Chen, Meindl, and Hunt, 1997); and now Hu, the current leader of the Communist party, has drawn from Confucian and Daoist traditions and proposed his theory of social harmony to address problems of growing inequality and conflict in China. It would not be surprising if Daoist philosophy of nature were used to address the emerging issues of the environment.

A holistic leadership approach tackles challenges and issues from multiple perspectives, recognizing their differential effectiveness but stressing their complementarity or balance. The ultimate ideal state is the balance rather than dominance or substitution of opposing forces although at any particular moment there may be temporary and shifting dominance. There is abundant rhetoric on a balance of opposing perspectives from Chinese leaders. Examples include building both material and spiritual civilization, following the logic of both reason and affect, competition and cooperation, and delegation and control. One striking characteristic of the interviews of Chinese executives reported in Chapter 8 is that they draw inspirations from multiple philosophical sources of East and West, from traditionalism and modernism. These seem to suggest that the Chinese leaders are more likely than their Western counterparts to adopt multiple, even conflicting, perspectives in the analysis of an issue, and to see more overlapping and complementary characteristics. In the case of incompatibility, Chinese leaders may be more inclined to compromise than to resolve it.

A variant of the holistic approach is the contingency approach, namely, choosing to apply a particular perspective from a variety of perspectives only to a particular situation. For example, a leader may use Confucianism as guidance in dealing with family relationships, modern management principles in dealing with work relationships, and Daoism in challenges of personal life. For example, the Chinese are more inclined to seek inspiration from Daoism when facing enormous uncontrollable adversity in work or in life. The active non-action perspective encourages the individual to accept calamity with peace of mind on one hand and to have hope and optimism on the other hand, because in Daoism ups and downs, fortune and adversity, are relative and transitory rather than fixed and permanent. The contingency approach gives the Chinese leader the freedom to deal with organizational complexities with flexibility rather than being overly concerned with consistency. For example, contingency-minded Chinese organizations may develop management systems which are responsive to factors such as regional cultural differences, business ownership types, and workforce characteristics.

In summary, philosophical diversity regarding leadership and management in Chinese culture provides rich ideological and intellectual resources for studying and practicing leadership in China. Eclectic and holistic approaches open up topic areas of research on China and cross-cultural comparative research and more effectively tap into a diverse set of resources to deal with complex and dynamic issues at a time of tremendous change.

*References*

Berling, J. 1985. "Self and whole in Chuang Tzu," in Munro (ed.), pp. 101–120.

Black, D. 1992. *Essentials of Chinese herbs*. Springville, UT: Tapestry Press.

Brewer, M. B., and Chen, Y. 2007. "Where (and who) are collectives in collectivism: toward conceptual clarification of individualism and collectivism," *Psychological Review* 114: 133–151.

Chen, C. C., Chen, Y. R., and Xin, K. 2004. "Guanxi practices and trust in management: a procedural justice perspective," *Organization Science* 15(2): 200–209.

Chen, C. C., Meindl, J. R., and Hunt, R. G. 1997. "Testing the effects of horizontal and vertical collectivism: a study of rewards allocation preferences in China," *Journal of Cross-Cultural Psychology* 28(1): 44–70.

Chen, Z. X., and Aryee, S. 2007. "Delegation and employee work outcomes: an examination of the cultural context of the mediating processes in China," *Academy of Management Journal* 50(1): 226–238.

Elvin, M. 1985. "Between the earth and heaven: conceptions of the self in China," in M. Carrithers, S. Collins, and S. Lukes (eds.), *The category of the person*, Cambridge: Cambridge University Press, pp. 156–189.

Fung, Y.-L. 1948. *A short history of Chinese philosophy*. New York: Free Press.

He, W., Chen, C. C., and Zhang, L. H. 2004. "Rewards allocation preferences of Chinese employees in the new millennium: effects of ownership reform, collectivism, and goal priority," *Organization Science* 15(2): 221–231.

Hofstede, G. 1980. *Culture's consequences*. Beverly Hills, CA: Sage.

House, R. J., Hanges, P. J., Mavidan, M., Dorfman, P., and Gupta, V. 2004 (eds.). *Culture, leadership, and organizations: the GLOBE study of leadership in 62 nations*. Thousand Oaks, CA: Sage.

Hsu, P. S. S. 1981. *Chinese discovery of America*. Hong Kong: Southeast Asian Research Institute.

Hui, C. and Graen, G. 1997. "Guanxi and professional leadership in contemporary Sino-American joint ventures in Mainland China," *Leadership Quarterly* 8(4): 451–466.

Hwang, K. K. 1987. "Face and favor: the Chinese power game," *American Journal of Sociology* 92(4): 945–974.

2000. "Chinese relationalism: theoretical construction and methodological considerations," *Journal for the Theory of Social Behavior* 30(2): 155–178.

King, A. Y. 1985. "The individual and group in Confucianism: a relational perspective," in Munro (ed.), pp. 57–70.

1991. "Kuan-hsi and network building: a sociological interpretation," *Daedalus* 120: 63–84.

Lee, L. O. 1985. "Romantic individualism in modern Chinese literature: some general explorations," in Munro (ed.), pp. 239–258.

Lee, Y.-T. 2000. "What is missing in Chinese–Western dialectical reasoning?," *American Psychologist* 55: 1065–1067.

    2003. "Daoistic humanism in ancient China: broadening personality and counseling theories in the 21st century," *Journal of Humanistic Psychology* 43(1): 64–85.

Lee, Y.-T., and Hu, P.-C. 1993. "The effect of Chinese Qi-gong exercises and therapy on diseases and health," *Journal of Indian Psychology* 11: 9–18.

Lee, Y-T., and Wang, D. 2003. "Aboriginal people in Taiwan, Continental China and the Americas: ethnic inquiry into common root and ancestral connection," in X. B. Li and Z. Pan (eds.), *Taiwan in the twenty-first century*, Lehman, MD: University Press of America.

Markus, H. R., and Kitayama, S. 1991. "Culture and self: implications for cognition, emotion and motivation," *Psychological Review* 98: 224–253.

Morris, M. W., and Peng, K. 1994. "Culture and cause: American and Chinese attributions for social and physical events," *Journal of Personality and Social Psychology* 67: 949–971.

Munro, D. 1985 (ed.). *Individualism and holism: studies in Confucian and Taoist values*. Ann Arbor: University of Michigan.

Nisbett, R., Peng, K., Choi, I., and Norenzayan, A. 2001. "Culture and systems of thought: holistic versus analytic cognition," *Psychological Review* 108: 291–310.

Parsons, T., and Shils, E. 1951. *Toward a general theory of social interaction*. Cambridge, MA: Harvard University Press.

Peng, K., and Nisbett, R. E. 1999. "Culture, dialectics, and reasoning about contradiction," *American Psychologist* 54: 741–754.

Poggi, C. 1983. *Calvinism and the capitalist spirit: Max Weber's Protestant ethic*. London: Macmillan.

Redding, S. G. 1993. *The spirit of Chinese capitalism*. New York: Walter de Gruyter.

Triandis, H. 1995. *Individualism and collectivism*. Boulder, CO: Westview.

Tsui, A. S., Wang, H., Xin, K. R., Zhang, L. H., and Fu, P. P. 2004. "Let a thousand flowers bloom: variation of leadership styles in Chinese firms," *Organization Dynamics* 33: 5–20.

Tsui, A. S., Zhang, Z. X., Wang, H., Xin, K., and Wu, J. B. 2006. "Unpacking the relationship between CEO leadership behavior and organizational culture," *Leadership Quarterly* 17: 113–137.

Walder, A. G. 1986. *Communist neo-traditionalism: work and authority in Chinese industry.* Berkeley: University of California Press.

Wang, H., Law, K., Hackett, R., Wang, D. X., and Chen, Z. X. 2005. "Leader–Member exchange as a mediator of the relationship between transformational leadership and followers' performance and organizational citizenship behavior," *Academy of Management Journal* 48(3): 420–432.

Whitman, C. 1985. "Privacy in Confucian and Taoist thought," in Munro (ed.), pp. 85–100.

Xu, X. Z. 1991. *The origin of the book Shan Hai Jing.* Wuhan: Wuhan Publishing House.

Yuan, K. 1988. *Chinese history of mythology.* Shanghai: Shanghai Literature Publishing House (in Chinese).

Yukl, G. 1998. *Leadership in organizations,* 4th edn. Englewood Cliffs, NJ: Prentice Hall.

Zhang, Y., Chen, C. C., and Wang, H. 2007. "Bounded empowerment: main and joint effects of supervisory power sharing and management control." Paper presented at the Academy of Management, Philadelphia.

# PART I

# The Confucian foundations

# 1 | *The Confucian and Mencian philosophy of benevolent leadership*

XIN-HUI YANG, YAN-QIN PENG, AND
YUEH-TING LEE

T HIS CHAPTER focuses on the major teachings of Confucius and Mencius as they relate to leadership. Confucianism has had a great influence on people not only in China and the rest of East and Southeast Asia, but also elsewhere in the world. Confucianism is broad and complex and has relevance to politics, philosophy, education, psychology, morality and ethics, but this chapter focuses on exploring Confucian ideas related to benevolent leadership. We first briefly introduce the biographical details and historical backgrounds of Confucius and Mencius. Next, we introduce the Confucian philosophy of benevolence, which includes the assumption of human goodness and the prescription of key Confucian virtues such as benevolence (*ren*), righteousness (*yi*), ritual propriety (*li*), wisdom (*zhi*), trustworthiness (*xin*), and filial piety (*xiao*). Third, we elaborate on a benevolent leadership model that includes self-cultivation and leading others. We conclude by discussing the significance of Confucian benevolent leadership for modern business organizations.

## Biographies and historical backgrounds

Confucius (551–479 BCE) is most widely known in China as Kongzi or Kongfuzi, with Kong being the family name, and *zi* or *fuzi* meaning master in Chinese. He is also known as Kong Qiu (Qiu is a given name) or Zhongni (a social name). We follow the latinized name of Confucius because it is well established in the literature outside China. Confucius was a native of the state of Lü (presently the city of Qufu in Shandong province, China) during the latter part of the Spring and Autumn Period (770–476 BCE). He was a great educator, thinker,

Thanks are extended to Chao-chuan Chen for his guidance and comments on earlier versions of this chapter.

philosopher, and political activist in ancient China, and the founder of
the Confucianist school. He lost his father at the age of three and grew
up under his mother's care. At thirty-two, he was engaged in teaching
the ancient rituals to the sons of a minister. At thirty-three, he went
to Lo Yang, the imperial capital, where he studied the customs and
traditions of the Zhou empire. According to Sima Qian (1994), the
most reputable official historian in ancient China, this empire was
dissected into numerous warring states of various sizes; its capital
remained solely a religious center. It was in Lo Yang that he met Laozi,
the founder of Daoism, and learned from him.

When Confucius was thirty-four, the prince of Lu, threatened by
powerful rivals among the local nobilities, was forced to flee to a
neighboring state. At the age of thirty-five, Confucius retired from
his official office. For the next fourteen years, he traveled from state to
state and presented his political ideas to different state rulers or kings.
Though he did not succeed in promoting his political philosophy to
the rulers, Confucius was esteemed as a great teacher and philosopher
of history. By the age of forty, he had set up an academy to popularize
Confucianism (Sima, 1994). The number of his students exceeded
3,000. In his career as a teacher, he advocated "education without
discrimination" and carried out school education among common
people, which used to be a privilege of the ruling class.

We can understand and appreciate the primary ideas of Confucianism
by reading the *Analects* (or *Confucian analects*), which his disciples
compiled. The book recorded what Confucius had said and done, and
it is the official literature for studies of Confucian thoughts, which
includes his ideas of leadership.

Another person who made a significant contribution to Confucianism
was Mencius. Mencius (372–289 BCE) was a disciple of Zi Si who
was also a great philosopher and a grandson of Confucius. In China,
Mencius was called "the Second Sage," or *Meng Zi*, with *zi* meaning
master. Like Confucius, Mencius was active in the politics of his times
and spent his life moving from one feudal court to another trying to
find rulers who would take his political advice. And, like Confucius, he
was largely unsuccessful in this endeavor. At last, he was invited to
meet with Prince Hui and was instrumental in promoting the welfare
of his people through his wise measures of reform. After the death of
the prince, Mencius retired to private life, and spent his last years
teaching his disciples, and preparing with them the book *Mencius*

(i.e. *The works of Mencius*). In both the *Confucian analects* and *The works of Mencius,* we find great ideas of governance and leadership.

During the Spring and Autumn (722–480 BCE) and the Warring States (480–221 BCE) periods of Chinese history, there were "a hundred schools of thought" competing for the attention of the kings and lords of the states. Different schools of thought, such as Confucianism, Mohism, Daoism, and Legalism all developed their own systems of theories of government. Although Confucianism was suppressed and abolished by the first emperor of Qin when he unified China (in 221 BCE), it became the dominant doctrine of government in the West Han dynasty (206 BCE), when it was proposed that all other schools of thought should be officially banned to uphold the supremacy of Confucianism. Since then the orthodoxy of Confucianism dominated Chinese ways of government and politics till the fall of the Qing dynasty (1911 CE).

Confucius and Mencius lived in periods of political and social turmoil that witnessed the degeneration of the feudal system from the central courts of the Zhou dynasties into the Warring States. There were debates in China as to whether Confucius and Mencius were political conservatives or reformists (Fung, 1948) because they advocated change and reform of the politics and government by means of restoring the rites, rituals, and music that were documented in the classics and attributed to sage-emperors of ancient times (Sima, 1994). Regardless of the differences in characterizing his political orientation, there is consensus that Confucius founded a philosophy of humaneness and benevolence by reinterpreting, reconstructing, and teaching the earlier Chinese classics.

## The Confucian philosophy of benevolence

A brief count of the frequency with which the Chinese character for benevolence (*ren*) appears in the *Analects* shows that it is the most important concept in Confucianism. The *Analects* contain 502 chapters of which 58 deal with *ren*, and the character *ren* appears 109 times. Forty-nine chapters deal with issues of *li* (rituals), which appears seventy-four times, and *yue* (music), which appears twenty-five times. In general, the Confucian philosophy focuses on human relationships instead of ontological and epistemological issues. The philosophical foundation of Confucian thoughts on leadership is in the central concept of benevolence, as it relates to human nature, human relationships, and human governance. This philosophy was expounded in part through employing homonyms and the ideographic features of the Chinese language. In Chinese, the pronunciation of human and benevolence (or humaneness) is the same, namely *ren*, and the word for benevolence is composed of two morphemes meaning two people. Literarily and philosophically, Confucius and Mencius believed that being human is being benevolent and that to be benevolent is to "be human" (*ren zhe ren ye*) and is to love humans (*ren zhe ai ren*).

## The original-goodness nature of human beings

The humane leadership philosophy is based on the assumption of the original goodness of human nature. Mencius said:

All humans have a mind which cannot bear to see the sufferings of others . . . When I say that all humans have a mind which cannot bear to see the sufferings of others, my meaning may be illustrated thus – even nowadays, if people suddenly see a child about to fall into a well, they will without exception experience a feeling of alarm and distress . . . The feeling of commiseration is the principle of benevolence. Such a commiserating mind of the ancient emperors guaranteed a commiserating government (Legge, 1970: 202).

Notice here, the goodness of human nature is defined in a human's natural feelings of empathy, compassion, and love for other human beings. Such benevolent feelings define and distinguish human beings from other beings. This human goodness lays the foundation for people to act altruistically as opposed to selfishly, according to social obligations and duties as opposed to individual instincts, morally as opposed to instrumentally to seek material benefits. Such inborn humane tendencies also lay the foundation for self-cultivation to become a superior person or even a sage. Lastly, and most importantly from a leadership perspective, such human goodness lays the foundation of benevolent leadership in terms of cultivating virtuous leadership characteristics, leading the followers, and forming a benevolent system of governance. Of course such a natural tendency does not automatically cause altruistic, responsible, and moral actions, which is why self-cultivation, moral education, and leadership are needed to sustain, extend, and institutionalize humaneness.

## Benevolence as the virtue of all virtues

As described above, the Chinese character for benevolence means "two interconnected people." According to Confucius, benevolence means loving others (see Legge, 1971: 167). In this narrower conception, benevolence represents one of the six major Confucian values and virtues, namely, benevolence (*ren*), morality or righteousness (*yi*), ritual propriety (*li*), wisdom (*zhi*), trustworthiness (*xin*), and filial piety (*xiao*). Righteousness refers to living and acting according to moral principles instead of pursuing self-interest and material gains. Ritual propriety refers to the observation of appropriate rituals and rules of conduct, which are social norms rather than formal laws and regulations. Confucius warned, "Look not at what is contrary to propriety; listen not to what is contrary to propriety; speak not what is contrary to propriety" (Legge, 1971: 250). Wisdom refers not only to learning, in the sense of understanding and appreciating the importance of benevolence, righteousness, and ritual propriety, but even more importantly to applying that abstract knowledge to real situations. Trustworthiness implies adherence and loyalty to moral principles, to ritual and social rules of propriety, and to one's superiors in hierarchical relationships. Finally, filial piety is a valuable virtue and concerns how to treat one's parents and ancestors. When asked by students about filial piety, Confucius replied that it means "not disobeying [one's] parents, serving and supporting them with loyalty and good-heartedness when they are alive and burying them with propriety when they are dead" (Legge, 1971: 147–148). Mencius gave specific examples of filial piety: "If, when their elders have any troublesome affairs, the young take the toil of them, and if, when the young have wine and food, they set them before their elders" (Legge, 1970: 148).

As one can see, these virtues are not mutually exclusive. Furthermore, benevolence is the most important of all virtues and is the source from which other virtues originate, or an overarching meta-value that unifies all virtues. For instance, the content of morality was largely defined in terms of being humane, the standards of ritual and rule propriety must be subject to the test of benevolence, and filial duty is an application of benevolence in relation to one's parents in particular and one's elders in general.

Despite the assumption of human goodness, Confucius considered it a supreme accomplishment to be truly benevolent. Benevolence is what distinguishes "the superior-minded" (*jun zi*) from the petty-minded people (*xiao ren*), the sage-rulers from poor and bad ones. Only individuals who are exemplary in all of these virtues are called *jun zi* (Ames and Rosemont, 1998) and only *jun zi* should be selected as leaders; and if all act like *jun zi*, that is, being righteous, following ritual propriety, exercising wisdom, being trustworthy, and being loyal to parents, there will be benevolence everywhere (Legge, 1971: 250; Yang, 1958).

## *The* Dao *of benevolent government* (ren zheng)

While benevolence was proposed as the fundamental defining characteristic of human goodness and as the guiding virtue of all virtues, more importantly it is the guiding principle of leadership, known as the *Dao* of benevolent government (*ren zheng*).

What does the *Dao* of benevolent government mean? First, it refers to human superiority over all other elements of the universe. The superiority of humans was argued on the basis of their intrinsic goodness through compassion and love for fellow-beings and their intelligence because they have the capacity to know and to be wise. Given this superiority, all activities, be they political, economic, or military, should be centered around human beings. Priority should be given to the interests of the people over material resources for the leaders. Confucius stated, "The government of King Wen and King Wu is displayed in the records. Let there be people and the government will flourish; but without people, their government decays and ceases" (Legge, 1971: 405). Mencius also remarked, "Opportunities of time vouchsafed by Heaven are not equal to advantages of situation afforded by the Earth, and advantages of situation afforded by the Earth are not equal to the union arising from the accord of Man" (Legge, 1970: 208).

Second, the *Dao* of benevolent government prescribes that the common people are the foundation (*min ben*) of governance and therefore take precedence over the government and the king. Mencius proposed that the common people are the most important, land and grain the next, and the sovereign the last. Therefore, benevolence toward the common people is the way to become sovereign and the way to maintain and extend sovereignty (Legge, 1970: 483–484). The distinction between benevolence and brutality is whether or not the rulers put the people's interests above their own interests and the *Dao* of benevolent government is a matter of surviving or perishing for the sovereign. In Chapter III of the first part of his essay on Li Lau (Li Liao), Mencius said,

It was by benevolence that the three dynasties [in ancient China] gained the throne, and by not being benevolent they lost it. It is by the same means that the decaying and flourishing and the preservation and perishing of States are determined. If the sovereign be not benevolent, he cannot preserve the throne from passing from him. If the Head of a State be not benevolent, he cannot preserve his rule. If a high noble or great officer be not benevolent, he cannot preserve his ancestry temple (Legge, 1970: 293–294).

Basing his historical account of the necessity of benevolent government on the vicissitudes of the dynasties of Xia, Shang, and Zhōu, Mencius asserted that because of their kindheartedness, the founders of these dynasties – Yu, Tang, Wen, and Wu – were able to have people's support. In contrast, the last emperors of the same dynasties – Jie and Zhòu – lost people's support as a result of their cruelty. So, if emperors are cruel, they are doomed to lose their territory; if dukes are cruel, they will fail to protect their states; if ministers and senior officials are cruel, they will fail to protect themselves. All in all, where there is no benevolent government there is no great peace or harmony throughout the land.

Lastly, the *Dao* of benevolent government refers to the rule of virtue. In Confucius' opinion, the rule of virtue is very important because "If the people be led by laws, and uniformity sought to be given them by punishments, they will try to avoid the punishment but have no sense of shame. If they be led by virtue, and uniformity sought to be given them by the rules of propriety, they will have the sense of shame, and moreover will become good" (Legge, 1971: 146). Ruling through punitive regulations will make people flee from you and lose their self-respect but ruling through virtue enables people to keep their self-respect and come to you of their own accord (Yang, 1958: 12). The rule of virtue through benevolence has two components: inward through self-cultivation of kindheartedness (*nei sheng*), and outward (*wai wang*) through extending virtues to others through role models and moral education and development, and establishing moral, social, and cultural norms and institutions. This is the essence of benevolent leadership, which we discuss further in the next section.

## Confucian theory of benevolent leadership

On the basis of the above discussion of the Confucian philosophy of benevolence we have constructed a model of benevolent leadership (Figure 1.1). This model starts with the foundational beliefs of human goodness and priority for people, which lead to benevolent leadership. Benevolent leadership has two interrelated components: cultivating oneself to be a sage (or superior) person and leading others as a sage-leader. These lead to the goal of building a harmonious and benevolent world.

### *Self-cultivation* (xiu ji) *and the sage person* (nei sheng)

Benevolent leadership starts from self-cultivation to acquire the virtues of a superior (or sage) person. According to Confucius, if you know how to cultivate your own character, you will know how to shape others and how to lead the family and the state. The cultivation of one's character is a prerequisite for leadership. Confucius and Mencius

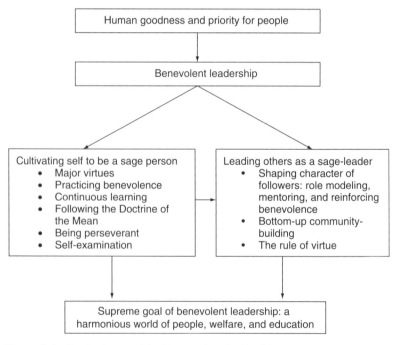

**Figure 1.1.** Confucian model of benevolent leadership.

prescribed a broad variety of virtues for individuals to aim at acquiring. Earlier we discussed six major virtues with benevolence as the core. In addition, the following virtues were prescribed as sub-virtues, or behaviors and processes that are instrumental to the cultivation of the major virtues, ultimately leading to a humane, sage person.

*Practicing benevolence and being an example.* As stated above, leaders must first and foremost lead in practicing the major virtues, the most important of which is benevolence. Confucius stated, "The most important component in governing is to love people" (Yang, 1958: 189). In general, benevolent rulers should take care of the people and extensively confer benefits on them. Specifically, benevolent rulers should know the living conditions of the people, be sympathetic to the poor, and take special care of the old and the young. Leaders take the lead in doing what they ask their people to do so as to set a good example. It should be noted that Confucius and Mencius insisted that leaders should strive to be examples in all virtues, in all spheres of life, and with regard to all relationships. That is to say leaders must be exemplary people in their hearts, minds, words, deeds, and manners, whether in their public or private lives.

*Learning by reading, listening, and seeing and being cautious and prudent.* Superior-minded people are learned people. Confucius promotes continuous learning as a major means of self-cultivation. He said, "There are three things of which the superior people stand in awe. They stand in awe of the ordinances of Heaven. They stand in awe of great people. They stand in awe of the words of sages" (Legge, 1971: 313). "Without recognizing the ordinances of Heaven," it is impossible to be a superior (exemplary) person. "Without an acquaintance with the rules of Propriety, it is impossible for the character to be established"; "without knowing the forces of words, it is impossible to know other people" (Legge, 1971: 354). In summary, one cannot be a leader without being always oriented toward learning and becoming learned.

With regard to the methods of learning, Confucius emphasized the importance of combining learning with independent thinking. Reading and learning without self-reflection, deliberation, or discussion could make one even more confused whereas thinking and self-reflection alone without learning can be dangerous as one can easily go astray without being enlightened by the accumulated wisdom and knowledge of the learned scholars. While book learning is the primary means of education, Confucius also encouraged listening and seeing.

"Listening a lot so as to select what is good to follow, seeing a lot so as to tell the right from wrong" (Legge, 1971: 151). Confucius held that leaders must not only have superior morality but also superior knowledge because only by being both moral and learned can a person be entrusted with leadership responsibilities. Confucius said, "not cultivating virtues, not deliberating on learning, knowing but not following righteousness, not correcting mistakes. These are the things that caused me concerns" (Yang, 1958: 72).

Superior persons should display a balance of concern and indifference, just like *yin* and *yang*. For example, seeing things clearly is fine, but seeing too much or too little is not optimal. Again, too much or too little respect for others is not optimal. This is consistent with the Doctrine of the Mean. There are nine things that they should take into serious consideration. Confucius said,

The superior man has nine things which are subjects with him of thoughtful consideration. In regard to the use of eyes, he is anxious to see clearly. In regard to the use of his ears, he is anxious to hear distinctly. In regard to his countenance, he is anxious that it should be benign. In regard to his demeanor, he is anxious that it should be respectful. In regard to his speech, he is anxious that it should be sincere. In regard to his doing of business, he is anxious that it should be reverently careful. In regard to what he doubts about, he is anxious to question others. When he is angry, he thinks of the difficulties (his anger may involve him in). When he sees gain to be got, he thinks of righteousness (Legge, 1971: 314).

*Following the Doctrine of the Mean and being fair and just.* In Confucianism, a state of balance and harmony has been considered a desirable state for all affairs, including interpersonal relationships. The Doctrine of the Mean dictates that "balance is the great root from which grow all of human actions, and harmony is the universal path that all should pursue. Let the states of equilibrium and harmony exist in perfection, and a happy order will prevail through heaven and earth, and all things will be nourished and flourish. No extremism should be practiced in one's manner of dealing with people" (Legge, 1970: 384–385).

Unity and harmony, of course, are founded upon principles of benevolence and righteousness, which was made clear by Confucius when he said that "the superior person is affable, but not adulatory; the small-minded is adulatory, but not affable" (Legge, 1971: 273). The superior person does not employ a person simply on account of words, nor put the person aside for the same reason. The superior person is dignified but does not wrangle, sociable but not partisan. From these sayings, Confucius emphasizes being objective and fair rather than selfish and showing favoritism.

*Being perseverant, ambitious, and optimistic.* Mencius emphasizes the importance of perseverance and optimism in the face of hardships and adversity. "When Heaven is about to confer a great office on any person, it first exercises his mind with suffering, and his sinews and bones with toil. It exposes his body to hunger, and subjects him to extreme poverty. It confounds his undertakings. By all these methods it stimulates his mind, hardens his nature, and supplies him with extraordinary competencies" (Legge, 1970: 447). What is more, leaders must have a heroic sprit, that is, they obtain the desire for office and practice principles for the good of the people. When that desire is unfulfilled they persist alone. And they are not to be corrupted by riches and honors, not to waver under poverty and humility, and not to yield under power and force.

*Self-examination and correcting mistakes.* Self-improvement cannot be made without self-examination and self-criticism. Confucius taught his disciples to self-examine in three aspects, as narrated by Confucius' disciple, Philosopher Zeng, in the Confucian *Analects*, "I daily examine myself on three points: whether, transacting business for others, I may have been not faithful; whether, in intercourse with friends, I may have been not sincere; whether I may have not mastered and practiced the instructions of my teacher" (Legge, 1971: 139). Daily examination of one's actions and behavior against moral standards and sage instructions reveals one's faults and mistakes. Confucius advised leaders to have a sense of shame and to be courageous to acknowledge and correct their mistakes. Knowing a fault but not correcting it is itself a fault and knowing and correcting a fault is a sign of a superior person. Zigong, one of Confucius' disciples, said, "The faults of the superior man are like the eclipses of the sun and moon. He has faults, and all men see them; he changes again, and all men look up to him" (Legge, 1971: 346).

## *Leading others* (an ren) *as the sage-leader* (wai wang)

*The supreme goals and tasks of benevolent leadership: population, welfare, and education.* According to Confucianism, there are three supreme goals for a benevolent government: the population should be large, rich, and well educated. As recorded in the *Analects*, "One day when Confucius went to the State of Wei, his disciple, Ran You, acted as driver of his carriage. The Master observed: 'How numerous are the people!' Ran responded: 'Since they are thus numerous, what more shall be done for them?' 'Enrich them,' was the reply. 'And when they have been enriched, what more shall be done?' The Master said, 'teach them, and promote education to enhance people's cultural quality'" (Yang, 1958: 144). With the accomplishment of all of the three objectives, there will be a harmonious society.

In this formula of "population–welfare–education," Confucius again based his philosophy of leadership on priority for the people and on their economic and cultural enrichment. A large population is both the objective and the measure of humane government as it signals stability and prosperity. Benevolence first and foremost means making sure a large population is well fed and well clad. Only when this is ensured can they be taught and cultured. In the benevolence philosophy, population is the prerequisite, economy, the foundation, and education, the vital line. The three interrelate and interact with each other: material abundance provides a foundation for mass education; enhancement of people's cultural quality may in turn help to promote the development of the state's economy. The Confucian *Dao* of governance therefore ultimately depends on education. Education does not stand narrowly in the form of teaching and learning but rather is part of the rule of virtue. For instance, Confucius insisted on government based on understanding. "The people may be made to follow the path of action (the Way). No, they may not be. Let them understand it" (Yang, 1958: 216–217). If people understand, then let them follow. If people have puzzles, then explain. Full understanding leads to better implementation.

Mencius prescribed similar government objectives when he said that "The precious things of a prince are three: the territory, the people, the government and its business. If one values as most precious pearls and stones, calamity is sure to befall him" (Legge, 1970: 492). To Mencius the territory is the land on which the livelihood of the people depend and the government's primary business is education because "Good government does not lay hold of the people so much as good instruction. Good government is feared by the people, while good instructions are loved by them. Good government gets the people's wealth, while good instructions get their hearts" (Legge, 1970: 455–456).

*Shaping the character of followers.* When Zilu, one of Confucius' disciples, asked what constituted the superior person (which to us stands for a leader), "the Master said: 'The cultivation of himself in reverential carefulness.' 'And is this all?' said Zilu. 'He cultivates himself so as to give rest to others,' was the reply. 'And is this all?' again asked Zilu. The Master said: 'He cultivates himself so as to give rest to all the people'" (Yang, 1958: 166). The phrase "to give rest to others" is translated from the Chinese phrase *an ren*. The verb *an* has different meanings depending on the object to which it is applied. It could mean, for example, "to help settle down," "to find a place/home for," "to appease," or "to bring peace and happiness to." When used in the context of self-cultivation and with the object being a person or people, it has the connotation of all of the above, which includes serving, helping, managing, governing, and leading. We use the term here to highlight the shaping of the character of followers as individuals and collectivities as well as to refer to general leadership functions.

In *The great learning*, the above ideas were summarized as cultivating the person (*xiu ji*), regulating the family (*qi jia*), governing the state (*zhi guo*), and making the empire peaceful and happy (*ping tian xia*). That is to say,

The ancient kings who wished to illustrate illustrious virtue throughout the kingdom first ordered well their own States. Wishing to order well their States, they first regulated their families. Wishing to regulate their families, they first cultivated their persons. Wishing to cultivate their persons, they first rectified their hearts. Wishing to rectify their hearts, they first sought to be sincere in their thoughts. Wishing to be sincere in their thoughts, they first extended to the utmost their knowledge. Such extension of knowledge lay in the investigation of things (Legge, 1971: 357–359).

Accordingly,

when things are investigated, our knowledge becomes complete. When our knowledge is complete, our thoughts are sincere. Our thoughts being sincere, our hearts may be then rectified. When our hearts are rectified, we may be cultivated. If we are cultivated, our families are regulated. If our families are regulated, our States are rightly governed. When our States are rightly governed, the whole kingdom or nation may be made tranquil and happy (Legge, 1971: 359).

From these teachings, it is clear that leadership of any size of a collectivity starts with leading each and every individual. And the core function of leadership rests in character-shaping followers and winning their hearts and minds. The character-shaping process unfolds primarily in the context of hierarchical and dyadic relationships. Confucius and Mencius identified five cardinal dyadic relationships and prescribed role requirements for each relationship. Confucius said, "The duties are those between sovereign and minister, between father and son, between husband and wife, between elder brother and younger, and between friends" (Yang, 1958: 135). Mencius specified that between father and son there should be affection, between sovereign and minister, righteousness, between husband and wife, attention to their separate functions, between old and young, a proper order, and between friends, fidelity (Legge, 1971). These relationships provide a basic social structure for character formation and the duties are the contents of character. One can see these duties as embodiments of various Confucian virtues or as different applications of the central virtue of benevolence to different relationships. As these relationships are assumed to be hierarchical (even close friends model a brotherly relationship) and the leader in a dyadic relationship is assumed to be of superior character, the leader–member relationship is one of teacher–student and mentor–protégé, with the leader serving as the role model of character and the member as the active learner. In summary, while all organizational members are expected to cultivate their own character it is leaders' moral and organizational responsibility to make clear that expectation and facilitate its accomplishment. The superior character of leaders qualifies and enables them to shape the character of the members they directly interact with and by extension the character of the organization.

*Building community from the bottom up.* As indicated in the above discussion, Confucian leadership boils down to the smallest unit of society, the individual, the dyadic relationship, the family, the state, the empire, and the universe. The most basic collective unit in the Confucian social system is the family. Mencius said, "People have this common saying, – 'the empire, the state, the family.' The root of the empire is in the state. The root of the state is in the family. The root of the family is in the person of its head" (Legge, 1970: 295). If people are filial toward their parents in their families, they may also respect others outside. If they respect others outside their families, chances are they may be good citizens. Being "Good citizens" in Confucius' times of disorder often means having respect for, and being obedient to, authority. In the Confucian *Analects*, one of Confucius' students, Youzi, said, "There are very few who, being filial and fraternal, are fond of offending against their superiors. There have been none, who, not liking to offend against their superiors, have been fond of stirring up confusion. The superior man bends his attention to what is radical (i.e. a root cause). That being established, all practical courses naturally grow up. Filial piety and fraternal submission!—Are they not the root of all benevolent actions?" (Legge, 1971: 138).

Confucius and Mencius therefore held that leadership originates from leaders' own characters, extends to dyadic interactions with others, begins to manifest more comprehensively in the basic unit of a community, and ends with a harmonious and benevolent world. One of the classical examples that Confucius used often is Emperor Shun (2255–2205 BCE) who managed his family so well that he was selected by Emperor Yao (2357–2255 BCE) as his successor. Shun displayed his benevolent character by being very filial to his blind father and step-mother and also by getting along with his step-brothers. Shun's magnanimous character stood out even more considering that his father and step-mother attempted to kill him several times. He nevertheless forgave them and remained steadfastly loyal to them (Sima, 1994). Furthermore, Shun was not only filial to his family members, but also very benevolent toward those in his village and tribe. The ultimate political goal of Confucianism is to carry on the traditions of Emperors Yao and Shun, namely "universal harmony" and "sharing a state with the people." This ideal was made clear in the *Book of history* (*Shang Shu*; see Zhou, 1996), which described how Emperor Yao was able to make both clans and families live in harmony by using his own personality and morality and how he subsequently was able to bring all the states of the empire into line.

*Rule of virtue as the primary means of leadership.* Benevolent leadership leads through virtue. Confucius said, "He who exercises government by means of his virtue, may be compared to the north polar star, which keeps its place and all the stars turn towards it" (Yang, 1958: 12). Only by means of virtue can leaders win the ardent support of their followers. Mencius stated that there is a way to get the empire, namely by getting people's support. There is a way to get people's support, namely, by getting their hearts (Legge, 1970: 299–300).

In Confucius' opinion, "if we govern the people by regulations, keep order among them by chastisements, they will flee from us, and lose all self-respect. On the other hand, if we lead or govern them by moral force, keep order among them by ritual, they will keep their self-respect and come to us of their own accord" (Yang, 1958: 12).

In the above discussion, by rule of virtue Confucius and Mencius referred to the building of a virtuous culture as well as personal role-modeling. Furthermore, the rule of culture differentiates moral persuasions, norms of ritual and propriety, and formal laws and regulations. Clearly, moral education and norms of propriety are an integral part of the culture whereas formal laws and regulations are looked upon with suspicion. The relationship between moral education and norms of propriety is more complementary than that between moral education and laws and regulations. While laws are viewed as primarily punitive and prohibitive and imposed from above, norms of ritual propriety are treated as behavioral embodiments of abstract internal moral virtues (*ren nei li wai*) which have emerged through practice within the community. Although Confucius and Mencius included both moral education and the establishment of norms of propriety as components of the rule of virtue, they focused more on moral education. It is Xunzi, the famous realistic Confucian, who further develops and elaborates the role of rule propriety as an important leadership function (see Chapter 2).

Moral education according to Confucius and Mencius focuses on the major virtues of benevolence, righteousness, ritual propriety, wisdom, trustworthiness, and filial piety. As pointed out earlier, the two masters emphasize the role model of the leader, the importance of direct dyadic teaching, and mentoring through behavioral performance of those virtues.

The rule of virtue is also a means of differentiating individuals and relationships on the basis of virtues. Confucius advocated universal kindness (*fan ai*) to all, but greater closeness to the more benevolent (*qin ren*) as a sign of good character and good leadership. It suggests that virtuous leaders should surround themselves with virtuous individuals and also employ, promote, and reward them accordingly.

The rule of virtue in practice entails leadership skills of balance, thoughtfulness, and consideration. For instance, Confucius listed five good and four bad practices of leadership and advised leaders to "honor the five excellent, and banish away the four bad things." The five good things were: "Being beneficent without great expenditure, laying tasks on the people without their repining, pursuing what one desires without being covetous, maintaining a dignified ease without being proud, and being majestic without being fierce" (Legge, 1971: 352). In contrast, the four bad things were: "To put people to death without having instructed them; this is called cruelty. To require from them, suddenly, the full tally of work, without having given them warning; this is called oppression. To issue orders as if without urgency at first and, when the time comes, to insist on them with severity; this is called injury. And, generally speaking, to give pay or rewards to men, and yet to do it in a stingy way; this is called acting the part of a mere official (Legge, 1971: 352).

## The significance of Confucian benevolent leadership theory

The Confucian leadership philosophy of benevolence needs to be evaluated in its historical context. In the Spring and Autumn and later the Warring Periods of Chinese history, the social, political, and cultural systems disintegrated and society was ridden with combats, violence, poverty, and instability. Rulers of the states were relying on brutal suppression and punishment to maintain social order. The Confucian philosophy of benevolence and the rule of virtue were in direct contrast to the practice of the rule of tyranny and of force and punishment. To be sure, Confucians valued hierarchy, obedience, and conformity, as these contributed to societal order and stability and, more importantly, were more complementary with and reciprocal to values of kindness, benevolence, and righteousness than disobedience and rebellion. Confucian benevolent leadership theory therefore represents the mutual interests of the ruling class and the common people, which may explain why Chinese feudal society under the dominance of Confucianism lasted for more than two thousand years.

Many Confucian thoughts and practices make more sense with reference to the fundamental values of benevolence and humaneness. For example, individuals are submitted to the discipline of character cultivation because doing makes good citizens and superior leaders who treat others kindly, morally, and fairly. And such benevolence-oriented character-, community-, and culture-building efforts, according to the Confucian vision, lead to a harmonious, benevolent, and just world (*shi jie da tong*).

Earlier Confucian thoughts on the rule of virtue and benevolence paid overwhelming attention to morality and education to the neglect of economic and military development and the establishment of laws and regulations, which led to the decline of those states that cherished Confucianism. But the other extreme, namely, government through coercion, as represented by the Zhòu of the Shang and Qin dynasties, also brought about disasters that led to the collapse of the dynasties. The early Confucian emphasis on the rule of virtue was later enhanced with rules of propriety and rule by law by Xunzi (Chapter 2) and by other Confucian scholars of the Han dynasty.

Confucianism has had a worldwide impact on leadership and management as well as on people's daily lives (Dai and Zheng, 2002; Fernandez, 2004; Lee, McCauley, and Draguns, 1999; Liu and Tu, 1970; Yang, Zheng, and Li, 2006). For example, in the last century, theories of management in the West went through some major changes. The period of the 1900s–1930s witnessed scientific management, which stressed every factor of production except workers themselves. Efficiency went up at the expense of people's sense of humanness. The subsequent phase of management theory tried to mend its predecessor's flaws by taking into consideration human feelings, motivation, needs, and self-value. But generally speaking, not until the 1970s did Confucian ideas enter modern management. Confucian theory of management, with its roots in the traditional doctrine of benevolence and centered around human beings gives special attention to ethics, moral education, and leader–member interactions (Graen and Uhl-Bien, 1995; Romar, 2002) so as to form harmonious human relationships and improve business and work effectiveness (see Chapter 6 on paternalistic leadership).

Through interpretation and transformation, Confucian theory of management and leadership has found its way into industrial and organizational activities in many East Asian and South-east Asian countries (see Cheung and Chan, 2005; Tan and Khoo, 2002). Since the 1960s, more and more neo-Confucianists and Sinologists have been active in Asian, European, American, Australian, and African countries, to apply the Confucian philosophy of benevolence and the rule of virtue to challenges of leadership and management.

One wonders what Confucius would say about many of the management and leadership practices in the world. Confucius would be very critical of the single-minded pursuit of economic profit by today's

CEOs and organizations, even with an understanding of the cut-throat competitive environment. The Confucian view of organizations is one of community than one of machines for profit and productivity. He would insist on evaluating leadership and organization on the standard of humaneness and benevolence rather than purely on financial performance on the stock market. Similarly, Confucius would lament and protest against how employees collectively are relegated to be the less, if not the least, important stakeholders compared to shareholders, the top management, or the customers. Confucius gave the top management a lot of power and status but he also required them to serve, not just to employ, the rank-and-file employees. When organizations are competing to innovate in today's era of change or perish, Confucius would want business leaders, in collaboration with governments, to make arrangements so that displaced workers are treated humanely. Confucius would be quite perplexed by some of the disorderliness of today's organizations such as the flattening of the hierarchy, the lack of a clear chain of command, and the increase in ambiguity of roles. However, our prediction is that he would adjust well because, for one thing, he valued benevolence more than hierarchy. And he valued education without discrimination, and his philosophy of the rule of virtue, education, and relationship-building would do well in a dynamic organization where some of the rigid Weberian rules cannot be established or consistently applied. Despite the flattening of the hierarchy, Confucius nevertheless would hold leaders accountable for problems under their supervision and he would be appalled at the corporate scandals in which CEOs abuse their authority to benefit their self-interest at the expense of employees and shareholders. He would point out that under his benevolent leadership philosophy, such scandals would be rare because such people would not get to the CEO positions in the first place and, should they be there, they would not survive long in a culture of benevolence.

*References*

Ames, T. A., and Rosemont, H. 1998. *The analects of Confucius: a philosophical translation*. New York: Ballantine.

Cheung, C.-K., and Chan, A. 2005. "Philosophical foundations of eminent Hong Kong Chinese CEOs' leadership", *Journal of Business Ethics* 60: 47–62.

Dai, C., and Zheng, Z. G. 2002. "Managing talent in China: Confucian origins," in C. B. Derr, S. Roussillon, and F. Bournois (eds.), *Cross-cultural approaches to leadership development*. Westport, CT: Quorum.

Fernandez, J. A. 2004. "The gentleman's code of Confucius: leadership by values," *Organizational Dynamics* 33: 21–31.

Fung, Y.-L. 1948. *A short history of Chinese philosophy*. New York: Free Press.

Graen, G. B., and Uhl-Bien, M. 1995. "Relationship-based approach to leadership: development of leader–member exchange (LMX) theory of leadership over twenty-five years: applying a multi-level multi-domain perspective," *Leadership Quarterly* 6(2): 219–247.

Lee, Y.-T., McCauley, C. R., and Draguns, J. 1999. *Personality and person perception across cultures*. Mahwah, NJ: Lawrence Erlbaum Associates.

Legge, J. 1970 [1895]. *The works of Mencius*. New York: Dover.
    1971 [1893]. *Confucius: Confucian analects, the great learning, and the doctrine of the mean*. New York: Dover.

Liu, J., and Tu, W. M. 1970. *Traditional China*. Englewood Cliffs, NJ: Prentice Hall.

Romar, E. J. 2002. "Virtue is good business: Confucianism as a practice business ethic," *Journal of Business Ethics* 38: 119–131.

Sima, Q. 1994. "Shi ji" (original work *c.*150 BCE), in *Records of the grand historian of China*, Yin-Chuan: Ninxia People's Press.

Tan, K. C., and Khoo, H. H. 2002. "The relevance of Confucianism to national quality awards in Southeast Asia," *International Journal of Cross-Cultural Management* 2: 65–82.

Yang, B., Zheng, W., and Li, M. 2006. "Confucian view of learning and implications for developing human resources," *Advances in Developing Human Resources* 8: 346–354.

Yang, B. J. 1958. "Lunyu yi zhu," in *Annotations and translation of Confucian analects*, Beijing: China Press.

Zhou, B. J. 1996. "Baihua shangshu," *Contemporary annotation of the Book of History in the pre-Zhou dynasty*, Changsha, Hunan: Mount Yue Lu Press.

# 2 | Bridging Confucianism and Legalism: Xunzi's philosophy of sage-kingship

YAN-QIN PENG, CHAO-CHUAN CHEN, AND XIN-HUI YANG

**K**NOWN AS AN "impure" or "realistic" Confucianist, Xunzi emerged as the great thinker who bridged Confucianism and Legalism. In this chapter, we first introduce Xunzi's philosophy of human badness and the importance of self-cultivation. We then analyze Xunzi's philosophy of community, social distinctions, and a system of ritual and conduct propriety. Third, we analyze Xunzi's philosophy of sage-kingship as the role model for self-cultivation, employing the virtuous and the talented, and building culture. Finally, we discuss his contributions to leadership theory and practice in China and in the world.

## Historical background: reconstructing order

Xunzi (*c.* 313–238 BCE) was a renowned thinker at the end of the Warring States Period and was the teacher of two eminent politicians, Hanfei (whose Legalistic perspective is featured in Chapter 4 of this book) and Li Si. Xunzi's last name was Xun and his first name Kuang. However, instead of Xun Kuang, he has been respectfully referred to as Xunzi, Master Xun, with the suffix *zi* meaning "master." Xunzi is also called Xun Qing, with Qing suggesting the status of a high official. In the Wade–Giles system, he is also referred to as Hsün K'uang, Hsün Ch'ing, Hsün Tzu, or Hsün-tzu.

Xunzi was both erudite and versatile, having studied in the town of Jixia in the state of Qi. The Scholars' Palace at Jixia was at that time the place where scholars of different groups gathered, and it thus became the center of academic studies. Xunzi was exposed to a variety of schools of thought, which laid the groundwork for him to combine the strengths of various schools of thinker. In the year 285 BCE, when the state of Qi was captured by the state of Yan, Xunzi left Qi for the state of Chu. Six years later when Qi took back the lost territory and restored the Scholars' Palace, Xunzi returned. Due to his scholarly achievement, he was chosen three times as the head of the palace and was revered as "the most superior teacher." He was appointed as the magistrate of Lanling County in the Chu state and was residing there when he passed away.

Xunzi has been widely viewed as the third most authoritative representative of Confucianism, after Confucius and Mencius (Fung, 1966). Nevertheless, he developed his own theoretical system by revising and enriching Confucianism and by incorporating some essential elements of various schools of thought of pre-Qin times, especially those of Daoism and Legalism. He is therefore labeled by some as an "impure" Confucian or "realistic" Confucian (Fung, 1966). Guo Mo-ruo (1956), a well-known modern scholar in China, asserted that "Xunzi is the last master among those in the pre-Qin times, who epitomizes not only the essence of Confucianism but also that of his contemporary hundred schools of thoughts." Studies of Xunzi in the West have also been gaining momentum with the publication of *Xunzi: a translation and study of the complete works* by Knoblock in 1998, who prefaced volume III by commenting that "The domain of knowledge traversed by his thought exceeds that of any other ancient Chinese thinker and bears comparison only with Aristotle in the West."

Xunzi lived in an era when slavery was coming to an end and feudalism was in its initial stage. During the Spring and Autumn Period and the Warring States Period, one of the main topics of debate was social order. What is the rationality of the existing social order (i.e. on what grounds could people be required to obey this order) and how could a rational order be reconstructed when the society was faced with the decomposition of the imperial system and the collapse of rituals and music? All these were central topics of concern for the rulers and the elite scholars who were part of the ruling class.

So far as these problems were concerned, different schools of thought fell roughly in two groups. One group believed that people have an inherent inclination to esteem order and comply with rules. It is this instinctive inclination that is the "goodness" of human nature by which excessive desires can be controlled and the rights of others observed. As is known, Mencius represented this group, which justified the rationality of the Confucian social order and defended

Confucian values on the ground of the goodness of human nature. Specifically, goodness lies in individuals' feelings and inclinations such as "compassion," "being ashamed of evil deeds," "declining compliments," and "distinguishing between right and wrong," all of which are intrinsic to human beings and are "picked up by human nature without necessary learning" and "understood without necessary pondering" (Yang, 1960: 258–259). All these are the fundamental bases for human beings to be considered human. Consequently, it is necessary to do nothing but extend the inborn existing qualities to external objects.

The other group, represented by Mohists, in contrast, argued for the reconstruction of social order on the basis of the observed evilness of human nature. It was argued that people only give consideration to their own and their relatives' belongings. Such selfish feelings and desires are bound to create extreme chaos in society. For instance, some "steal into others' gardens to filch the peaches and plums of others"; some boldly rob others of their property and even murder others for that purpose; to top it all, some rulers "never hesitate to go on punitive expeditions to satisfy their desires to enjoy all the benefits under the sun." Thus it seems all people in the world "harm each other by evil-minded means" (Zhang, 1937). According to this school of thought, conscience and morality are merely ornaments that have little effect on people's behavior; people and society therefore have to be managed strictly by means of legal systems and regulations.

Although the Legalist school of thought was not fully established at the time (Hanfei, the ultimate master of the Legalist school, emerged a little after Xunzi), Xunzi became the great thinker who epitomized the thoughts of various schools of the pre-Qin times, although he steadfastly claimed to be within the classic tradition of Confucius and refuted other schools of thought (Xunzi, Book 6)[1] especially in his earlier writings. Xunzi picked and chose from the opinions of both groups by incorporating what he considered reasonable and useful, but rejected their extreme positions. According to Xunzi, too much emphasis on the self-consciousness of human nature was too idealistic and would be hard to apply in social practices; conversely, too much dependence on legal restriction would result in excessive utilitarianism, which would lead to indifference in human relationships. Xunzi would like to take a moderate two-stranded approach, on one hand insisting on the significance of rituals and the powerful self-regulating function of human conscience, and on the other, adhering to the implementation of institutionalized laws. In so doing, Xunzi turned philosophical and intellectual discussions by scholars into social practices by practitioners, thereby contributing to a Chinese philosophical tradition of being practically oriented.

Facing the grave problem of reconstructing social order, Xunzi brings forward a series of interrelated concepts regarding the requirements of good governance and kingship. Xunzi's philosophy has been studied in the West primarily from a moral and ethical perspective (e.g. Cua, 1978, 1979). In this chapter, we seek to examine the theoretical implications of Xunzi's philosophy for leadership and organization. Although we do not find the exact terms "leader" or "leadership" in Xunzi, there are equivalent terms. Xunzi argued that "from birth all men are capable of forming societies. If a society is formed without social divisions, strife would result; if there is strife, disorder ensures; if there is disorder, fragmentation results; if there is fragmentation, weakness comes; if there is weakness, it is impossible to triumph over objects" (Xunzi, Book 9: 9.17). "To be able to use them [ritual and moral principles] in commanding one's subordinates is called being lordly. A lord is one who is accomplished at causing men to form societies" (Xunzi, Book 9: 9.17). In Xunzi's time formal leaders were rulers of states (kings and lords), assisted and counseled by civil servants comprising scholars and officials. The ruled are the common people, primarily the mass of peasants. In addition, Xunzi addressed leader–subordinate relationships between kings and their ministers and he often gave scholars and teachers the status of leadership (Xunzi, Books 9, 12, and 13).

In Xunzi's writings, two labels frequently used in the same breath for superior leaders are "sages" (*sheng ren*) and the "noble-minded" (*junzi*). These are people equipped with supreme moral character and wisdom, and, therefore, are held up as models of leadership. According to Xunzi (Book 8: 8.7), these superior leaders are vital for the survival of society and as leaders, they must have the knowledge of the success and failure of generations of predecessors as clearly as they know black and white; they must be good at making decisions according to the changing social reality; and they must be able to stabilize the political situation, calm people, and unite millions of them as one person.

For achieving his political ideal, Xunzi put forward a wealth of ideas, concepts, and principles that enable us to develop a theoretical model of leadership. Xunzi (Book 23: 23.2a) stated:

The sage accumulates thoughts and ideas. He masters through practice the skills of his acquired nature and the principles involved therein in order to produce ritual principles and moral duty and to develop laws and standards. This being the case, ritual principles and moral duty, laws and standards, are the creation of the acquired nature of the sage and not the product of anything inherent in his inborn nature ... Thus the sage by transforming his original nature develops his acquired nature. From this developed acquired nature, he creates ritual principles and moral duty. Having produced them, he institutes the regulations of laws and standards.

These statements are compacted with much of Xunzi's philosophical thought on the evilness and transformability of human nature, the process of self-cultivation, the requirements of great leaders, and their role in establishing rituals and righteousness in order to create an effective system of organization and administration. In the following we seek to build a framework of leadership by elaborating and connecting these concepts.

## Philosophical foundation: the nature of human beings

As summarized in Figure 2.1, we examine Xunzi's philosophy of human nature by depicting four components and their relationships. First, we analyze what Xunzi means when he proposes that human nature is evil. We then point out that despite its evilness, Xunzi believes that human nature is transformable into goodness through the endowment of the mind and its capacity to reason, reflect, and consider. Third, we identify the major virtues constituting human goodness, emphasizing conduct propriety. Finally, we identify the major ways in which human nature is transformed through self-cultivation.

## *The evilness of inborn human nature*

One of the philosophical debates at Xunzi's time was whether human beings are born good or evil. This debate had urgent practical implications for the building of social order either through the morality and conscience of humans or through the external constraint of

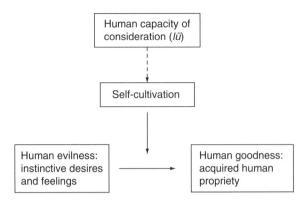

**Figure 2.1.** Xunzi's philosophy of human nature.
Note about self-cultivation (*xiu sheng*): (1) all human beings should self-cultivate; (2) the more self-cultivation, the more goodness; (3) leaders are differentiated from non-leaders not in terms of human nature but in terms of goodness.

regulations and systems. While Xunzi upheld the Confucian ideal of benevolent and moral government, which he shared with Mencius, he nevertheless severely criticized the theory of human goodness as explicated by Mencius and proposed his thesis of human evilness in direct refutation of Mencius' thesis of human goodness (for a summary, see Xunzi, Book 23 [Introduction]: 139–150). Xunzi's positions on human nature are primarily presented in "Man's nature is evil" (Book 23), but relevant arguments can also be found in his writings on ritual principles, honor and disgrace, the correct use of names, self-cultivation, and exhortation to learning (Xunzi, Books 1, 2, 4, 19, 22, and 23). In "Man's nature is evil" (Xunzi, Book 23), the opening sentence states: "Human nature is evil: any good in humans is acquired by conscious exertion." In defining human nature, Xunzi distinguishes two terms, *xing* (human nature) and *wei* (human artifice).[2] The essential distinctions Xunzi made between *xing* and *wei* are summarized by Lau (1953: 558). *Xing* (human nature) is that "which is (1) made what it is by heaven, (2) cannot be learned, (3) cannot be improved through application, and (4) is not the result of reflection by the mind," while *wei* (human artifice) is that "which is (1) invented by the sages, (2) can be learned, (3) can be improved through application, and (4) is the result of refection by the mind." According to the definition of *xing*, the most instinctive and spontaneous elements of human nature are feelings (*qing*) and desires (*yü*). Cua (1977) categorizes Xunzi's feelings into three types: moods such as joy, sorrow, and pleasure; emotions such as love, hate, anger, and envy; and bodily feelings such as feeling hungry and cold. Experiencing these feelings naturally inclines people to take certain actions to express or to satisfy desires aroused by those feelings. Xunzi argued that "it is the inborn nature of man that when hungry he desires something to eat, that when cold he wants warm clothing, and that when weary he desires rest – such are essential qualities inherent in his nature" (Xunzi, Book 23: 23.1e). Besides feelings, people are born with basic desires; for example, the sensory desires such as those of the ear and the eye for music and beauty. More importantly, people are born with a desire for gain (*hao li*), that is, a propensity to seek benefits to satisfy their desires. Feelings and desires are intimately and closely related in that desires may arise in response to feelings, both of which stimulate purposeful albeit reactive and instinctive actions for their expression and satisfaction. Cua (1977: 378; 1978) therefore insightfully frames Xunzi's inborn human nature as the "basic motivational structure" in that it is made up of feelings and desires that incline people to engage in self-benefiting activities in order to satisfy those feelings and desires.

Contradicting Mencius, who believed that humans are born good, but become bad when they lose their human goodness, Xunzi held that humans are born evil, but become good when they modify their evilness through learning. While Mencius viewed learning as evidence of human goodness and as a means of preserving and nurturing human goodness, Xunzi restricted human nature to what cannot be learned and human goodness to what is learned and acquired through intervention after birth. Mencius held that children do not have to learn to love their parents. Xunzi argued that when a son goes hungry so his father can eat and labors tirelessly so his father can rest, the son is violating his natural instincts so as to follow social and moral requirements of righteousness. Mencius asserted that reason and moral principles please our minds just as fine meats please our mouths. Xunzi reasoned that preferences for fine smell and good taste are inborn but preferences for reason and morality are learned. A poor person who knew only coarse foods and was satisfied with them would nevertheless like and choose fine meats because of the latter's better smell, taste, and nourishment. However, a tyrant who was used to tyranny and indolence would not naturally choose reason and morality; only sage-kings who have acquired goodness through self-cultivation would. The point is that people's moral attributes, particularly those of leaders, are not naturally inherited but require concerted learning and acculturation. Such being the case, why are the human instincts to pursue benefits and avoid harm necessarily evil rather than simply natural or morally neutral? Xunzi argued that "men are born with desires which, if not satisfied, cannot but lead men to seek to satisfy them. If in seeking to satisfy their desires men observe no measure and apportion things without limits, then it would be impossible for them not to contend over the means to satisfy their desires. Such contention leads to disorder. Disorder leads to poverty" (Xunzi, Book 19: 19.1a). In other words, although the basic human feelings and desires are neither good nor bad, pursuing them without social and moral constraints will inevitably result in combats, disorder, and poverty, which in turn will hinder the satisfaction of human desires and threaten the very existence of human beings. It is thus clear human nature is not evil in that people are inherently wicked, malicious, and hopeless, but it is evil because the unconstrained pursuit of those desires leads to deplorable consequences such as violence, disorder, and poverty.

## *Consideration* (lü) *as the foundation for self-cultivation*

Although Xunzi was emphatic on the evilness of inborn human desires and feelings, he did not claim that all inborn human attributes are evil. He believed human evilness is capable of being transformed into goodness through a process of self-cultivation (Xunzi, Book 2). The psychological foundation for self-cultivation lies in some of the human's naturally endowed capabilities. The first natural endowment of humans that allows for cultivation is the commanding ability of the mind, which has the capacity to think, reason, and be concerned (*lü*). "The mind is the lord of the body and master of the spiritual intelligence. It issues commands but does not receive commands. On its own authority it forbids or orders, renounces or selects, initiates or stops" (Xunzi, Book 21: 21.6a). Desires generate opposite emotions such as liking and disliking, love and hate, and sorrow and joy, but it is the mind that thinks, considers, reflects, and decides on a course of action based on the calculation of social, economic, and moral appropriateness. The capacity of *lü* therefore lays the foundation for human beings to learn and develop a cultivated nature. Xunzi went even further by saying that human beings, in comparison with the rest of nature, have a sense of what is right, which puts Xunzi close to Mencius' human goodness argument. However, Xunzi did not mean that humans are naturally inclined to good deeds and averse to wrong deeds, but rather they are capable of developing human goodness because they have a basic sense of propriety (Xunzi, Book 8).

## Acquired human goodness

Given the evil nature of inborn desires and emotions, human nature has to be modified and transformed in order for human beings to develop and survive in a resource-limited world. "Following this nature will cause its aggressiveness and greedy tendencies to grow and courtesy and deference to disappear ... Indulging these feelings causes violence and crime to develop and loyalty and trustworthiness to perish" (Xunzi, Book 23: 23.1a). Since good human attributes are not inborn, they are learned through conscious exertion of self-cultivation, socialization, and rules and regulations. In time, the acquired attributes become the second nature of humans, the acquired nature. Xunzi used the term *wei* to refer to both acquired human attributes and the process of concerted cultivation of human nature.

What then are the central characteristics of acquired good human nature? Xunzi's writings list numerous virtues such as benevolence (*ren*), righteousness (*i*), ritual propriety (*li*), wisdom (*zhi*), filial piety, loyalty, trustworthiness, modesty, courtesy, and respectfulness, etc. Of these virtues, the first four on the above list have been considered the central values of classical Confucianism as expounded in the *Analects of Confucius* (Ames and Rosemont, 1998) (see also Chapter 1 of this book).

Benevolence as a general virtue is kindness to and love of others. It consists of all other-oriented pro-social virtues such as empathy, compassion, and concern with others' well-being. The benevolence of the sage-king refers to love and care of the people, primarily in terms of securing people's economic well-being. Xunzi distinguished the following three types of ruler according to their benevolence toward the people (Xunzi, Book 10: 10.11). True sage-kings are the first type. They love the people and provide them with benefits without asking anything in return. These kings will win the world. The second type of ruler loves the people and offers them benefits before taking benefits from them. In order to survive, a society must have at least this type of ruler. The third type of ruler takes benefits from the people without providing any benefits in return. This type of ruler is bound to perish.

Righteousness receives less individual consideration from Xunzi and is often used in conjunction with propriety (e.g. in Xunzi, Books 2 and 12). When used on its own, it has various meanings depending on the context, including a moral sense of right and wrong as opposed to pursuing material benefits and satisfying desires (Xunzi, Book 2), uprightness in terms of following moral and social rules and norms (Xunzi, Book 2), and justice in terms of impartiality (Xunzi, Book 12).

Ritual propriety refers to the conscientious observation of the rituals established and passed down from ancient sage-kings, but Xunzi broadened the concept to the establishment and observation of rules of proper conduct (Cua, 1979; Dubs, 1927) in accordance to the Dao of humanity. Central to the Dao of humanity are virtues of benevolence and righteousness. Propriety rules are wide-ranging, elaborate, and mostly explicit for occasions ranging from court ceremonies of tribute and sacrifices to ancestors, to rules of good manners and details of costume and dress. Because most of these rules are highly ritualized, propriety is known as "ritual propriety" in the classical Confucian literature. We call it "conduct propriety" to stress a broader definition and conscientious performance and practice.

The last one of the four virtues is wisdom, which is conceived as knowledge that is harmonious with experience (Xunzi, Book 22). In addition to emphasizing accumulated historical knowledge of antiquities, Xunzi sees wisdom resulting from continuous practical applications of rules of proper conduct and morality in emergent and changing circumstances. Wisdom is therefore a "repository of insights derived from the proper exercise of *i* (righteousness) in exigent situations" (Cua, 1987: 392), in other words, wisdom is the accumulation and application of the three virtues of benevolence, righteousness, and propriety.

Of the four central virtues, Xunzi gave the greatest prominence to conduct propriety, which was also considered his major contribution to Confucianism (Cua, 1979). In a narrow sense, propriety as a personality virtue represents a person's disposition to be conscientious and compliant with social, cultural, and moral rules. But more broadly, propriety is a unifying virtue that is capable of integrating benevolence, righteousness, and wisdom (Cua, 1977, 1978) in operational and behavioral terms. It is the means by which relatively more abstract virtues are translated into personal conduct. In the most general sense, propriety is the way in which a virtuous person conducts life, and is a comprehensive measure of culturedness. Looked at this way, conduct propriety is not about conforming to external rules imposed on individuals, but about acquiring a new character that seeks to live a noble-minded life.

## Self-cultivation: transformation of instinctive desires

As discussed earlier, Xunzi on one hand steadfastly argued for the evilness of human instinctive desires and emotions, but on the other believed in the human potential to be thoughtful, reflective, and rational. This potential paves the way for the possibility of humans to acquire pro-social, rational, and moral ways of thinking so as to balance or counteract instinctive desires and emotions. To the extent individuals engage in conscientious and continuous self-cultivation, they become superior, qualifying them to be better humans and better leaders. The key to acquiring good human nature is the process of self-cultivation.

In general, noble-mindedness and sageness result from continuous and conscientious mental and behavioral exertions, which involves continuous learning, thinking, and performing goodness (Xunzi, Book 8). "By accumulating earth you can create a mountain; by accumulating water you can make a sea ... A man in the street, one of the hundred Clans, who accumulates goodness and achieves it completely, is called a sage" (Xunzi, Book 8: 8.11). In Book 2 on self-cultivation, Xunzi prescribes specific domains of self-cultivation ranging from cultivating one's thoughts, aspirations, and temperament, to keeping good physical health and good life habits, to attending to the etiquette of postures and mannerisms. Furthermore, Xunzi proposes major ways of self-cultivation in Books 2 and 23. The first is to learn and follow the model of rituals and rules that came down from past sage-kings that have been tried and proven right. Second, one must learn from teachers, absorbing their knowledge and following their advice because they are in the best position to know those ritual traditions and norms and are able to interpret them in the light of new circumstances. "Having a teacher and the model is man's greatest treasure and lacking a teacher and the model his greatest calamity (Xunzi, Book 8: 8.11). Third, self-cultivation requires the initiative to keenly observe and emulate behavior of propriety in others, seeking critical feedback and being willing and ready to inspect and correct imperfect conduct. In summary, self-cultivation, according to Xunzi, involves primarily education, learning, and practice to accumulate consciousness and habit about conduct propriety, and in so doing people become knowledgeable, reasonable, virtuous, and, in a word, cultured.

The profundity of Xunzi's theory of human nature, as we see it, exists not just in his insight into the distinction between "inborn nature" and "cultivated nature" and in proposing a quite comprehensive and rigorous process of cultivation, but also in the great significance of combining inborn and acquired human natures, although most researchers emphasize their distinctness rather than their integration. Xunzi argues that without the innate basis there would be no support for the acquired and the innate nature cannot be perfected without cultivation. Only the combination of the two can help achieve sageness and happiness in human life. He foresees that the combination of heaven and earth induces the growth of all things in the universe; the joining of *yin* and *yang* leads to varieties of changes in things; the integration of nature and culture makes the world governable. Without nature, there would be no precondition and basis for cultivation; without culture, there would be no possibility for nature to reach perfection gradually. Only the combination of the two can make it possible for the individual to develop and for society to be stable, orderly, and prosperous.

## Philosophy of human society and governance

Largely on the basis of, and to some extent parallel to, the philosophy of human nature, Xunzi proposed his philosophy of society and governance, which can best be illustrated by a compact paragraph in Book 9, "On the regulations of a king" (9.16a). Here Xunzi stated that water and fire have energy but no life; plants have life but no awareness; animals have awareness but know no ritual and moral principles. People have all of these. Xunzi asked why are oxen and horses driven by humans even though they are physically stronger or faster than humans. The answer is that humans alone possess the ability to form society (*neng qun*), to assemble in groups, communities, and larger societies. How do humans form society? Through social distinctions. How could social distinction work? Through ritual and moral principles. The very reason that collectives of humans can survive is that, under the constraint of social norms, an otherwise chaotic collective acquires a social structure in which individuals and groups enjoy rights and carry out corresponding obligations.

## *Humans' ability to assemble* (neng qun)

By the ability to assemble, Xunzi referred to the ability to build a prosperous and peaceful society in which people perform different tasks but maintain harmonious relationships. If the ability to assemble is what differentiates humans from animals, does it mean it is an inherent part of human nature? The answer is no, because as we see from his philosophy of human nature, humans differ from animals not primarily because of their inborn nature, which Xunzi judged to be evil, but because of their cultivated attributes. Xunzi did acknowledge that humans have an inherent need or desire to form associations with others and have the cognitive ability to make and understand distinctions including that between right and wrong. Yet while these endowed natural attributes lead to the formation of societies, they do not lead to stable and functional societies. The latter requires conscious personal and societal efforts to intervene. The ability to assemble is therefore a manifestation of human goodness because what enables humans to form a well-functioning society is human culture on the basis of rules of proper conduct, which belongs entirely to the acquired nature of human beings.

In Xunzi's philosophy, human culture or the culture of any society does not emerge naturally, but requires the sageness and the noble-mindedness of the leaders. Indeed, Xunzi uses ability to assemble as a defining attribute of kingship. To the question of what makes a lord, Xunzi answered that it is "one who can assemble" (Xunzi, Book 12: 12.6). The human superiority in assembling therefore lies in sage leaders' superiority in assembling. Knoblock (1998, vol. II: 5) points out that "In Western thought the position of humanity is secure, having at creation been given dominion over the beasts, but in Chinese thought there is no such divinely sanctioned superiority. Thus, humanity's present position of superiority is attributable to the sages, who invented the various cultural objects that now give people superiority." Indeed, sage-kingship in Xunzi's philosophy of human society, itself accomplished through personal and societal cultivation, is the source, the culmination, and the model of human cultivation. Without sage-kings and noble-minded ministers and scholars, human society would be impoverished, violent, and chaotic, which in Xunzi's point of view, is not much different to the world of animals and beasts.

## Social distinctions (fen)

Xunzi holds that nature is inherently diverse and unequal. From nature, there are old and young, odd and even, primary and secondary. Furthermore, because the life necessities of members of society are varied, a wide range of skills and vocations is required to satisfy people's needs, and one individual cannot be proficient in all skills and be qualified for all vocations. Consequently, to meet the needs of society as a whole, work must be reasonably divided among its members. Social hierarchy as a means of economic collaboration is therefore absolutely necessary for humans to survive and triumph in the natural universe.

Xunzi elevates the role of social distinction to the Way (*Dao*) of rulership (Xunzi, Book 12). In Book 10, he states that the principle of governing the universe is social distinction and the essence of conduct propriety is also social distinction. "Conduct propriety means that there should be rankings according to nobility or baseness, disparities between the privileges of old and young, and modes to match these with poverty and wealth, insignificance and importance" (Xunzi, Book 10: 10.3a).

Given social distinctions are natural and necessary for basic human society, what distinguishes good and successful from bad and failing governance is not so much the presence or absence of distinctions, but the bases on which distinctions are established. Social distinctions without just bases will leave the weak, the less intelligent, and the less powerful bullied and taken advantage of by the strong, the intelligent, and the more powerful, which will lead to poverty, violence, and disorder. Xunzi therefore proposes a system of rules of proper conduct to be the guiding principles of social distinctions.

Xunzi's social distinctions have horizontal and vertical dimensions although more attention and emphasis have been given to the latter.

Horizontal distinctions refer to those between different occupations, be they different trades practiced by commoners or specialties of government by court administrators. Vertical distinctions are unequal distributions of wealth, power, status, and prestige. Xunzi advocated the creation of a hierarchy of distinctive ranks, titles, and honors for structuring, stabilizing, and harmonizing society. "Where the classes of society are equally ranked, there is no proper arrangement of society; where authority is evenly distributed there is no unity; and where everyone is of like status, none would be willing to serve the other" (Xunzi, Book 9: 9.3). Clearly, Xunzi favored hierarchy because he believed that its absence leads to conflict, fragmentation, and disorder. There are other reasons why Xunzi advocated hierarchical social distinctions. First, he observed that "desires are many and the things that satisfy them relatively few" (Xunzi, Book 10: 10.1) and it is completely futile to try to eliminate human desires, be they moral education or brutal suppression. Therefore, human desires should be satisfied where resources are available and be channeled and modified through moral education and social and legal regulations where resources are limited. Social distinctions become institutional mechanisms to channel and regulate human desires from unconstrained conflict and strife into collaborative and productive efforts. Second, social distinctions, especially those of an honorary and symbolic nature, serve as rewards to encourage and reinforce acquired human goodness and to divert desires for material wealth to desires for social status. Furthermore, social distinctions are important artifacts and conduits of the underlying ritual and moral principles and norms. In summary, Xunzi advocated social distinctions for symbolic and moral, as well as material and instrumental, reasons.

What then are the bases for social distinctions? The question in essence is about how desired resources are allocated in ways that promote social harmony and economic prosperity. Xunzi provided his answers in his theory of conduct propriety, which we discuss in more detail in the next section. Here we outline a few major criteria by which social distinctions are made. The first is moral character. Xunzi distinguishes people by three broad categories of moral character: small-minded, noble-minded, and sage, and held that power, position, and status should be allocated according to moral distinctions. He insists that descendants of kings and dukes should be relegated to the position of commoners if they have not observed principles of propriety, while descendants of commoners, if they have accumulated culture and study and rectified their character and conduct, should be promoted to the rank of a prime minister, knight, or grand officer (Xunzi, Book 9: 9.1). This position is extraordinary as it opposes hereditary succession and selection, the hallmark determinant of feudal distinctions.

The second basis for social distinctions is ability and accomplishment. "Those without morality shall be without honored status, those without ability shall be without office, those who lack accomplishment shall go unrewarded ... The worthy shall be honored and the able employed, each assigned a position of appropriate rank, with none overlooked" (Xunzi, Book 9: 9.12). Of the two merit bases, moral character is held as more important than ability because when juxtaposed, noble character is most often associated with eminent position and status, and talent with employment and rewards.

Besides bases for social distinctions, there are other points worth making. First, in a benevolently governed society, all members are entitled to a basic level of economic well-being and a minimal share of the state's resources regardless of their social position. A society in which some enjoy extravagant wealth while others suffer dire poverty is not a benevolent one and will not last long. For example, Xunzi proposed that those with crippling physical defects should be cared for by social welfare services. Second, symbolic social distinctions are elaborate and clearly marked whereas material social distinctions are less so. In fact, Xunzi cautioned against offering excessive material rewards because it could benefit small-minded individuals just as excessive punishment could hurt noble-minded individuals. Third, commoners could rise to high position and status through acquiring proper conduct. Social ranks are therefore penetrable and mobile in that individuals can attain and lose their social distinctions on the basis of character and ability. Lastly, although the standards of distinction are universally applied to all individuals of a given rank (e.g. all kings should have the loftiest moral character and know how to identify and use talents), standards of distinction differ among social ranks and are judged to be proper relative to a given rank. Standards of excellence, especially for moral character, are different for commoners, for officials, and for kings. Importantly, the more eminent social rankings require higher standards of character and conduct. For instance, honesty and diligence are the standards of low-level bureaucrats; uprightness in thought and conduct and respect for rules of conduct and social distinctions are the standards of heads of bureau; and knowing and assisting the greater purposes of observing rituals, honoring the upright, loving the people, and employing the talented to honor the king and enhance the reputation and strength of the country are the standards of the prime ministers and councils of the king (Xunzi, Book 12: 12.13).

## Systems of ritual and conduct propriety (li)

Earlier we discussed ritual and conduct propriety (*li*) as a core personal virtue. It is important to note, however, that Xunzi also views *li* as external social institutions. Here we examine how Xunzi uses the concept of *li* as a set of cultural, legal, and administrative systems and procedures that leaders can create to cultivate the individuals and to transform society (which is operated on the basis of instinctive human nature) from a state of conflict, poverty, and disorder to one of cooperation, wealth, and stability.

*Symbolic and cultural rituals.* Rituals are the most fundamental and central elements of *li* governance. Rituals are, first and foremost, embodiments of morality and justice and are major responsibilities of the sage-kings. They are performed to exemplify and honor the prevailing moral and cultural values handed down from ancient sage-kings and to instill them into all members of the society. As elaborate and meticulous as were the ceremonies to worship and make sacrifices to heaven, earth, and ancestors, Xunzi did not believe in any supernatural or substantial functions of these ceremonies in terms of bringing about material benefits and protections. The purpose of rituals is primarily symbolic and cultural. In ceremonies honoring social distinctions, Xunzi insisted that the purpose was not to enhance and highlight the distinctions *per se*, but to glorify and cultivate virtues such as benevolence, righteousness, and conduct propriety in social relationships.

*Laws and regulations.* As a pure Confucianist, Xunzi's views of the legal system, according to Knoblock (1998, vol. I: 18–35), evolved from cynicism to affirmation as he personally witnessed the stabilizing effects of laws in the state of Qin. While rituals, emanating from Confucian social and moral principles, were positive and promotive, laws, in Xunzi's conception, were tilted toward being punitive and prohibitive. Because of the great variation in the process of self-cultivation, Xunzi believed that although it was sufficient to appeal to rituals to enforce conduct propriety for the noble-minded, for the small-minded, coercive measures were needed to prohibit immoral and antisocial behaviors (Xunzi, Book 9). Because laws are primarily punitive, Xunzi cautioned that they should used only as a last resort, that is, after moral and ritual education has been tried but proved ineffective. Furthermore, when people violate propriety norms, the legal system must consider intentions so as to punish only those transgressors with bad wills. In summary, Xunzi's incorporation of laws into his philosophy of governance was a significant departure from the classic Confucianism that preceded him. Although narrowly conceived, his inclusion of laws and regulations as part of the system of propriety laid the foundation of legal governance, which was carried forward by his student Li Si, who was to be chancellor of the Qin empire.

*Administrative and organizational principles.* In Xunzi's system of *li*, this subcomponent deals with operational norms and practices of government administration especially with regard to personnel management. His prescriptions of these principles reminds us of what are known today as human resources practices. Here we highlight three of his expositions, which are consistent with his belief in social distinctions. First, Xunzi proposed hierarchical ranking and differential rewards instead of egalitarianism in administration. He believed that is the only way to attract and motivate talented people to serve and to establish and maintain stable relationships. Second, he insisted that the fundamental criterion of personnel administration with respect to selection, assessment, promotion, and reward is merit in terms of moral character, ability, and work performance relative to the objectives and requirements of the post. Extraneous factors such as one's birth, age, looks, or current social and economic status are of no relevance. He believed that merit-based administration is the most benevolent and the most righteous: "Esteeming the worthy is humaneness; deprecating the unworthy is humaneness as well" (Xunzi, Book 6: 6.9); "Thus, giving important responsibility to those whose abilities are few is like giving a man whose strength is slight a heavy load. He will have to let it go, break down under the load, and not go far" (Xunzi, Book 8: 8.6). He proposed that "The ruler should dangle the prospect of noble rank and substantial incentives in order to entice them to come. Within the palace it would be impermissible for him to show favoritism for his sons and brothers. Without, it would be impermissible for him to keep in obscurity those who have come from afar" (Xunzi, Book 12: 12.9). "Conduct and deportment, activity and repose, were measured by the standards of ritual principles. Knowledge and thought, choosing or setting aside, were tested by what they in fact did" (Xunzi, Book 12: 12.8c). Third, Xunzi paid great attention to how to develop and assess officials systematically and rigorously in diverse conditions.

"As the days and months piled up over a long span of time, they were compared in terms of their accomplishments . . . Thus, rulers compare their ministers with the standards of ritual principles, so as to observe their ability to remain at ease while taking strict reverent care in the execution of their tasks. They alternately promote and dismiss them, transferring them from position to position so as to review their ability to respond to changing circumstances. They bestow ease and comfort on them so as to observe their capacity to avoid wayward and abandoned conduct. When ministers were exposed to the pleasures of music and women, to the privileges and benefits of power, to angry indignation and violent outbursts of fury, and to misfortune and adversity, the ruler observed their capacity not to depart from strict observance of their duties. Since comparing those who genuinely had such abilities with those who truly did not was like comparing black and white, could there be any distortion or perversion of the truth! Accordingly, just as Bole could not be deceived about horses, the gentleman cannot be deceived about men. Such is the way of the intelligent ruler" (Xunzi, Book 12: 12.8c).

Lastly, Xunzi emphasized that the propriety of a system should be measured not by the presence but by the actual use of talents. To him, it is the worst breach of duty on the part of the ruler that able and virtuous persons are found but not assigned to post (Xunzi, Book 6).

Apart from these administrative principles, Xunzi also prescribed rules of interaction in work relationships, especially hierarchical ones in which both parties observe their respective responsibilities and obligations. The legitimacy and effectiveness of these hierarchical rules of conduct ultimately rely on the essential Confucian values of benevolence and righteousness, that is, there will be no propriety in the hierarchical principles of conduct if they are executed without benevolence and righteousness. However, although held as a long-term sustaining foundation, values of benevolence and righteousness were not seen as the precondition of establishing an effective administrative system. This is another indication of how Xunzi departed from the strict and pure moralistic tradition of Confucianism to be closer to more rule-oriented governance.

## Philosophy of the sage-kingship

Xunzi proposed that one cannot rule the world unless one is a sage and only when the most virtuous, wise, and capable are in the authority positions can a society be well governed and prosperous. Nothing is more important than kingship because it is the source from which flows the *Dao* of governance or the rules of proper conduct (Xunzi, Book 12). The *Dao* of governance is therefore the *Dao* of kingship. When asked what state administration is, Xunzi answered, "I have heard about cultivating character, but I have never heard about administering the state" (Xunzi, Book 12: 12.4). It can therefore be argued that in Xunzi's philosophy, governance boils down to kingship, and kingship boils down to self-cultivation, which in turn is the foundation and exemplification of a well-cultivated society. Xunzi's kingship can therefore be analyzed in terms of self-cultivation for individual conduct propriety and social cultivation for institutional propriety.

*Serving as a model of self-cultivation.* As discussed earlier, so far as basic human desires are concerned, there is no difference between the noble- and the small-minded and between the sage and the tyrannical king. What differentiates them is that the sage and the noble attained the highest standards in the self-cultivation process and its results. Self-cultivation requires being methodical, stern and strict with self, resolute in undertakings, adept in applying wisdom, upright, rich with refinement, delighted in others' strengths, and concerned with others' improprieties (Xunzi, Book 8: 8.7). Xunzi further insisted on well-roundedness and character perfection. He argued that just as the sun sheds its light and the earth spreads its width, the noble-minded are supposed to develop in all aspects. The noble-minded know that impurity is imperfect. So they read continually to connect different pieces of knowledge already acquired and ponder to further integrate and synergize the knowledge; they interact with others to learn the way of being a good person, to remove weaknesses, and to cultivate good character. A sage-king and a noble-minded person should hold themselves to the loftiest standards of character and conduct and serve as examples of the core virtues of benevolence, righteousness, conduct propriety, and wisdom.

*Assembling the worthy and the competent.* To Xunzi, social, cultural, and legal principles and norms of propriety could not and would not be effective without those who design, execute, and sustain them. That is the primary responsibility and privilege of the sage-kings. But sage-kings are few and far between and by themselves will not be able to accomplish the task. The sage-king needs a contingent of well-cultivated people as standard-bearers, pace-setters, and exemplars. The key to successful kingship lies therefore in attracting, employing, and assessing the talents of the worthy and the competent according to the administrative principles. Xunzi (Book 16: 16.1) stated that great kingship "exalts ritual principles and honors worthy men [and] stresses law and loves the people."

*Building a culture of conduct propriety.* In his system of conduct propriety, Xunzi put leadership as the source of the system and he focused on the enculturation of individuals and society through the establishment and promotion of norms of conduct propriety. To Xunzi, a society will not survive and prosper without a superior culture and it is the most critical responsibility of the leader to build a successful culture. Culture-building involves the enculturation of core values through models of conduct propriety exemplified in the leader and the leader's core contingent and embodied in the systems of *li* of rituals, of laws and regulations, and of administrative and interpersonal relationships.

Based on moral virtues, the ability to assemble, and success in enculturation, Xunzi classified rulers into four types: true (sage-) kings, protector lords, secure lords, and endangered or perished lords. The first striking distinction is between those who survived and those who perished. The perished ones had no self-cultivation, no ability to assemble, and no institutions of enculturation. However, among those who survived, there are still critical differences between the sage-king and the other two types of surviving lord. The sage-king governs through winning the heart and soul of the people by demonstrating superior virtues, attracting superior talents, and building superior cultural institutions, in addition to possessing superior military and material resources; the protector lord had superiority in attracting talents, building a system of rewards and punishment, and building up military strength internally and externally through alliances; the

secure lord survived through following ordinary measures of governance and attracting ordinary talents. It goes without saying that
the superiority of the sage-king lies primarily in serving as a model
of self-cultivation and building enculturation institutions.

## Historical significance of Xunzi

There has been considerable discussion on the practical significance
of Xunzi's work in his own time and in modern times (Cua, 1992;
Knoblock, 1998, vol. I). Some scholars regard Xunzi as a typical
Confucian theorist but overlook some striking differences between
him, Confucius, and Mencius (Dubs, 1927), while some amplify their
differences by viewing Xunzi as the originator of the Legalist theory
and overlooking the Confucian aspects of his philosophy (Lu, 2003).
We seek to examine Xunzi's leadership philosophy according to how it
was proposed to answer social issues raised at the time. As was discussed at the beginning of this chapter, one of the primary topics of
Xunzi's time was how to provide a theoretical basis and an operational
method for a dynasty to reconstruct order following the disintegration
of moral and ritual orders. Xunzi did it in the following two ways.

### *Inheriting Confucianism and creating a unique school of thought*

Confucianism, with a mission to serve government and politics, has a
tradition of active participation in the reconstruction of social order.
As the last master of Confucianism of pre-Qin times, Xunzi inherited
some key thoughts of his predecessors. Even though he replaces
Mencius' thesis of the "goodness of human nature" with a thesis of
the "evilness of human nature," Xunzi nevertheless endorses the
Confucian virtues of benevolence, righteousness, ritual propriety,
and wisdom and shares the same vision of a virtuous society. Liang
Qi-chao (1925), a Chinese scholar during the period of the late Qing
dynasty and the early Republic of China, comments that Xunzi and
Mencius were both Confucian masters; their political theories lead
to the same result in spite of the minor difference at the beginning.
For example, Xunzi embraced the Confucian proposition that the way
to be a sage-king is to be sage person, what is known as "being a sage
within so as to be an emperor without." In this fundamental aspect,

Confucius, Mencius, and Xunzi develop their theories following one continuous thread, although Xunzi, in our view, significantly enriches and diversifies Confucianism, thus reflecting the complexities and vicissitudes of the times.

Nevertheless, Confucian as he is, Xunzi exhibits some major differences from Confucius and Mencius. Confucius and Mencius stress individuals' innate goodness arguing that individuals' self-conscious endeavors are more important than external forces. In contrast, based on the original evilness of human nature, Xunzi held that people may not willingly and consciously remold themselves. According to followers of Mencius, good governance involves merely extending human conscience and its inherent virtues in order to transform the social chaos and the collapse of conduct propriety. The times that Xunzi lived in, however, denied him the possibility of simply striving for "benevolent administration" as advocated by Mencius. Xunzi therefore draws upon the perspectives of the Legalists and further explicates social and administrative rules and regulations to supplement the moral and ritual governance previously advocated by orthodox Confucians, thus making his theory more relevant and applicable to the reality of his time.

Xunzi contended that people follow propriety rules not because of the self-discovery of some innate conscience but because of the cultural, legal, and administrative systems created by leaders. Hegel, the distinguished German philosopher, was quoted (Marx and Engels, 1972: 233) as saying that "people believe that they express a great idea when they say human nature is good; but they forget that they bring out an even greater idea when they say human nature is evil." The recognition of the evil side of human nature broadens and legitimizes social interventions that include prohibitive and coercive governance measures. For example, while strengthening education and enculturation to foster virtuous outlooks, values, and behaviors, kings and lords can also strengthen the legal system to keep crimes within limits. Xunzi therefore did not merely express "an even greater idea," but brought forward a series of feasible frameworks for governance and leadership. For this,

the thoughts of Xunzi were more influential than those of Mencius in an era of prevalent disorder and universal utilitarianism. This is why Xunzi held a significant position in the emergence of an ideology during the period of the Qin and Han dynasties. Although Mencius transformed the school of Confucianism, and its descendants increasingly rise in their status in the field of ideology in China, making Mencius "the sub-saint" since the Tang and Song dynasties, Xunzi is all the more significant in the ideological transformation and finalization in China from the end of the Warring States Period to the Qin and Han dynasties (Ge, 1999).

## Bridging Confucianism and Legalism

In sharp contrast to orthodox Confucianism the Legalists emphasize law, tactics and power and attach importance to the exterior controlling force of organization and authority. There exists, however, no unbridgeable gap between the courteous and tender Confucianism and severe-looking and iron-handed Legalists. It can be argued that the transition from rituals to law is a natural extension of the social order reconstruction perspective of the time, when both schools of thought are seriously concerned with establishing social order (Ge, 1999). Indeed, both of the seemingly contradictory perspectives were industriously pursued by the rulers of pre-Qin times. Xunzi's injection of Legalistic thinking into Confucianism both reflects and influences governance practices of his times and his impact is obvious throughout the development of Confucianism during the periods of the Han and Tang dynasties. In particular, the ideological propositions by Confucianists Lu Jia and Jia Yi at the advent of the Han dynasty are virtually a direct inheritance and continuation of Xunzi. In both Lu's (1986) drawing on the Daoistic theory of "inaction" and Jia's (1976) development of the thoughts of Shen Buhai and Shangyang, we see the continuation of the theoretical synthesis initiated by Xunzi. This trend reaches perfection and maturity at the hand of Dong Zhong-shu (1985), who eulogized Xunzi and mirrored his political writings. It is safe to say the thoughts of Xunzi on governance and leadership constitute the core and soul of the Chinese traditional socio-political ideology. It is in this sense that Tan Si-tong, a modern Chinese thinker at the end of the Qing dynasty, concludes that "Theoretical thinking in the past two thousand years has been dominated by Xunzi" (Tan, 1981: 337).

## Significance of Xunzi in modern leadership and administration

Besides the great importance of Xunzi's philosophy of leadership and governance in the history of Chinese philosophy, its relevance and significance with regard to leadership theories and practices in modern and contemporary Chinese and Western business organizations should be considered. Much of relevance can be drawn directly from the discussions of the philosophy of human nature and human society. In the following we draw attention to theoretical and practical implications in three major areas: transformational leadership, bureaucracy, and culture-building.

## Sage-kingship and transformational leadership

Xunzi's theory of kingship in the context of reconstructing a new social order should shed light on transformational leadership theories and practices. Both Xunzi's theory of kingship and Western theories of transformational and charismatic leadership place the greatest importance on leadership for organizational success, especially the success of organizational change (e.g. Bass and Avolio, 1994; Conger and Kanungo, 1998). Although Xunzi viewed both character and talents as important for good governance, he clearly put greater emphasis on character, especially for those in higher leadership positions. He insisted that the highest position-holders must be selected and appraised according to the highest standards of moral character and conduct propriety. Such insistence on moral leadership over 2000 years ago turns out to be also the most essential characteristic of Chinese business leadership, especially in Chinese family businesses (Farh and Cheng, 2000; see also this volume, Chapter 6). However, the concept of moral character is not prominent in major transformational leadership theories in the West. If it were, it would save a lot of scandals and demises of organizations led by highly talented CEOs with weak moral character. There clearly needs to be more theory and research on how the character and conduct of top management have a cascading effect on the character and conduct of middle-level managers and rank-and-file employees.

A related striking difference lies in the emphasis by Xunzi on the necessity of the leader being transformed first and foremost, whereas in Western theories, transformation is rarely inwardly of the self, but mostly outwardly for the organization as a whole or downwardly for lower-level organizational members. One component of Western transformational leadership is to subjugate followers' self-interest to the collective interest of the organization. The question Xunzi would ask is of the extent to which the leader's own self-interest has been subjugated and how that affects the effectiveness of the follower transformation (Chen *et al.*, 2007).

## Distinctions, conduct propriety, and Weber's bureaucracy

In reading Xunzi's theory of social distinctions and the ability to assemble, and noting his detailed attention to administrative propriety through division of labor, a clear chain of command, and impartial rules for the allocation of rewards, we are reminded of Weber's theory of bureaucracy, which incorporated Chinese ancient bureaucracy. In his "ideal administrative system of organization," Weber (1947) laid out, among other principles, work division, hierarchy in command, and impersonal administrative rules and regulations. The difference, however, is also striking in that Xunzi, while advocating rational merit-based impartiality, nevertheless insists on maintaining ritualized conduct propriety in accordance to roles and positions. While Weber criticized clanship and excluded personal relationships in an organization for the sake of efficiency and rationality, Xunzi took personal relationships for granted in organizations and sought to establish mutual and reciprocal obligations between managers and subordinates through defining and operationalizing propriety in interpersonal and administrative affairs. In so doing, Xunzi sought to maintain social bonds and harmony in an otherwise impersonal bureaucracy.

## Defining and building organizational culture

The ideal Confucianist society is one that is most humane, and the Way (*Dao*) of humanity is primarily defined and manifested in terms of benevolence, righteousness, and ritual propriety. More noteworthy of Xunzi's theory of kingship, humanity means culturedness resulting from persistent and concerted cultivation, which differentiates not only sage and noble individuals from small-minded ones, but also sage leadership from mediocre or tyrannical styles, and humane, harmonious, and prosperous societies and organizations from those that are merely surviving or in peril. From the logic of the evilness of human nature, culture is by definition humane, hence positive. Negative or dysfunctional cultures as conceived by Western organizational researchers (e.g. Trice and Beyer, 1993) are extensions and manifestations of base, instinctive human nature (which displays a lack of benevolence, righteousness, and conduct propriety).

The paramount responsibility of a leader is therefore one of defining and building an organizational culture under the principles of benevolence, righteousness, and propriety. While these three principles are inherited from teachings of Confucius and Mensius, Xunzi emphasized and perfected the role of propriety and systematically theorizes its function of enculturation. Whereas most Western organizational culture theories regard beliefs and values as the essence of culture (e.g. Schein, 1992), Xunzi's concept of propriety focused on practices as the best markers of culture in the daily mundane organizational life, through rites and ceremonies on one hand and behavioral enactment on the other. Rites and ceremonies are designed to promote and reward people and behaviors that exemplify social and cultural values of the organization. These symbolic (as opposed to financial and material) means of enculturation serve to maintain social distinctions without causing too much social conflict arising from competition for limited material resources. Xunzi's prescriptions of propriety are ultimately behavioral and practical. The role of the leader is not only to display exemplary behaviors for followers to emulate, but also to develop behavior norms and expectations and provide followers with inspiration and guidance in practicing cultural principles in specific and uncertain circumstances. Xunzi's behavioral perspective on culture and enculturation is especially important when organizations increasingly profess homogeneous values that are universally good and virtuous, but lack behavioral and practical import in the real operations of business.

## Conclusion

Xunzi's philosophy of governance and kingship can be summarized as cultural leadership. He inherited the fundamental values of benevolence, righteousness, propriety, and wisdom, but rejected the notion of goodness of human nature, and emphasized and expanded the role of propriety both as a central value and as means of social and cultural cultivation. In doing so, Xunzi bridged major philosophical schools of thought regarding leadership and developed a more dynamic and complex theory of leadership. His major contributions to leadership theories and practices, in addition to enriching the Confucianist philosophy of leadership, lie in his conceptions of the dark side of human nature, in both equalizing and distinguishing leaders and followers in terms of self-cultivation, and in placing culture-building at the center of leadership and providing ways of enculturation through ritual and behavioral propriety.

## Notes

1 All citations of the books of Xunzi refer to Knoblock's (1998) work, which is composed of three volumes, with Books 1–6 in volume I, Books 7–16 in volume II, and Books 17–32 in volume III.
2 There are two different, although identically pronounced (transliterated as *wei*), Chinese characters associated with the concept of human artifice. One has been rendered into English as human activity, conscious activity, conscious exertion, acquired training, or human artifice, and the other as disguise or factitiousness. The common thread of both translations is that these human attributes are not innate in humans, but artificially created after birth. Because of the obvious negative connotation of the latter, the former has generally been preferred to the latter in modern Chinese writing.

## References

Ames, T. A., and Rosemont, H. 1998. *The analects of Confucius: a philosophical translation*. New York: Ballantine.
Bass, B. M., and Avolio, B. J. 1994. *Improving organizational effectiveness through transformational leadership*. Thousand Oaks, CA: Sage.
Chen, C. C., Belkin, L. Y., McNamee, R., and Kurtzberg, T. R. 2007. "In the eyes of the follower: construction of charisma in response to organizational change." *Academy of Management Proceedings*: 1–6.
Conger, J. A., and Kanungo, R. N. 1998. *Charismatic leadership in organizations*. Thousand Oaks, CA: Sage.
Cua, A. S. 1977. "The conceptual aspect of Hsun-Tzu's philosophy of human nature," *Philosophy East and West* 27(4): 373–389.
1978. "The quasi-empirical aspect of Hsun-Tzu's philosophy of human nature," *Philosophy East and West* 28(1): 3–19.
1979. "Dimensions of *li* (propriety): reflections on an aspect of Hsun-Tzu's ethics," *Philosophy East and West* 29(4): 373–394.
1987. "Hsun Tzu and the unity of virtues," *Journal of Chinese Philosophy* 14: 381–400.
1992. "Competence, concern, and the role of paradigmatic individuals: Chun-tzu in moral education," *Philosophy East and West* 42(1): 49–68.
Dong, Z. S. 1985. *Chun qiu fan lu*. (The luxuriant dew of the Spring and Autumn annals). Shanghai: Shanghai Ancient Classics Publisher.

Dubs, H. H. 1927. *Hsuntze: the moulder of ancient Confucianism*. London: Arthur Probsthain.

Farh, J. L., and Cheng, B. S. 2000. "A cultural analysis of paternalistic leadership in Chinese organizations," in J. T. Li, A. S. Tsui, and E. Weldon (eds.), *Management and organizations in the Chinese context*, London: Macmillan, pp. 94–127.

Fung, Y. L. 1966. *A short history of Chinese philosophy* (ed. Derk Bodde). New York: Free Press.

Ge, Z. G. 1999. *Qi shiji qian zhong guo de zhishi, sixiang yu xingyang shijie* (Knowledge, thoughts and beliefs in China before the seventh century). Shanghai: Fudan University Press.

Gerth, H. H., and Mills, C. W. 1946 (eds. and trans.). *From Max Weber: essays in sociology*. New York: Oxford University Press.

Guo, M. R. 1956. *Shi pipang shu* (Ten critiques). Beijing: Science Publications.

Marx, K., and Engels, F. 1972. *Ma Kesi En Gesi xuan ji (Selected works of Marx and Engels)*, vol. III. Beijing: People's Press.

Jia, Y. 1976. *Jia Yi ji, xin shu, xiu zhen* ("Rectification," in New Book in Collections of Jia Yi). Shanghai: Shanghai People's Press.

Knoblock, J. 1998. *Xunzi: a translation and study of the complete works*, 3 vols. Stanford: Stanford University Press.

Lau, D. C. 1953. "Theories of human nature in Mencius and Shyuntzyy," *Bulletin of the School of Oriental and African Studies* 15: 558–570.

Liang, Q. C. 1925. *Shu xue xia, Xun Qinzi tong lun* (Annotation and interpretation of the theory of Xunzi), Jiangdu Wangshi series. Shangai: China Books.

Lu, D. D. 2003. "Shi lun Xunzi zhexue de tezhi ji qi dui rujia Daotong zhi yiy" (On Xunzi's philosophy and its significance in the Confucianist tradition), *Confucian Philosophy* 2: 81–90.

Lu, J. 1986. *Xin yu jiaozhu* (Annotations of Lu Jia's New Discourses). Beijing: China Publisher, pp. 30–36.

Schein, E. H. 1992. *Organizational culture and leadership*. San Francisco: Jossey Bass.

Tan, S. T. 1981. "Renxue: 29" (On Benevolence: 29), in *Collected works by Tan Si-tong*. Beijing: China Press, p. 337.

Trice, H. M., and Beyer, J. M. 1993. *The cultures of work organizations*. Englewood Cliffs, NJ: Prentice Hall.

Weber, M. 1947. *Theory of social and economical organization*, New York: Free Press.

Yang, B. J. 1960. *Mengzi Yi Zhu* (Interpretation of Mencius). Beijing: China Publications.

Zhang, C. Y. 1937. *Mozi Ji Zhu* (Collections of interpretations of Muzi). Beijing: International Books.

# PART II

# Alternative traditional
# Chinese leadership philosophies

# 3 | Daoist leadership: theory and application

## YUEH-TING LEE, AI-GUO HAN, TAMMY K. BYRON, AND HONG-XIA FAN

T HIS CHAPTER is in four parts. First, we address the historical and philosophical context of Daoism (or Taoism). Second, we explore the nature of Daoism. Daoism is a philosophical way to understand human existence and the meaning of the universe in relation to human existence. Third, we demonstrate that a Daoist leadership style is distinctive but useful. One of the philosophy's metaphors is of being like water. An example of the use of this metaphor is the description of a water-like leadership style (with attributes which are known as the Eastern or Daoist leadership Big Five – altruistic, modest, flexible, transparent, and gentle but persistent). Also, leading a big organization is like cooking a tiny fish (*wei wu wei*). Eastern and Western cultures and leadership styles and theories are discussed along with Chinese Daoism. We conclude with practical applications and implications related to Daoist leadership.

## Daoist leadership: theory and application

According to Craig Johnson (1999), a Western scholar of Daoist philosophy, Daoist leadership cannot be divorced from the philosophy's underlying world-view. Leaders may decide to adopt only certain Daoist practices. However, they should first be aware that Daoism is a complex, comprehensive, integrated system of beliefs, not a set of unrelated concepts (see Lee, 2003). Daoism seems to speak most directly to a leader's use of power and position.

Thanks are extended to the late Professor Jim Meindl and to Diane Dreher, Chao Chen, Julie Carlson, and Kan Shi for their helpful comments on various versions of this chapter. Part of this research was funded by the National Institute of Mental Health, the National Institute of Alcohol Abuse and Alcoholism, and the Fogarty International Center (Grant No. NIH AA014842-01) and by a Minnesota State University research grant (Grant No. 211555) given to the first author.

At the outset, two notes are in order. First, throughout this chapter, the standard system of Chinese pronunciation, the Pinyin system, is used for the transliteration of proper nouns from the original Chinese. Those quoted from other sources, however, may have been translated by their original authors using an alternate system. For example, Laozi, Daoism, and *Dao de jing* are used to replace the older Wade-Giles English expressions of Lao-tsu (or Lao-tzu), Taoism and *Tao te ching*. Second, *Dao de jing* is better known and has been translated more often than any other work except the Bible. There are many English versions of Laozi's *Dao de jing*, which may be different from each other in their translations because of the philosophical and linguistic difficulty and complexity of the book. For the purpose of accurately understanding and comprehending Laozi's ideas, this article quotes *Dao de jing* using the translations of Wing (1986) and Shi (1988), which provide readers with both English and Chinese versions. These authors also modified and adjusted their translations when investigating other original versions of Laozi's *Dao de jing* in either modern or classic Chinese (e.g. Fei, 1984; Lao-tzu, 1993; Laozi, 1961). Thus, to the best of our knowledge, the modified translations and quotations below are consistent with Laozi's intentions, as was verified by other research (see also Lee, 1993, 2003).

## The historical and philosophical context of Daoism

We address two issues in this section. First, what is the historical context of Daoism in relation to other philosophies? Second, how is the philosophy of the *Dao* (Daoism or *Dao jia*) different from the worldly religion of the *Dao* (*Dao jiao*)?

To understand and appreciate Daoist ideas of leadership, one must understand two major texts of Daoism, Laozi's *Dao de jing* and *Zhuang zi* (also known as *Nan Hua Jing*; see Li, 1999a). Though Liezi, author of *Wen shi jing* (see Li, 1999b), is also considered an influential Daoist scholar, our focus will be primarily on the work of Laozi who was the pioneer of Chinese Daoism. We will refer to the ideas of Zhuangzi, another famous Chinese philosopher, where necessary.

Next is an issue related to the differentiation between *Dao jia* and *Dao jiao*. Although some concepts or ideas in Daoism had existed long before his time (e.g. shamanism), Laozi has been recognized as the founder or father of Daoism. According to the famous Chinese historian

Sima Qian (145–86 BCE) and recent research (Lee, 1991, 2000; Sima, 1994; Yan, 1999), Laozi was born Li (or Lee) Er (Name of Laozi) around 604 BCE in Ku county of the state of the Chu, which is close to today's Lu Yi of Henan province in the central part of China. Laozi served as the Keeper of Royal Archives for the Zhou dynasty, and, according to Sima Qian, Confucius, traveled from the state of Lu to visit Laozi and seek his advice. After his visit, reflecting on the profoundness of Laozi's talk, Confucius described Laozi's speech to his disciples: "When I met Laozi today, it was like meeting a dragon." In China, a dragon is the most powerful of all species. Meeting Laozi was like meeting the most powerful person of all in the eyes of Confucius.

According to historians, Laozi left his job as the Keeper of Royal Archives in 516 BCE and traveled west to the state of Qin. When he reached the pass of Han Gu Guan leading to the state of Qin, the warden of the pass, Yin Xi, persuaded Laozi to write down his teachings, now known as the book *Dao de jing*. According to Daoist record, Laozi stayed in Lou Guan Tai, which is southwest of today's city of Xi An, the capital city of Shannxi province. Laozi stayed in Lou Guan Tai for some time and passed on his teachings. He then left and continued westward, traveling through the pass of San Guan and entering Shu, which is today's Si Chuan province. Legend holds that it was here that Laozi became hermitical and lived to over a hundred years (i.e. he achieved anonymity and immortality).

According to Laozi's *Dao de jing*, life followed by death is nature's course and man should follow this course calmly. This aspect of *Dao de jing* is known as *Dao jia*. The Daoist School as a religion, or *Dao jiao*, however, was developed much later and focuses on how to avoid death. This, of course, is against nature and Laozi's philosophy. Thus, this chapter focuses only on *Dao jia*, i.e. Daoism as a philosophy or the Way of life.

## Daoist views of general human existence – the way of living

One of the most significant aspects of Daoist views is the role of the universe or general human existence (Dreher, 1991, 1996, 2000). Daoism is a way of life and human existence in relation to the universe rather than simply an ethical or religious way of behaving. We can appreciate it more if we examine the meaning of *Dao*, and the similarities and differences between *Dao*, its influence and development, and other general principles.

## *The meaning of* Dao *(the Way) and* De

Laozi's Daoism has two meanings. One meaning is that human beings must follow natural laws and the way it is. The other is that humans must be very humanistic or humanitarian (or *de*) by following human laws. The former means that humans are in harmony with nature and the latter means that they are in harmony with each other. These are the backbone of Laozi's Daoism.

More specifically, the *Dao* also means a road, a path, the way it is, the way of nature, the Way of Ultimate Reality, the rules/laws of nature. According to Blakney (1955), in the eyes of the Chinese, *Dao* does not only refer to the way the whole world of nature operates, but it also signifies the original undifferentiated Reality from which the universe has evolved. *De* means humanistic behavior/ virtues, character, influence, or moral force. The character *de* has three parts: an ideograph meaning "to go"; another meaning "straight"; and a pictograph meaning "the heart." Together, these imply motivation by inward rectitude (Blakney, 1955: 38; Lee, 2003).

In another translation (Addiss and Lombardo, 1993), *Dao* means a "way" in both literal ("road") and metaphysical ("spiritual path") terms. It can also, more rarely, mean "to say," "to express," or "to tell." According to Burton Watson (Addiss and Lombardo, 1993: xiii), *Dao* literally means a "way" or "path" and is used by other schools of Chinese philosophy to refer to a particular calling or mode of conduct. But in Daoist writing, it has a far more comprehensive meaning, referring rather to a metaphysical first principle that embraces and underlies all being, a vast Oneness that precedes and, in some mysterious manner, generates the endlessly diverse forms of the world. Thus, it is difficult to use language to describe the *Dao* completely. Burton Watson (Addiss and Lombardo, 1993: xiii) defined *de* as the moral virtue or power that one acquires through being in accord with the *Dao* (Lee, 2003).

## *What does the* Dao *follow?*

According to Laozi there is a clear hierarchy or order among humans (*ren*, human beings), earth (*di*, land), heaven (*tian*, sky), nature (*zi ran*), and the *Dao*. Conceptually, as in shamanism (Lee, 2001; Lee and Wang, 2003; Wang, 2000; Xu, 1991; Yuan, 1988), earth is the Mother Nature, or *yin*, and is parallel to heaven, the Father Nature, or *yang*. Another meaning of heaven is the natural world (i.e. *zi ran*) outside individuals (*ren*). Nature can also mean the principle of nature, the way of the universe, or the way of life, including Mother Nature, Father Nature, i.e. anything external to human beings. Being very complicated, the *Dao* is part of nature, follows nature, and produces almost everything in the universe (i.e., the Way), as can be seen throughout the chapters of *Dao de jing*. For example, in Chapter 25, it is held that the way humans act should follow or be consistent with the way earth works (*ren fa di*) whereas the way earth works follows or is consistent with the way heaven works (*di fa tian*). Also, the way heaven works follows or is consistent with the way the *Dao* works (*tian fa dao*), and the way the *Dao* works follows or is consistent with the way nature, or the universe, works (*dao fa zi ran*). In other words,

Humans model themselves on earth,
Earth on heaven,
Heaven on the Way,
And the Way on that which is naturally so.

While Westerners tend to believe that humans are the center of all things or above all things, and that humans can conquer almost everything (see Fung, 1948; Johnson, 1985), Laozi's opinion is that humans should be humble in the face of nature, the universe, or the *Dao*. People should follow the principles of nature and strive to conduct themselves in such ways that their behaviors are in complete harmony with the *Dao*. The Chinese call this optimal state *tian ren he yi*, which means man and external natural world (i.e. *tian*) are united into one. In this sense, Eastern humanism seeks the harmonious integration of human society and nature (see Lee, 2003; Lee, McCauley, and Draguns, 1999; Lee *et al.*, 2003; Tu, 1985) and has no intention to conquer with human ambitions.

## What does the Dao generate?

Unlike many other philosophical schools, Daoism addresses how everything in the world begins and what the meaning of life is for everything. For example,

> The Dao produced the One.
> The One produced the Two.
> The Two produced the Three.
> The Three produced All Things.
> All Things carry Yin and hold to Yang.
> Their blended influence brings Harmony.
>                            (Laozi, Chapter 42)[1]

What did Laozi mean by the One? One which is produced by the *Dao* (or the natural course) means the entire universe. Two means the *yin* and *yang*, and Three means heaven, earth, and humans, which produced all things (Fei, 1984).

After being created, all things in the world have their own cycle of destiny (i.e. life-time or development). For example, it is very natural for a person to be born, to grow up, to become old and senile, and finally to die. As described by Laozi, harmony means a cycle of destiny or change:

> Empty your mind of all thoughts,
> Maintain the deepest harmony.
> Become a part of All Things,
> In this way, I perceive the cycles.
>
> Indeed, things are numerous;
> But each cycle merges with the source.
> Merging with the source is called harmonizing;
> This is known as the cycle of destiny.
>
> The cycle of destiny is called the Absolute;
> Knowing the Absolute is called insight.
> To not know the Absolute
> Is to recklessly become a part of misfortune.
>
> To know the Absolute is to be tolerant.
> What is tolerant becomes impartial;
> What is impartial becomes powerful;
> What is powerful becomes natural;
> What is natural becomes Dao.
>                            (Laozi, Chapter 16)

As can be seen above, the Absolute may also imply regularity or universal laws. Those who comprehend regularity or universal laws are those who understand and appreciate the *Dao*.

## *The* Dao *means change like* yin *and* yang

The *Dao* is not static but dynamic as a universal principle. How does it change? Regarding the *yin–yang* principle, we can read the following in Laozi's book:

> Polarity is the movement of the Dao.
> The receptivity is the way it is used.
> The world and All Things were reproduced from existence.
> Its existence was produced from nonexistence.
> (Laozi, Chapter 40)

In other words, *yin–yang* reasoning is part of the *Dao*, and the constant change and reversal between opposites are the core movements of the *Dao*. When things reach one extreme, a reversal to the other extreme takes place (*wu ji bi fan* in Chinese, or *fan zhe dao zhi dong* in Laozi's Chapter 40), which is similar to a statistical regression. According to *The book of change*, "When the cold goes, the warmth comes; when the warmth goes, the cold comes" (Fung, 1948: 19), and "when the sun has reached its meridian, it declines; when the moon has become full, it wanes" (Fung, 1948: 19). Consistent with Daoism and *The book of change*, Sunzi observed in the *Art of war* in 550 BCE, "The thinking of the wisest leaders lies in considering both pluses and minuses. Think positively of yourself when in difficulty or in crisis; consider your weaknesses when in a strong position" (Sun, 1977: 79). In other words, the *Dao* is not static but dynamic, and it is similar to the *yin–yang* principle described in other Chinese philosophies.

## *Fundamental way of living: other universal values and existence*

Simplicity and altruism (or serving others) are two examples of the fundamental way of living. Human beings should keep life simple and easy and try not to be too selfish. In Chapter 19, Laozi stated, "But be plain, and embrace simplicity and truth; reduce selfishness, and eschew many lusts." Simplicity clears our vision, frees us from false values, and brings greater beauty to human life (Dreher, 1991: 77; Dreher, 2000: 79). Serving others and being altruistic are other general universals of human existence. This is addressed at greater length when we deal with various features of water metaphorically in the following section.

Based on Johnson's (1999) work, individuals who follow the *Dao* (including those who are leaders): (a) exert minimal influence on the lives of followers; (b) encourage followers to take ownership of tasks; (c) employ "soft tactics," such as persuasion, empowerment, modeling, teamwork, collaboration, service; (d) reject the use of violence; (e) demonstrate creativity and flexibility; (f) promote harmony with nature and others; (g) live simply and humbly; (h) reject the trappings of status and promote equality; (i) recognize the underlying spiritual dimension of reality; and (j) give to and serve others. These principles appear to provide an ethical framework for many of the latest trends in the literature: empowerment, teamwork, collaboration, servant leadership, spirituality in the workplace, and rapid innovation.

## Daoism and water-like ("wateristic") leadership style

The most effective way to comprehend Daoism is to focus on a metaphor that links Daoism with water (i.e. water-like, or "wateristic," personality features). For Laozi, the best human qualities reflect the properties of water. We human beings, especially leaders, should learn from water because water always remains in the lowest position and never competes with other things. Instead, water is very helpful and beneficial to all things. Laozi observed that, at that time, human conflict (e.g. fighting, killing, wars) occurred very often. Less conflict might occur if everyone was less likely to compete and go after his or her interest (e.g. moving or fighting for more material, more fame, or higher rank). Thus, if we are altruistic and humble or modest, human conflict might be reduced.

Why is the best like water? In his writings, Laozi used water as a metaphor many times to explain the leadership style of a sage. More specifically, water is altruistic and always serves others; water is modest, flexible, clear, soft, yet powerful (or persistent) (Lee, 2003, 2004).

*First, water is altruistic.* All species and organisms depend on water. Without water, none of them can survive. What does water get from us? Almost nothing. A good Daoist leader should be as altruistic as water. For example, Laozi advocated a "water personality." We, as human beings, including leaders, should learn from water because it always remains in the lowest position and never competes with other things. Indeed, water is very helpful and beneficial to all things.

The highest value (or the best) is like water,
The value in water benefits All Things
And yet it does not contend,
It stays in places that others despise,
And therefore is close to Dao.
(Laozi, Chapter 8)

Daoism recognizes that the ultimate goal of leaders is to serve their people without the desire to gain for personal benefit or to receive gratitude. Laozi stated that "The best are like water, good at benefiting all things without competing for gain" (Laozi, Chapter 8). This entails selflessness as an essential attribute of a leader, which is realized in accepting people's aspirations as one's own. "The sage does not have aspirations but adopts those of the people as his own" (Laozi, Chapter 49). Only when a leader does not have his own ambitions can he truly serve his people instead of competing with them.

*Second, water is very modest and humble.* It always goes to the lowest place. As we can see from the earlier quotation (i.e. Laozi, Chapter 8), although water benefits all things, it does not contend and always stays in the lowest places that others despise. Being humble and modest is necessary for good leaders to appreciate and understand the *Dao* of things, and to always be ready to learn and be alert to overconfidence in the self. While many Westerners often value and enjoy a sense of authority, assertiveness, aggressiveness, and competitiveness, Laozi encouraged people to have a water-like characteristic – that is, to maintain a low profile and to be humble and modest, especially in the face of the *Dao* or nature, and to be very helpful and/or beneficial to others.

To Laozi, modesty or humbleness, willingness to help and benefit others, and the ability to maintain a low profile (just like water) are qualities essential to a leader who wants to influence others:

The rivers and seas lead the hundred streams
Because they are skillful at staying low.
Thus they are able to lead the hundred streams.
(Laozi, Chapter 66)

In Laozi's opinion, those who are humble and modest not only exist in good harmony with others, but are effective leaders, just like the rivers and seas.

The sea, for instance, can govern a hundred rivers because it has mastered being lower. Being humble is important for leaders because it enables them to accept people's goals as their own and to attract and unite people around themselves. Just as the sea accepts and embraces all rivers coming its way – muddy or clear, large or small – leaders who humble themselves before people draw people towards them and gain their trust. This does not belittle leaders, but strengthens them instead. When leaders do not discriminate against those coming their way, they will have people of all abilities around them. When they place themselves below people and praise them for their abilities, leaders will boost the self-esteem and confidence of the people, who will in return be more eager to carry out tasks to their full potentials. That is why Laozi said "He/she who knows how to motivate people acts humble. This is the virtue of no rival and uses the strength of others" (Laozi, Chapter 68).

*Third, water is very adaptable and flexible.* It can stay in a container of any shape. This flexibility and fluidity lends a great deal of wisdom to leadership. Good leaders can adjust themselves to any environment and situation just as water does to a container. Lu Jin Chuan, a contemporary Daoistic master and philosopher, once said that water has no shape but that of the container (Lu, 2001: 280). Maintaining flexibility and adapting to the dynamics of change, like water following its path, are probably the best options for a leader. There is no such thing as the best leadership style or governing method across time and space in the world; rather, the best principle is being flexible and fluid, finding the appropriate way for here and now.

*Fourth, water is transparent and clear.* Effective leaders should be honest and transparent to their followers. The most honorable individuals (not only leaders) are usually honest and transparent like water. Though Western Machiavellian or other deceptive approaches might work temporarily, being honest and transparent is one of the big ethical concerns in modern management. Water itself is very clear and transparent if you do not make it muddy. In Chapter 15, Laozi stated, "Who can (make) the muddy water clear? Let it be still, and it will gradually become clear." Metaphorically, human beings by nature are naïve and honest. Social environment and competition (like muddiness) make them unclear. Water's clarity, transparency, and honesty are much appreciated by Laozi.

*Finally, water is very soft and gentle, but also very persistent and powerful.* If drops of water keep pounding at a rock for years, even the hardest rock will yield to water. Over time, water can cut through the hardest rock, forming valleys and canyons. The style of leaders should be similarly gentle and soft, but also persistent and powerful. Here is an example of what we could learn from water:

> Nothing in the world
> Is as yielding and receptive as water;
> Yet in attacking the firm and inflexible,
> Nothing triumphs so well.
> (Laozi, Chapter 78)

Since there is nothing softer than water, yet nothing better for attacking hard and strong things, there is no substitute for it. Its softness enables it to tolerate all kinds of environments, gathering strength without wearing it off at an earlier stage. And the resolute and perseverance of water help it to cut its path through hard rocks and wear away mountains. It is very important for a leader to know the dialectical relationship as such and to acquire the resolute and persevering characteristics of water.

In summary, water has five features which are essential to all individuals including leaders. This is what we call the Daoist model of "wateristic" personality (Lee, 2003, 2004; Lee *et al.*, 2005; Watts, 1961, 1975) which includes five essential components: altruism, modesty/humility, flexibility, transparency and honesty, and gentleness with perseverance (Lee, 2003, 2004; Lee *et al.*, 2005). This model is summarized in Figure 3.1.

## Leading a big organization is like cooking a tiny fish: *wei wu wei*

As a philosophy of the way of life and beyond, Daoism intends to explain the principles of the universe and to embody all aspects of human existence and experience, including the issue of leadership. Using major principles of Daoism – *zi ran* (to adhere to the principle of nature), *wei wu wei* (practicing active non-action) – Daoist masters or sages like Laozi not only outlined the characteristics of a desirable leader, but also discussed the goals and strategies of assuming leadership roles in many aspects of human activities, from managing state affairs to cultivating the morals and virtues of individual citizens. Therefore, the analysis of Daoist notions about leadership can be a valuable source of information for many.

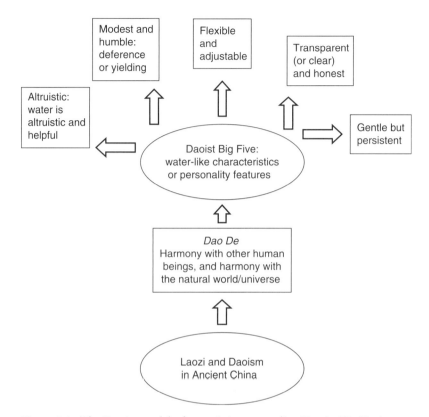

**Figure 3.1.** The Daoist model of wateristic personality (Daoist Big Five).

In the opinion of Laozi and many other Daoists, leaders are those *sheng ren* (or sages or saints) who are actually no more than servants or followers (see Li and Zhu, 2001; Zhu, 1999). The more one serves, the more one leads. Leadership first means follower-ship or service-ship just like water. Second, leadership means non-intrusiveness or non-interference (by practicing *wu wei* or by following natural laws or *Dao*), and it also refers to change, as discussed at length below.

Laozi strongly emphasized the principle of *wei wu wei*, or "spontaneity and the natural way" throughout his book. "*Wei* (follow or do) *Wu-Wei* (without doing or without action; *wu* = not)" adheres to the principle of "noninterference" in the natural course of things or events, allowing things to be or to act within the true nature of the *Dao*. *Wu wei* "flows naturally from the holistic vision of Tao" (Dreher, 1991: 213; Dreher, 2000: 223). For example, if individuals see themselves as part of the larger whole, they cooperate with the rhythms of life. According to Chinese research on leadership (Ge, 1994), *wei wu wei* has three meanings, or principles, with regard to governance or leadership. Principle 1 is "doing something while not doing something else." Principle 2 is noninterference or following a natural course. Principle 3 is symbolic leadership or governance. For example, the following is consistent with Principle 1:

> The Dao never acts,
> And yet is never inactive.
>     (Laozi, Chapter 37)

> To pursue artificial discovering (to learn), add to it daily,
> To pursue the Dao, subtract (interfere less) from it daily
> Subtract and subtract again,
> To arrive at non-action.
> Through non-action nothing is left undone.
>     (Laozi, Chapter 48)

> Act without action; work without effort.
> Taste without savoring.
> Magnify the small; increase the few.
> Repay ill-will with kindness.
> Plan the difficult when it is easy;
> Handle the big where it is small.
> The world's hardest work begins when it is easy;
> The world's largest effort begins where it is small.
> Evolved/Wise Individuals (or Sages/Saints), finally take no
>     great action,
> And in that way the great is achieved.
>     (Laozi, Chapter 63)

As can be seen above, *wei wu wei* does not mean being inert, lazy, or passive. Based on counseling and psychotherapy research (Knoblauch, 1985; Maslow, 1971, 1998; Watts, 1975), noninterference can be helpful and important in certain circumstances. For example, too much care or being too concerned for other people or clients (or things) may lead to too much intervention or control. It is important and necessary that Daoistic leaders be aware that too much action or intervention in the affairs of other humans (or things) may produce opposite or negative outcomes (e.g. in counseling or management). As was discussed previously, man follows earth which follows heaven;

heaven follows the *Dao* which follows nature. This means that we should be natural, and should not intervene too much – *wei wu wei*.

In Chapter 60 of the *Dao de jing*, Laozi wrote, "Leading a large organization or state is like cooking a small fish." In other words, in order to support an organization or state, a leader must follow the *Dao* by "cooking a small fish" appropriately. Just as too much stirring will cause a delicate fish to fall apart, too much interference will unbalance the situation and one's place within it (Wing, 1986). The major concern of leaders is to cultivate the *Dao* in organizational affairs (e.g. adding flavor to the fish and taking care of the temperature and cooking time) and to allow natural forces, the *Dao*, to produce problems and point the way toward solutions by themselves. Cooking a small fish is just an example of *wei wu wei*, which is consistent with Principles 1 and 2 above.

Primarily based on Principle 2, *wei wu wei* means "going with the grain, rolling with the punch, swimming with the current, trimming the sails to the wind, taking the tide at its flood, and stooping to conquer" (Watts, 1975: 75). It is the flow or well-being that allows one to be in harmony with all things or people, which is similar to the Western religious saying, "Letting God be God in you."

*Wei wu wei* (practicing positive inaction) also means letting events take their own course of complying with the forces of nature. There is an excellent example of swimming with the current. Zhuangzi (or Chuang-tzu) illustrated the power of *wei wu wei* in a story in which an old man fell into a great waterfall. By the time rescuers reached him, he had already climbed back onto the bank. When asked how he survived his ordeal, the gentleman replied: "I go down with the swirls and come up with the eddies, following along the way the water goes and never thinking about myself. That is how I can stay afloat" (Johnson, 1999, 2000).

In the physical world many things move and change, but underlying principles remain the same. Therefore, leaders should be able to observe fundamental principles while adapting to change. It is essential for leaders to reconcile between *wu wei er zhi* (doing nothing to interfere with the natural course and things will settle themselves) and *you wei er zhi* (making an effort and things will change with it), two seemingly contradictory approaches that are both present in Laozi's book, *Dao de jing*, which are consistent with Principles 1 and 2.

For example, in Chapter 57 Laozi stated, "When I do nothing, people will transform themselves. When I remain still, people will adjust themselves. When I do nothing, people will prosper themselves. When I do not desire, people will simplify their lives." Here he clearly advocated doing nothing to intervene in leadership style. On the other hand, he emphasized early preventative action (i.e. to be proactive): "It is easy to maintain it while it is peaceful. It is easy to deal with it before it materializes. It is easy to break it while it is fragile. It is easy to disperse it while it is tiny. Take action before it comes into existence and govern before it rebels" (Laozi, Chapter 64). This is consistent with Principle 1. According to Daoism, while too much interference is not good, not taking action when needed is equally problematic.

Consistent with Principle 3 (symbolic leadership or governance), Laozi wrote with regard to *wei wu wei*:

> When the Master governs, the people
> Are hardly aware that he exists.
> Next best is a leader who is loved.
> Next, one who is feared.
> The worst is one who is despised.
>
> If you don't trust the people,
> You make them untrustworthy.
> The Master doesn't talk, he [she] acts.
> When his [her] work is done,
> The people say, "Amazing:
> We did it, all by ourselves!"
>                     (Laozi, Chapter 17)

First, according to research by Ge (1994), a philosopher now in China, "when the Master governs, the people are hardly aware that he is leader." In other words, the leader leads strategically without micro-managing his or her followers, lets his followers do their work, and does not interrupt what they do naturally. The Master here implies *sheng ren* (or sage) whose style is to follow *Dao* or the natural course (noninterference). Second, according to Ge (1994), "next best is a leader who is loved," which means the leader whose style is to follow *de* (leading people based on their needs – i.e. humanistic). Third, "next, one who is feared" which means relying solely on *fa*, that is rules and regulations and punishment. Finally, "the worst is one who is despised" which means the leaders who are not only incompetent, but also do not follow any *Dao*, *de* or *fa*. Thus, their followers despise them. The first of these, *Dao*-based leadership is an example of *wei wu wei* leadership, which is the best (see also Fan and Zhu, 2003; Ge, 1994).

## Applications and implications

### Chinese cases related to Daoism

Here are several examples of Daoistic leadership, management, and conflict resolution. The first case is that of Zhou Gong Dan. About 3200 years ago, Zhou Gong Dan assisted his brother King Wu in defeating the Shang dynasty (Sima, 1994). When King Wu passed away, his son and successor, King Cheng, was too young to rule, so Zhou Gong Dan served as regent. He managed the nation very well, but when King Cheng grew up, Zhou Gong Dan stepped aside and let King Cheng exercise full control of state affairs. In the opinion of Laozi and Kongzi (or Confucius), Zhou Gong Dan was a typical *sheng ren* (or sage or saint) because, just like water, he was humble and served the interest of the nation instead of his own desires or interests (Sima, 1994).

*Wei wu wei*'s Daoism was also followed and practiced in the Han and Tang dynasties (Ai, 1996). About 2000 years ago, China was in chaos after years of warfare. Cao Can, a statesman in the Han dynasty, followed Daoism and let people work for their living without any taxation or without drafting them to any big governmental projects. In the Han dynasty, one of the emperors was Wen Jing. He practiced Daoism so well in his leadership that during his tenure, people were very happy and society was very prosperous. The society was peaceful, and people were happy and well fed. It was called "Wen Jing Days" (Xiong and Yuan, 1999). In the Tang dynasty (about 1400 years ago), Emperor Li Shimin also followed Daoism as the state ideology. He redistributed the land-holdings among the Chinese people and had an "in-kind" system of minor taxation whereby farmers could pay in goods or food. This period is historically called the Happy Days of "Zhen Guan" (the Year of his Governance) in which everything was in harmony and everyone was happy (Wing, 1986). Moreover, Li Shi Ming was very careful about his own behavior as leader. He was open to others' advice and learned from history.

Among his recorded sayings, the best known is, "By using a mirror of brass, you may see to adjust your cap and clothes; by using antiquity as a mirror, you may learn to foresee the rise and fall of empires; and by using others as your mirror, you will learn about your own strengths and weaknesses" (Wing, 1986: 52–53).

Another case is that of Xue Yong Xin and his En Wei Corporation, a Chinese skincare product manufacturer (Xue, 2003). Xue Yong Xin uses Daoism to educate his employees on a weekly basis. Specifically, their slogan is not to compete against other companies, but to serve people by filling the market niche. To serve people, one of their most reputable products is Ji Er Yin which is used as a very effective Chinese medicine to clean skin. Today En Wei is one of China's top twenty private and successful corporations. As CEO of the company, Xue Yong Xin says that both he and the corporation strictly follow Laozi's Daoism (Xue, 2003).

## Burton's case

Daoism can also be used to build a harmonious relationship between a leader and a follower (i.e. conflict resolution). For example, Robert Rosen made a cogent case that twenty-first-century success will belong to CEOs who develop a "global mindset" that goes beyond the limits of any single country's culture or approach. Daoism may challenge people to go beyond "either–or" thinking to achieve "both–and" thinking. The following case is illustrative (Burton, 2000):

An association CEO found herself with a seemingly unsolvable dilemma. Her new president, whose company recently dominated the industry, asked her to do something blatantly unethical: use association funds to pay for travel of his four top Latin American customers to the association's trade show. Her supporters on the board secretly advised her to comply because they felt their businesses would be at risk; the association's attorney advised her to go along – after all, what he was suggesting wasn't "illegal." What to do? She could make a grand stand and lose her job – the president had already subtly threatened her on another occasion – or she could comply but lose her soul. It was a clear either–or dilemma. She chose non-action – first, by deliberately not responding for several days and, second, by meditating on the situation. She stilled her mind; she allowed her outrage to dissolve. An hour later in the meditation, she heard the words, "Turn it on its head." She had it! These four individuals could put on a seminar about trade issues in Latin America. The association needed an international focus: why not start with Latin America? The resulting program was the genesis of a major international initiative. Going beyond either–or thinking (and the self-righteousness that accompanies a "right" and "wrong" approach) and cultivating "non-action" enabled her to act within her ethical limits and develop something new and creative.

From the above case, there are at least two implications from the practice of Daoistic leadership style. First, sometimes it is wise to decide not to act (i.e. positive non-action). Time and patience (i.e. *wei wu wei*) are important characteristics of Daoistic leaders. Second, Western leadership thinking is based on an either–or style while Daoism is holistic, or both–and. The Western approach is that you cannot have it both ways. However, the Daoistic style is that you can have both. Research has shown a difference between the East and West in reasoning styles, which will be illustrated in greater detail in the part that follows.

According to Peng and Nisbett (1999), Western thinking or reasoning is more Aristotelian, while Chinese thinking is more dialectical. Patterns of causal attribution and conflict resolution can vary tremendously from culture to culture (Lee and Seligman, 1997; Nisbett *et al.*, 2001; Takaku, Weiner, and Ohbuchi, 2001). Recent studies by Richard Nisbett and his colleagues (2001) showed that the East Asian view of causality is *holistic*, marked by a tendency to attend to the entire field when making causal attributions. This way of viewing causality has been labeled *dialectical reasoning* (or *yin–yang* thinking as by Lee, 2000). It includes the principles of change, contradiction, and inter-relation based on Chinese Daoism or traditional culture. For example, an unpleasant situation can become a peaceful one (i.e. change); a conflict can be viewed as something positive (i.e. contradiction); and any problem or dilemma involves two parties (i.e. interrelation).

Thus, it is safe to assume that some conflict situations become very difficult to resolve because of a tendency of both parties to perceive victims and wrongdoers as separate entities. They hold that if one is a wrongdoer he or she cannot be anything other than a wrongdoer. The same holds true for their perception of a victim. If both parties involved in a conflict were to follow the principles of Eastern dialectical reasoning, however, these conflict situations could be resolved more easily (Takaku *et al.*, 2003; Takaku, Weiner, and Ohbuchi, 2001). Daoistically, "it takes two to tango," or "one hand cannot clap."

## Leadership based on Theory X, Theory Y vs. Daoistic humanism

Western management theories often neglect the benefits of Daoism. The common Western leadership theory, Theory X, was developed by Douglas McGregor (1960, 1966). It is a traditional management approach that emphasizes control and compliance. Specifically, managers or leaders make a number of assumptions, such as: subordinates or followers dislike work and consequently will avoid it; they do not or will not accept responsibility; they are not ambitious and desire to be led; and they must be closely supervised if organizational goals are to be attained (see also Miller, Catt, and Carlson, 1996: 326–327).

McGregor developed another theory, known as Theory Y. This stresses management or leadership through input, collaboration and delegation. According to Theory Y, people want to work, they are willing to accept responsibilities, and they are ambitious and demonstrate initiative to achieve an objective. People can attain goals with positive motivation.

Based on McGregor's Theory X and Theory Y, William Ouchi (1981) developed Theory Z and Abraham Maslow (1970) developed humanistic or hierarchical need theory. Theory Z, as proposed by Ouchi, combines the best parts of both Japanese and American firms and focuses on sharing, collaboration, trust, teamwork, and inclusive decision-making, which is in line with Daoistic management or leadership. Similarly, Maslow's approach also focuses on human dignity and self-actualization, and was much influenced by Daoism and Native American culture (see Maslow, 1998). According to Lee (2003), Maslow is not only a great humanistic psychologist, but also a great Daoist. In his books *Motivation and personality* (1970) and *The farther reaches of human nature* (1971), Maslow cites the concept Daoism/Daoistic numerous times.

Maslow's being values and perception/cognition are also based on Daoism (Maslow, 1971: 129). Daoistic listening is much appreciated and emphasized in his writing. In one of his bestsellers, *Eupsychian management*, Maslow (1965) expressed displeasure with "the materials on leadership in the management literature" (p. 122) that focus on McGregor's Theory X or Y rather than functional leadership:

The kind of B-leadership [i.e. Being leadership] which would emerge would be the same kind of functional leadership that I saw in the Blackfoot

Indians, or that I see in a group of youngsters who form a basketball team, perhaps, and who have good team spirit and who are not selfish prima donnas. The Blackfoot Indians tended not to have general leaders with general power, for instance, like our President of the United States, but rather had different leaders for different functions. For instance, . . . in any group of hundreds of people, we should not expect that the person who is best suited to arrange the Sun Dance must be exactly the same person who is best suited to be the political representative to the Canadian government . . . Another aspect of B-leadership in the Blackfoot was that the leader had absolutely no power whatsoever that wasn't deliberately and voluntarily given to him *ad hoc* by the particular people in the particular situation. That is to say, he didn't really influence anyone or order anyone around (Maslow, 1965: 123–124).

Maslow's leadership model above is similar to Fiedler's contingency model (1967) that holds that any individual's leadership style is effective only in certain situations. For another, Maslow's eupsychian leadership style is very daoistic or wateristic – it is characterized by refraining from giving orders and having no power (but being modest and gentle). In brief, we can observe direct connections between humanistic psychology and Daoism through Maslow's work.

In summary, Daoism is very complex, and this chapter provides only a preliminary overview of Daoism and Daoistic leadership perspectives, including its historical and philosophical context, its general/universal approach to human existence, the idea of water-like (or wateristic) personality (or leadership style), and the *wei wu wei* approach as well as its application. But what are its implications?

First, rediscovering the meaning of *Dao* and *de* is still useful in management and leadership studies. Times may change, but human nature remains largely unchanged. In fact, Maslow was one of the very few researchers in management and psychology who realized and appreciated the value and significance of Daoism. Though Daoist leadership was briefly touched on by Maslow (1971), mainstream management scientists pay little attention to Maslow's work (see Drucker, 2001: 77), which is a major regret in the field of leadership and management. Reintroducing Laozi and Daoism to the leadership and management field will broaden its research outlook not only in the specific academic discipline, but also in the social and behavioral sciences in general (Lee, 2003).

Second, Daoism may help leaders to lead more effectively and happily in the practical world. Most managers and leaders in the West behave and function on the basis of Western philosophy or religious beliefs. Eastern philosophy or beliefs (e.g. Daoism) may complement what is missing in the West and help managers and leaders function more effectively and with more satisfaction (see also the parables of leadership by Kim and Mauborgne, 1992).

Third, the theoretical research on Daoist leadership here may throw some light on empirical investigations in management science and social and behavioral sciences. For example, much research suggests that leaders who display self-sacrificial altruistic behavior lead their followers more effectively than those without self-sacrificial altruism (Choi and Mai-Dalton, 1998, 1999; van Knippenberg and van Knippenberg, 2005), which is consistent with our Daoist wateristic model. It is hoped that this chapter provides management researchers and scholars with some theoretical ideas to test Daoist perspectives in their future research.

Fourth, studying Daoism theoretically may help us to reduce ecological problems and human conflict. Following *Dao* and *de* may help us to be peaceful and in harmony with Mother Nature and other human beings. In this day and age, the world is like a small village and human issues, such as interpersonal and intergroup/ cultural relationships, ethnic conflict or ethnic cleansing, hate crimes, discrimination against females or minorities, violence against women, and ecological/environmental ones are major concerns for all global citizens. Perhaps Daoism may be useful and valuable to most global citizens, including those leaders who understand and appreciate Laozi's *Dao* and *de*.

Finally, some Chinese scholars and managers are so preoccupied with Western management theories and applications that they have paid little attention to Daoistic leadership style (see the review by Li and Zhu, 2001). Rediscovering and promoting Daoism will not only enhance research in Chinese management but also help to apply Daoism to Chinese management and leadership style in a way that is more effective than the Western Theory X or Theory Y. Because Daoism is part of the Chinese traditional culture and belief systems, it is much easier for Chinese scholars and CEOs to learn, practice, and benefit from it. Besides, Chinese scholars and leaders must develop their own identity in research and its application to leadership. Perhaps Daoistic leadership is one area where they can start. Although this may pose major challenges and difficulties for some Chinese scholars and managers because little has been done in this endeavor, we must begin now to achieve its great promise. As Laozi stated in Chapter 64, "A journey of a thousand miles begins with a single step."

*Note*

1 Throughout this chapter, quotations of Laozi's *Dao de jing* are taken from Wing's (1986) translation.

*References*

Addiss, S., and Lombardo, S. 1993. *Lao-Tzu Tao Te Ching*. (trans.) (introduced by Burton Watson). Indianapolis, IN: Hackett.

Ai, Qi 1996. "Dao jia de wu wei ling dao si xiang" (Ideas of Daoist Wu-Wei leadership), *Leadership Sciences* 5: 43–44.

Blakney, R. B. 1955. *The way of life: Lao Tzu (a new translation of the Tao Te Ching)*. New York: New American Library.

Burton, S. 2000. "The Tao of leadership: beyond action and non-action," www.gwsae.org/ExecutiveUpdate/2000/August/Tao.htm

Choi, Y., and Mai-Dalton, R. R. 1998. "On the leadership function of self-sacrifice," *Leadership Quarterly* 9: 475–501.

1999. "The model of followers' responses to self-sacrificial leadership: an empirical test," *Leadership Quarterly* 10: 397–421.

Dreher, D. 1991. *The Tao of inner peace: a guide to inner and outer peace*. New York: HarperCollins.

1996. *The Tao of personal leadership*. New York: HarperCollins.

2000. *The Tao of inner peace*. New York: Penguin Books.

Drucker, P. 2001. *The essential Drucker*. New York: HarperCollins.

Fan, T. W., and Zhu, Y. X. 2003. "On Taoist managerial psychological thoughts," *Advances in Psychological Sciences* 11(1): 116–119.

Fei, W.-Z. 1984. *Investigating and editing Laozi's Dao De Jing*. Taipei: Meizhi Library Press.

Fiedler, F. 1967. *A theory of leadership effectiveness*. New York: McGraw-Hill.

Fung, Y.-L. 1948. *A short history of Chinese philosophy*. New York: Free Press.

Ge, R. J. 1994. "Dao jia wu wei er zhi de si xiang dui xian dai guan li de qi shi" (Daoist wu-wei's governance helps in modern management), *New Perspective* 4: 51–54.

Hsu, P. S. S. 1981. *Chinese discovery of America*. Hong Kong: Southeast Asian Research Institute.

Johnson, C. E. 1999. "Emerging perspectives in leadership ethics," www.academy.umd.edu/ila/Publications/Proceedings/1999/cjohnson.pdf

2000. "Taoist leadership ethics," *Journal of Leadership Studies* 7(1): 82–91.
Johnson, F. 1985. "The Western concept of self," in A. J. Marsella, G. DeVos, and F. L. K. Hsu (eds.), *Culture and self: Asian and Western perspectives*, New York: Tavistock Publications, pp. 91–138.
Kim, W. C., and Mauborgne, R. A. 1992. "Parables of leadership," *Harvard Business Review* 70: 23–128.
Knoblauch, D. 1985. "Applying Taoist thought to counseling and psychotherapy," *American Mental Health Counselors Association Journal*, Special issues on attitudes toward counseling and mental health in non-Western societies, 7(2): 52–63.
Lao-tzu 1993. *Tao te ching*, introduced by B. Watson, trans. by S. Addiss and S. Lombardo. Indianapolis, IN: Hackett.
Laozi 1961. Laozi's *Dao de jing*. Its notation by Wang Bi in the Jin Dynasty [*c.* 150 CE] and review by Yan Fu in the Qing dynasty [*c.* 1800 CE]. Taipei: Kuang Wen Press (in Chinese).
Lee, Y.-T. 1991. "Psychological theories in Ancient China: a historical view." Paper presented at the 99th Annual Convention of the American Psychological Association, San Francisco.
1993. "Psychology needs no prejudice but the diversity of cultures," *American Psychologist* 48: 1090–1091.
2000. "What is missing on Chinese–Western dialectical reasoning?", *American Psychologist* 55: 1065–1067.
2001. "'Unique' similarities between Ancient Chinese and Native American cultures: paleo-psychological beliefs and cultural meanings beyond time and space." Paper presented at the Annual Conference of the Association of Chinese Social Scientists (in USA) at University of Bridgeport, October 26–27. Bridgeport, CT.
2003. "Daoistic humanism in ancient China: broadening personality and counseling theories in the 21st century," *Journal of Humanistic Psychology* 43(1): 64–85.
2004. "What can chairs learn from Daoistic/Taoistic leadership? An Eastern perspective," *The Department Chair* 4(4): 25–32.
Lee, Y.-T., McCauley, C. R., and Draguns, J. 1999. *Personality and person perception across cultures*. Mahwah, NJ: Lawrence Erlbaum Associates.
Lee, Y.-T., McCauley, C. R., Moghaddam, F., and Worchel, S. 2003. *Psychology of ethnic and cultural conflict: looking through American and global chaos or harmony*. Westport, CT: Greenwood.
Lee, Y.-T., Norasakkunkit, V., Liu, Li, Zhang, J., and Zhou, M. 2005. "Taoist altruism and wateristic personality: East and West." Paper presented at the 34th Annual Conference of the Society for Cross-Cultural Research, February 23–27, Santa Fe, NM.

Lee, Y.-T., and Seligman, M. E. P. 1997. "Are Americans more optimistic than the Chinese?," *Personality and Social Psychology Bulletin* 23: 32–40.

Lee, Y.-T., and Wang, D. 2003. "Aboriginal people in Taiwan, Continental China and the Americas: ethnic inquiry into common root and ancestral connection," in X. B. Li and Z. Pan (eds.), *Taiwan in the Twenty-First Century*, Lehman, MD: University Press of America.

Li, A. G. 1999a. *Zhuangzi's Nan Hua Jing*. Beijing: Chinese Social Press (in Chinese).

    1999b. *Liezi's Wen Shi Jing*. Beijing: Chinese Social Press (in Chinese).

Li, Y., and Zhu, Y. X. 2001. "Ideas of *wu wei* and management and modern values," unpublished manuscript, Jiangsu University.

Lu, J. C. 2001. *Yuan rong de tai ji miao li: Hua sheng, dui dai, liu xing* (Tai ji: a seamless theory about life, relativity, and change). Taipei: Third Nature.

Maslow, A. 1965. *Eupsychian management: a journal*. Homewood, IL: Richard Irwin.

    1970. *Motivation and personality*. New York: Harper & Row.

    1971. *The farther reaches of human nature*. New York: Viking Press.

    1998. *Maslow on management* (with D. C. Stephens and G. Heil). New York: Wiley.

McGregor, D. 1960. *The human side of enterprise*. New York: McGraw-Hill.

    1966. *Leadership and motivation*. Cambridge, MA: MIT Press.

Miller, D. S., Catt, S. E., and Carlson, J. R. 1996. *Fundamentals of management: a framework for excellence*. Minneapolis–St. Paul, MN: West.

Nisbett, R., Peng, K., Choi, I., and Norenzavan, A. 2001. "Culture and systems of thought: holistic versus analytic cognition," *Psychological Review* 108(2): 291–310.

Ouchi, W. 1981. *Theory Z*. Reading, MA: Addison-Wesley.

Peng, K., and Nisbett, R. E. 1999. "Culture, dialectics, and reasoning about contradiction," *American Psychologist* 54: 741–754.

Shi, J. 1988. *Selected readings from famous Chinese philosophers*. Beijing: People's University of China Press.

Sima, Q. 1994. "Shi ji" (original work *c.* 150 BCE), in *Records of the Grand Historian of China*, Yin-Chuan: Ninxia People's Press.

Sun, Tsu 1977. *Sunzi binfa* (The art of war, *c.* 550 BCE). Beijing: China Book Bureau.

Takaku, S., Lee, Y.-T., Weiner, B., and Ohbuchi, K. 2003. *A cross-cultural examination of people's perceptions of apology, responsibility, and justice: The U.S.S. Greenville accident and the EP-3 airplane accident*. Los Angeles: Soka University of America.

Takaku, S., Weiner, B., and Ohbuchi, K. 2001. "A cross-cultural examination of the effects of apology and perspective taking on forgiveness," *Journal of Language and Social Psychology* 20: 144–166.

Tu, W.-M. 1985. "The selfhood and otherness in Confucian thought," in A. J. Marsella, G. DeVos and F. L. K. Hsu (eds.), *Culture and self: Asian and Western perspectives*, New York: Tavistock, pp. 231–251.

van Knippenberg, B., and van Knippenberg, D. 2005. "Leader self-sacrifice and leadership effectiveness: the moderating role of leader prototypicality," *Journal of Applied Psychology* 90(1): 25–37.

Wang, D. Y. 2000. *The times of Shan Huang Wu Di*. Beijing: Chinese Society's Press (in Chinese).

Watts, A. W. 1961. *Psychotherapy East and West*. New York: Pantheon.
    1975. *Tao: the watercourse way*. New York: Pantheon.

Wing, R. L. 1986. *The Tao of power: a translation of the Tao Te Ching by Lao Tzu*. Garden City, NY: Doubleday.

Xiong, L. H., and Yuan, Z. G. 1999. *Laozi and modern management*. Beijing: Xuelin (in Chinese).

Xu, X. Z. 1991. *The origin of the book Shan Hai Jing*. Wuhan: Wuhan (in Chinese).

Xue, Y. X. 2003. "Da Dao Wu Wei," http://dd.sharebook.net/main.htm.

Yan, L.-S. 1999. "Dao De Jing xin li xue sixiang: jingshen jieyue lun" (Psychological ideas in *Dao De Jing*: conservation of psychological energy), *Academic Bulletin of Social Sciences at Hunan Teaching University* 28(1): 116–121.

Yuan, K. 1988. *Chinese History of Mythology*. Shanghai: Shanghai Literature Publishing House (in Chinese).

Zhu, Y. X. 1999. *Chinese management wisdom*. Jiangsu: Suzhou University Press.

# 4 | Leadership theory of Legalism and its function in Confucian society

## KWANG-KUO HWANG

**T**HIS CHAPTER reorganizes Hanfei's theory of leadership from the perspective of social science and explains its implications in contemporary Chinese society. It begins with a brief biography of Hanfei and the origins of his thought. His theory of leadership is then presented as a formal theory and its meanings are explained in terms of modern organizational theories. Based on Hwang's (1995; 2001) analysis of the deep structure of Confucianism, a conceptual framework is proposed to illustrate the dialectical relationship between Hanfei's theory and Confucianism. Finally, operation of the firm and state in Taiwan are used as examples to explain how this conceptual framework may be used to study Chinese organizational behavior.

## Introduction

Among the various Chinese indigenous leadership theories, the importance of Legalism is second only to Confucianism. *Fa Jia* (the Legalist school) emerged during the Warring States Period (403–222 BCE) and its main thoughts were refined against the cultural background of Confucianism, although its contents are in direct opposition to Confucianism in many respects.

During the Han dynasty, Tung Jong-shu (179–104 BCE) proposed integrating the two systems with the idea of "making judicial sentence by the Confucian classic of *Spring and Autumn*"[1] and "utilizing Legalism as an instrument to consolidate the Confucian social system." (Chu, 1961). Rulers of China began to use Legalist methods to defend their power and position and to control people, but retained Confucian doctrine to educate and discipline people. Chinese society became characterized by the feature of "Confucianism in public and Legalism in private." Strictly speaking, there were neither pure Confucian scholars nor pure Legalists after the Han dynasty; their philosophies became mixed to some extent.

This mixture remained while China was in a period of order and prosperity, and the emperor's power was strong and stable. But when Chinese society fell into turmoil and disturbance, struggle between Confucianism and Legalism frequently appeared. Those who got involved in power struggles tended to use related cultural slogans to attack their opponents. For example, during the period of the Cultural Revolution from 1966 to 1976, the Red Guards used the slogan "denounce Confucianism and support Legalism" to mobilize the masses to participate in political struggle.

Hanfei is a representative figure of the Legalist school. He used many idioms and metaphors to explain his principles of organization, which, along with his principles of leadership, are well known to modern Chinese intellectuals. If Hanfei's principles of leadership are reorganized into a formal theory, they are applicable not only to a feudal state but also to a modern organization. Moreover, if Confucianism is conceptualized as the deep structure of Chinese culture, and its dialectic relationships studied with respect to Legalism, greater understanding of the operation of Chinese organizations is possible.

## A brief biography of Hanfei

According to his biography in *Shih ji* (Records of the Historian), Hanfei (280–233 BCE) was a prince from a royal family in the small state of Han during the Warring States Period. The ruling family of Han had formerly been high ministers in the state of Jin, but they gradually usurped power and divided the territory of Jin with two other noble families to create three new states, Han, Jao, and Wei. The domain of Han was small and its territory located in a mountainous area, so they were constantly threatened by their strong neighbors, especially the powerful state of Chin.

Worrying about the dangerous condition of his own native state, Hanfei devoted himself to studying the course of the rise and fall of a state. Because of his stutter, Hanfei was unable to articulate his ideas with eloquence. He repeatedly submitted suggestions to his ruler, but the ruler ignored his advice. So he decided to take another course and wrote them into a book (Liao, 1939–59).

Some of his works were sent to the king of Chin, a young ruler with an ambition to conquer all the country. The king read the chapters and expressed great admiration for them to his minister Li Ssu, a former classmate of Hanfei under Xunzi's tutelage: "If I have a chance to meet this author and make friends with him, I would die without any regrets!"

Li Ssu identified the author and persuaded the king to send troops to launch a fierce attack on Han as a way to meet Hanfei. At the moment of crisis, the ruler of Han dispatched Hanfei as his peace envoy to call on the king in the hope of saving Han from being destroyed.

The king received Hanfei with great delight. But, before Hanfei could earn the full confidence of the king, Li Ssu incriminated him by warning the ruler that, since Hanfei was a prince of the royal family of Han, he would always be loyal to Han against Chin. As Chin had a plan to annex other states including Han, if Hanfei were allowed to return home, he might become a barrier to the plan. The king was persuaded. He ordered officials to arrest Hanfei for investigation. Before the ruler had a chance to regret his decision, Li Ssu sent poison to Hanfei who was confined in prison and unable to communicate with the ruler to defend himself against the accusation of duplicity. Eventually, Hanfei was forced to commit suicide.

## Origins of Hanfei's thought

As a major school of philosophy, *Fa Jia* emerged in a tumultuous and chaotic age in Ancient China. In the earlier Zhou dynasty, the rights and duties of the ruler and his vassals were clearly defined by a feudal system. During the Western Zhou period (1027–771 BCE), the sovereign not only commanded universal allegiance and tribute among his vassals, but also exercised considerable control over their social affairs. He might even punish an offending vassal with armed force. After the Zhou capital was invaded by barbarians in 771 BCE, the ruler fled and established his court at Loyang in the East. The power of the Eastern Zhou dynasty waned rapidly, and the rulers of the feudal states were left with increasing freedom to ignore their customary duties to the sovereign and to expand their territories and domains of power.

Gradually, five powerful feudal leaders emerged. They were eager to influence or even to control the Zhou king and to impose their will on the other feudal lords. Many intellectuals began suggesting ideas to the rulers on how to attain their goals of state. This historical context fostered the formation of the Legalist school. Unlike the Confucians, the Legalists had no interest in preserving or restoring the customs or moral values of the past. Their only goal was to teach the ruler how to survive and prosper in a highly competitive world through various measures of administrative reform, such as strengthening the central government, increasing food production, enforcing military training, and replacing the old aristocracy with a team of bureaucrats.

Hanfei's theory of leadership was formulated in this context. The tragedies of Hanfei's life made him concentrate on understanding the previous Legalist literature and develop a theory of leadership which is scattered in his writing but has been integrated in this chapter by the author. His thoughts were profoundly influenced by several preceding Legalists, including Guan Zhong, Shang Ian, Shen Bu-hai, and Shen Dao. Guan Zhong was a minister of Duke Huan of Chi (685–643 BCE). He suggested the ruler carry out a series of administrative reforms that would enrich the state, strengthen the army and make Chi one of the five hegemons of the time. From Guan Zhong's chapter on *xin-shu* (literally, art of mind) in his book *Guan Zi*,[2] Hanfei adopted the ideas of *xu* (emptiness), *yi* (one mind), and *jin* (calmness).[3] *Xu* means getting rid of one's subjective prejudice to recognize the objective facts of an event with an empty mind. *Yi* means concentrating one's mind on a single thing. *Jin* means waiting for the occurrence of an event with a calm and peaceful mind. Hanfei adopted the doctrine of *xu-yi-er-jin* and argued that it is necessary for an enlightened ruler to cultivate mental capability for recognizing the objective facts of an event by concentrating on them with a calm and peaceful mind and an attitude of waiting.

Shang Ian was originally from Wei. He worked for a minister of Wei, Gong-xuen Tuo, who recommended Shang Ian to the king of Wei, but the ruler rejected the recommendation. He then went to serve Duke Xiao of Chin as a high minister, and helped Chin to carry out a series of reform programs. Hanfei adopted many fundamental concepts of *fa* (law) from Shang Ian's *Book of Lord Shang*.[4] He also noted some shortcomings in Shang Ian's thoughts. In ruling the state of Chin, Shang Ian strongly emphasized the strict control of people by harsh laws, as well as the encouragement of agriculture and aggressive warfare. These policies enriched the state within a short period of time. But he paid less attention to *shu* (the art of manipulation) and was unable to discriminate the cunning ministers from the loyal ones. Thus Chin's reform program enhanced the ministers' power, but it brought few benefits to the state.

Shen Bu-hai was a Legalist who served at the court of Hanfei's native state. Han Fei also critiqued him in that although he taught the ruler how to manipulate subordinates with *shu*, he was careless about the consistency of the law. Eventually there were many contradictions between newly issued rules and old laws, and many people took advantage of the confusion and used it to defend their own misconduct. Hanfei therefore advocated the necessity of both *fa* and *shu*.

From Shen Dao, a Daoist-Legalist philosopher, Hanfei recognized the importance of *shih* (power). He agreed with Shen's viewpoint that for a ruler, power is like claws and teeth for a tiger. If a tiger has no claws or teeth, it cannot catch other animals. By the same token, a ruler without position and power cannot control his subjects.

In addition to these Legalists, Hanfei followed his teacher Xunzi, an eminent Confucian scholar who served as magistrate of Lan-Ling, in adopting the idea that human beings are born evil, in direct opposition to Mencius' theory that men are born good.[5] However, unlike his teacher, he made no attempt to preserve or restore the moral values and ceremonies of the past, and looked upon the fondness for such ceremonies as an indicator of a doomed state.

## Hanfei's theory of leadership

Hanfei argued that all human behaviors are motivated by a ruthless pursuit of self-interest, not by moral values:

A physician will often suck men's wounds clean and hold the bad blood in his mouth, not because he is bound to them by any tie of kinship but because he knows there is profit in it. The carriage maker making carriages hopes that men will grow rich and eminent; the carpenter fashioning coffins hopes that men will die prematurely. It is not that the carriage maker is kindhearted and the carpenter a knave. It is only that if men do not become rich and eminent, the carriages will never sell, and if men do not die, there will be no market for coffins. The carpenter has no feeling of hatred toward others; he merely stands to profit by their death. (Guarding against the interior)[6]

Farming requires a lot of hard work but people will do it because they say, "This way we can get rich." War is a dangerous undertaking but people will take part in it because they say, "This way we can become eminent." (The five vermin)[7]

Hanfei proposed his theory of leadership on the presumption that all human behaviors are based on the pursuit of self-interest.[8] His principles of leadership are reorganized into a formal theory in what follows.

## Shih: *resources for influencing others*

Hanfei's theory of leadership was constructed around three core concepts, namely, *shih* (power), *fa* (law), and *shu* (management technique). According to Hanfei's theory, a ruler has to occupy the position of leader with substantial power (*shih*) before he is able to use law (*fa*) and management techniques (*shu*) to manipulate his subordinates. Therefore, the concept of *shih* is discussed first.

In Hanfei's theory, *shih* is conveyed by the resources controlled by a ruler that can be used to influence subordinates. It is very similar to the Western concept of power. French and Raven (1959) classified power into five categories, namely, legitimate power, reward power, coercive power, information power, and referent power. Hanfei also discussed some of these five forms of power in his own way.

### Position: legitimate power

"Position" (*wei*) can be viewed as a basis of legitimate power which may be exercised by a person who occupies the position through a specified procedure that is recognized as legitimate by members of the group. This form of power was widely emphasized by Chinese philosophers during the period before the Chin dynasty (246–207 BCE). For example, Confucius said, "Don't comment on something that is not one's concern at a particular position."[9] In other words, he implied that only those who occupy a particular position have the right to make certain decisions.

Hanfei elaborated the concept of position power and argued that it is very difficult for a wise man without a high position to display his talents. For example, the sage-philosopher Yao was unable to influence his neighbors before he became king because he had an inferior position, not because he was incompetent. In contrast, when the tyrannical Jie became king, he was able to command the whole country and to entice talented people to do things for him. This was not because of his competence or moral standing, but because of his superior position of influential power. It is crucial for a person to occupy an important position in order for him to be able to display his talent for leadership and command followers to achieve organizational goals.

A man of talent but without positional advantage, cannot, even if he is worthy, control the unworthy. Therefore a foot of timber that is placed on top of a high mountain will overlook a thousand-fathoms deep ravine; it is not that the timber is long but that its position is high. When Jie was the Son of the Heaven he could rule the whole world; it was not that he was worthy, but that his positional advantage was great. When Yao was a commoner he could not make three families behave properly; it was not that he was unworthy, but that his position was low . . . Therefore, a short thing can overlook a tall one because of its position; the unworthy can control the worthy because of his positional advantage. (Achievement and reputation)[10]

### Two handles: reward and punishment

It is unlikely one can influence others merely by occupying a position in an organization. There are many positions without real power. To Hanfei, real power means ability of the position-occupier to utilize tactics of influence by meting out reward and punishment, termed *reward power* and *coercive power,* respectively, by Western psychologists (French and Raven, 1959). Hanfei called them "two handles" and proposed that a ruler has "to hold handles while situated in his position."

The enlightened ruler controls his ministers by means of two handles alone. The two handles are punishment and favor. What do I mean by punishment and favor? To inflict mutilation and death on men is called punishment; to bestow honor and reward is called favor. Those who act as ministers fear the penalties and hope to profit by the rewards. Hence, if the ruler wields his punishments and favors, the ministers will fear his sternness and flock to receive his benefits. (The two handles)[11]

In ancient times in East Asia, the ruler held the absolute power of taking or sparing life, so the power of punishment was defined as the power "to inflict mutilation and death on men." In the modern age of capitalism, the relationship between employee and employer is established on the basis of market exchange, the employer has no absolute power over the employee. Therefore, the meaning of punishment must be redefined in a more humanistic way. Nevertheless, the employer can still utilize the two handles of reward and punishment to manipulate the subordinate's behavior. This principle is very similar to that advocated by scholars who adhere to the Skinnerian school of management, which is applicable to most commercial and industrial organizations.

### Capability

Hanfei did not blindly believe in power. He also emphasized the importance of the ruler's capability as well as the necessity of assigning talented people to the key positions of an organization:

> Is it enough to rule a state by power only without any consideration of the ruler's capability? I don't think so . . . When Jia and Jou were the King, they were able to exercise the power with their prestigious position as Son of the Heaven, but the whole country was unavoidably to fall in great turmoil, because their capabilities were very poor . . . When the power is well exercised by a capable person, the whole country may have prosperity and order; when an incompetent one abuses it, the country may be subject to turmoil and upheaval. (Critique of the doctrine of position)[12]

A leader's capability can be viewed as his expert power, or referent power in the terminology of Western psychology. The preceding quotation indicates that Hanfei advocated compatibility between a leader's capability and his position. When the same position is occupied by persons with different capabilities, the consequences of their ruling practices are likely to be completely different. Therefore, he strongly suggested the ruler appoint capable persons to high-ranking positions in the government:

> If a ruler wants to initiate the useful and to abolish the harmful, but he doesn't know how to assign the talented and capable persons to the key positions, this is a shortcoming in ability to classify people into the right categories. (Critique of the doctrine of position)[13]

If an official is incompetent with respect to his duties, it is a matter of course that the ruler should dismiss him. But, what should be done if the ruler himself is incompetent in a specific domain? The capability to use talents suggests that a leader who lacks expertise in a given area may still have great power if he employs and uses people with expertise. This might be the unique aspect of Hanfei's concept of *shih* in addition to its overlapping with the Western concept of power bases.

## Fa: *rules of regulation*

Hanfei advocated that a ruler with power should manipulate his subordinates by *fa* and *shu*. *Fa* means law or rules of regulation, while *shu* means skills of manipulation that can be used by the ruler to control subordinates to attain organizational goals. Though Hanfei argued that *fa* (law) should be initiated by the ruler, he did not think that a ruler should establish law at his own will. In one of his important works, *The way of the sovereign*, he said:

The Way is the beginning of all beings and the measure of right and wrong. Therefore the enlightened ruler holds fast to the beginning in order to understand the wellspring of all beings, and minds the measure in order to know the source of good and bad. (The way of the sovereign)[14]

Just like other Chinese philosophers of his time, Hanfei believed that the *Dao* (the Way) is the origin and fundamental principle of operation for everything in the universe. An enlightened ruler should realize it and use it as a basis for constructing rules to judge right and wrong. In the chapter called "Achievement and reputation" he argued that an enlightened ruler should follow the natural Way so that his subordinates may regulate their own behavior without external urging. In the chapter entitled "Main thing" he also argued that an enlightened ruler should

construct law in accordance with the *Dao* that gentlemen are happy with it and evil persons are prohibited by it. He should follow the order of heaven and insist on the fundamental principle of nature with an easy and relaxed attitude, so as to let people never commit crime by violating the law on purpose. (The principal features of Legalism)[15]

In a society of permanent stability, the law has been constituted in such a natural way that nobody is dissatisfied with it or complains about it. (The principal features of Legalism)[16]

It is quite obvious that Hanfei supported natural law established with the consensus of all group members. His concept of following "the order of heaven," "the fundamental principle of nature," or "the natural Way" means that a leader has to study the principles of operation in the state carefully and use them as the foundation for constituting rules. Because all rules are constituted on the basis of the equity rule, or *gong-dao*, people are willing to follow them without complaint. Thus, "the superior never express malicious anger, and the subordinates have no hidden dissatisfactions in their minds" so that "the superior and the subordinates may interact smoothly" and the state may acquire "long-term profits." (The principal features of Legalism)[17]

Hanfei said that "law is used for regulating ordinary operation" of a state. It must be characterized by several important features which are organized and explained in the following subsections.

## Publicity

Law is the standard of behavior for people of a state, so it must be publicized and made known to everybody.

Law should be edited as charts or records, established by the governmental office, and publicized to the people. (Criticisms of the ancients, series three)[18]

"Law should be edited as charts or records" means that Hanfei advocated statutes that are constant over time. They must be publicized to let the masses in the state know of them. He even advocated that "law should be used as teaching materials" and "officials should serve as teachers." Officials should be able to teach and to explain details of the law to the people, and make them understand the importance of following the law.

## Objectivity

According to Hanfei, laws must be objective and fair to everybody. They must be consistent with the *gong-dao* or principle of fairness, and can be used as standards of behavior for the masses, with intellectuals enjoying no special privileges.

Unifying the standards of the people, nothing can compare to law. (Having regulations)[19]

He argued that the main purpose for establishing law is to eliminate private interest.

If the superior is unable to insist on *gong-dao* (the principle of fairness), then the intellectuals may propose their biased arguments, the wise men may strive for their personal gain, the superior may do favors privately, and the inferior may struggle for their own selfish desires. [Eventually,] the intellectuals may form their own cliques to create rumors and to incite incidents (Absurd encouragements)[20]

and the whole organization may suffer from a crisis of struggle between cliques and factions.

### Feasibility
Laws and regulations should be feasible and possible for people of the state to carry out:

The enlightened ruler provides rewards that are achievable and establishes punishments that are avoidable. His charts are obvious to see, so his restraint works; his teachings are clear to know, so his words are followed; his laws are easy to practice, so his orders are obeyed. If the superior insists on these three things without any selfish motive, than the subordinates will be ruled by the law and act in accordance with the instruction of charts . . . By doing so, the superior will never show any cruelty or anger, and the subordinates will never be punished for their ignorance or stupidity. (How to use men)[21]

Rules in an organization must be so simple and feasible that they can be carried out by everybody in order to achieve rewards and avoid punishment. It is absolutely not proper to use a complicated doctrine that cannot be understood easily by ordinary people as the basis of law:

Doctrines that only the wise men can understand should not be used as a basis for official order, because people are not all wise men. Disciplines that only the talents can practice should not be used as a part of law, because people are not all talents. (Eight fallacies)[22]

### Enforceability
Once the law is announced, it must be compulsory. Behaviors of obeying or disobeying the law must be followed by reward or punishment:

The best laws are those which are uniform and inflexible. (The five vermin)[23]

Rewards should be reliable to encourage the talents to do their best; punishment should be certain to inhibit the wicked from their evils. (Outer congeries of sayings, the upper left series)[24]

If rewards and punishments are not reliable, then the order of inhibition will never be followed. (The two handles)[25]

Theoretically, the rules should be the most appropriate procedures for regular operations in the state and are designed to achieve goals of the state. Behaviors that make substantial contributions to the achievement of national goals should be reinforced with reward, while those that are detrimental should be met with punishment. These principles exactly reflect what Hanfei meant when he wrote that a ruler should use two handles to manipulate subordinates to achieve goals of the state.

## Universality

In contrast to the Confucian idea that penalties should not be applied to high officials of state, and rites should not be used by ordinary people (Li Chi, Chu Li),[26] Hanfei argued that once the law was announced, it should be applicable to everybody in the state without any exceptions:

The law no more makes exceptions for men of high position than the plumb line bends to accommodate a crooked place in the wood. What the law has decreed the wise man cannot dispute nor the brave man venture to contest. When faults are to be punished, the highest minister cannot escape, when good is to be rewarded, the lowest peasant must not be passed over. (Having regulations)[27]

This passage invites the question of what happens if the faults are those of the ruler who is author of the law and holds the absolute power of the state? Hanfei's works provided no answer to this question. However, he did insist that the ruler should also follow the law in dealing with the public affairs of the state:

Even though the ruler is intelligent and competent, he should not be tyrannical and disregard the law in commanding his ministers. (Facing the south)[28]

The way of an enlightened ruler makes clear distinction between private and public, emphasizes the priority of ruling by law, and eliminates the practice of doing private favor. (On pretensions and heresies: a memorial)[29]

The ruler should also evaluate subordinates' performance with reference to standards as defined by the rules instead of according to subjective impressions. If the leader tends to distort rules and damage public affairs through personal interest, it is very likely the state will be drawn into crisis.

## Practicability

In addition to these features, rules should be practicable. Whenever they are found impracticable, they should be revised with reference to the real situation to make them appropriate and practicable. Hanfei said:

The tasks to be accomplished will change when the world changes, so the method for doing the task should be changed as a result. (Surmising the mentality of the people)[30]

In order to secure peace and order of state, the law has to be adjusted to fit the changes of time; in order to achieve extraordinary merits, the regulation has to be modified to fit conditions of the world. (Surmising the mentality of the people)[31]

It seems to Hanfei that law is just an instrument or method for solving problems to achieve goals of the state. Because the external environment of a state changes from time to time, the methods or procedures for doing tasks in the state must also be adjusted accordingly.

The kingdom may fall into a state of chaos, if the rules of regulation cannot be adjusted to the changes of time; the power of a leader may be weakened if he attempts to control his subordinates by himself without modification of the regulations. (Surmising the mentality of the people)[32]

## Shu: *art of manipulation*

Based on this concept of *fa*, Hanfei proposed three main techniques, defined as *shu*, for a ruler to manipulate subordinates:

*Shu* means assigning the competent talents to right positions of the government, checking results of performance with what had been stated in their proposals, controlling the power of sparing and killing to evaluate competencies of ministers. Those should be held by a ruler. (Deciding between two legalistic doctrines)[33]

These three *shu* are discussed in the following subsections.

### Assigning competent talent to the right position

In his chapter "How to use men" Hanfei wrote a paragraph to describe his main ideas about assigning competent talent to the right position:

The minister of an enlightened government occupies a position for his contribution to the state; gets appointment for his talents to serve the government; assumes his office for his ability in making judgments. All ministers have appropriate talents, are competent in their positions, and can carry out their duties easily. They need neither to worry about second jobs nor to assume responsibility for dual duties to the ruler. An enlightened ruler ensures the responsibilities of each office do not overlap with those of another, so there is no argument; does not make officials responsible for two or more jobs, so they are specialized in their skills; makes everybody have his own responsibility, so there is no conflict. (How to use men)[34]

The conflicts and arguments are ceased, every official has his own specialized skills, then there is no confrontation between the strong and the weak, and there will be no infighting between those in the government. This is the best state of regulation. (How to use men)[35]

The operations of bureaucratic officialdom are designed to accomplish routine tasks. In addition to routine tasks, the changing environment may cause a state to encounter many new problems that demand action to solve them. In this case, Hanfei suggested the ruler use another *shu* in supervising subordinates to solve the problem and achieve the national goal.

### Following up the project and checking the results

Han Fei emphasized that a state is destined to face many problems in pursuing its goals. A leader has to ask subordinates to propose their projects for problem-solving, while the leader's own job is to follow up the project and check its effectiveness.

All words must be evaluated by their effectiveness to attain goals. Listening to subordinates' words and observing their deeds, if they have nothing to do with the effectiveness of attaining goals, though their words are sound and deeds are firmly determined, they are all wild speeches and useless acts. (Inquiring into the origin of dialectic)[36]

Hanfei was a utilitarianist. He strongly suggested that in examining subordinates' words and conduct, the first thing for a leader to consider is their effectiveness in attaining goals of the state. Eloquent speeches and high-minded deeds that make no substantial contribution to the attainment of national goals are useless and should not be encouraged. He advocated that:

Listening to a subordinate's words, an enlightened ruler will ask for their usefulness; Observing the subordinate's deeds, he will ask for their effectiveness. (Six contrarieties)[37]

If the ruler of men wishes to put an end to evil-doing, then he must be careful to match up names and results, that is to say, words and deeds. The ministers come forward to present their proposal; the ruler assigns them tasks on the basis of their words, and then concentrates on demanding the accomplishment of the task. If the accomplishment fits the task, and the task fits the words, then he bestows reward; but if they do not match, he doles out punishment. (The two handles)[38]

Hanfei's proposal is a kind of project management: names (_ming_) or words (_yan_) can be conceived of as a project, while results (_xing_) or tasks (_shi_) are the final results of executing the project. The idea of examining the match between names and results (_shen he xing ming_) is exactly the same as the idea of project management. The leader asks the staff to propose a project. Once the project has been approved by the leader, the staff are authorized to execute the project, and the leader checks the match between the project's goals and the final results of its execution.

### Evaluating contributions and granting rewards accordingly

As a consequence of checking the match between names and results, or words and deeds, the most important step for a leader in manipulating subordinates is to evaluate their contributions and grant rewards accordingly. The leader should establish an objective standard for evaluating subordinates' performance. If there is a match between performance and proposal, that is if the names and results correspond or if the words fit the deeds, the subordinate should be rewarded; otherwise, the subordinate should be punished. Only those who make substantial contributions to attainment of national goals should be eligible to be promoted to higher positions in the government:

A truly enlightened ruler uses the law to select people for him; he does not choose them himself. He uses the law to weigh their merits; he does not attempt to judge them for himself. Hence men of true worth will not be able to hide their talents, nor spoilers to gloss over their faults. Men cannot advance on the basis of praise alone, nor be driven from court by calumny. Then there will be a clear understanding of values between the ruler and his ministers, and the state can be easily governed. (Having regulations)[39]

Being servants of an enlightened ruler, a prime minister is selected from local officials, while commanders are promoted from soldiers. Because men of merit always win recognition, the higher one's degree of nobility is, the greater one's effort will be. Only officials with achievement are promoted;

the higher one's position is, the better one's performance will be. Matching the degree of nobility with the official's contribution, this is exactly the great Way of the king. (Learned celebrities)[40]

## Confucian cultural tradition

Hanfei's theory of leadership has been presented in the previous section. Traditional Chinese society was organized on the basis of Confucian ethics rather than Legalist principles. The struggle between Confucianism and Legalism occurred many times at the state level in Chinese history, and it may continue to happen either at the state level or at the firm level in the future. As a social psychologist, my major interest is the effect of cultural tradition on the daily operation of individuals in modern Chinese society. In order to explicate the relation of Legalism to modern life, an analysis of Confucian cultural tradition is presented, followed by a conceptual framework to expound the essential nature of the struggle between Confucianism and Legalism from the perspective of social science. Finally, social change in Taiwan after World War II is taken as an example to illustrate the meaning of the struggle between Confucianism and Legalism in understanding the operation of Chinese society.

Confucianism was the traditional orthodox ideology formulated in Ancient China. In order to understand the emergence of the antithetic Legalism, it is necessary to study the possible influence of Confucianism on Chinese social behavior. I first constructed a theoretical model of Face and Favor on the basis of scientific realism (Hwang, 1987). Using it as a framework, I analyzed the deep structure of Confucianism by the method of structuralism (Hwang, 1995; 2001). According to this analysis, the deep structure of Confucianism has three major components: (1) *rendao*, (2) self-cultivation with the *Dao*, and (3) benefiting the world with the *Dao* (Hwang, 2001).

## Rendao: *ethics for ordinary people*

The essential component of Confucianism is the *ren-yi-li* (benevolence–righteousness–propriety) ethical system, with the cardinal idea being *ren*, which is generally called *rendao*. This ethical system requires everybody to interact with the other party in each dyad of the "five cardinal relations"[41] according to different standards of conduct. It proposes a principle of respecting superiors as the guideline for procedural justice. This advocates that the individual who occupies the higher position among interacting parties should have the power to make decisions. It also proposes a principle of favoring intimates as the formula for distributive justice. This principle demands the decision-maker distribute resources on the basis of *rendao*, i.e. should adopt the need rule for interacting with family members, and the *renqing* (affective) rule for interacting with acquaintances in his network of *guanxi* (relationships) outside the family (Figure 4.1). The principles of favoring the intimate and respecting the superior are Confucian ethical requirements for everybody, so they can be termed "ethics for ordinary people." The practice of such ethics is elaborated in the following subsections.

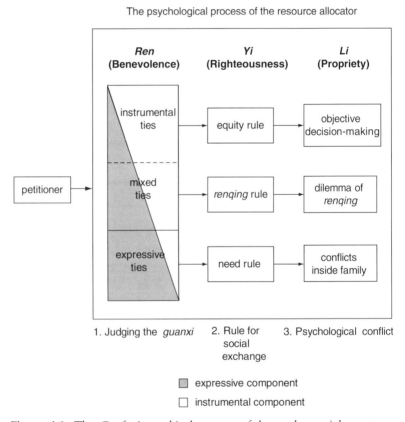

The psychological process of the resource allocator

**Figure 4.1.** The Confucian ethical system of benevolence–righteousness–propriety for ordinary people.

*Source:* Adapted from Hwang (1995: 233).

## Familism

The Confucian view assumes that one's life is inherited from one's parents as well as one's ancestors, and that the lives of one's offspring are continuous with one's own life, so the family is viewed as an inseparable entity. This is the cardinal component of the ideology of East Asian familism, which is dramatically different from the individualism of Western culture originating from Christianity. In traditional Chinese society, the family is the fundamental social unit with a very tight structure, emphasizing the hierarchical order of seniority, age, and sex (Cheng, 1944; Hsu, 1967). It satisfies its members by serving such functions as production, education, recreation, and religion (Lang, 1946; Winch, 1966). As Chinese society has gradually transformed from an agricultural society of mechanical solidarity to an industrial/commercial one of organic solidarity (Durkheim, 1984 [1933]), the Chinese family system has experienced drastic changes. Family size has shrunk, the power distance between the dyadic roles in the family has decreased, and many functions of the family have been replaced by those of other social institutions. Nevertheless, most Chinese still have a strong affective attachment to their families (Yang, 1988). The family is still highly valued and viewed as an inseparable entity, and Chinese still tend to interact with their family members according to the need rule.

## *Guanxi* network

In addition to familism, Confucianism also includes a social philosophy encouraging individuals to maintain harmonious relationships with people outside their own families. Viewed from the conceptual framework of Face and Favor, when individuals interact with relatives, friends, or acquaintances within the network of *guanxi*, they must be polite and hospitable. According to the rule of *renqing*, when an acquaintance encounters difficulties, one must behave as considerately as possible and do favors for him as far as possible. By the same token, when individuals receive favors from acquaintances, they must remember to try to reciprocate.

The operation of a *guanxi* network might be either beneficial or harmful to the operation of a firm or a state, depending on the nature of resources involved in the *renqing* event. A leader may utilize *guanxi* to solve many problems; in contrast, the *guanxi* network may become a breeding-ground for nepotism, factionalism, and cliquism in an institution.

## *Self-cultivation with the* Dao

Because Confucians believe that the way of humanity (*rendao*) corresponds with the way of heaven (*tiendao*), it is one's obligation to cultivate oneself with the *Dao*. Therefore, one must learn *rendao* with diligence and practice it with effort. When conduct deviates from the principle of *rendao*, one should feel shame.

Since the examination system for the Civil Service was abolished during the Qing dynasty in 1905, Confucian classics have been replaced by Western science and knowledge as the major subjects of education in schools. As a consequence, many Chinese youths may transfer their enthusiasm for pursuing metaphysical *Dao* to a particular system of knowledge about the physical world, and learn a particular technology, science, or social science by the traditional practice of self-cultivation. This is a way by which the Confucian cultural tradition may possibly contribute to the modernization of East Asian societies.

## *Benefiting the world with the* Dao: ethics for scholars

In addition to the *ren-yi-li* ethical system for ordinary people, Confucianism confers upon intellectuals (scholars) a mission to benefit the world by the *Dao* with which they have identified. The larger the group one has benefited, the greater the moral merit one attains. This can be termed "ethics for scholars."

When a Chinese society is transformed from an agricultural into an industrial/commercial one, Confucian ethics for scholars may encourage intellectuals to identify a particular system of knowledge originating from the West as their *Dao* (way), to work in a firm or a governmental institution, and to utilize their knowledge, which may eventually benefit that firm or the whole of society.

## Struggle between Confucianism and Legalism in Chinese society

As discussed earlier in this chapter, Legalism is essentially an organizational theory formulated in the authoritarian culture of Ancient China. It has been used by many rulers in Chinese history to consolidate their power, but it can also be used by managers of organizations in contemporary society. Legalist ways of organization are akin to Western ideas of bureaucracy that became widespread after the Renaissance.

The cultural traditions of Confucianism emphasizing the values of benevolence and affection (*qing*), and especially ethics for ordinary people, are constantly in conflict with those of Legalism, which might result in dialectical dispute over political, social, or cultural issues between centripetal and centrifugal elites in the societal center. This constitutes the so-called struggle between Confucianism and Legalism in Chinese history, and decision-makers in power are frequently urged to make a choice between the *renqing* rule and the equity rule. Even in contemporary Chinese society, the struggle between these two value systems is repeated, and may have direct or indirect influence on the operation of a firm or a state.

## A conceptual scheme

In order to elucidate the essential nature of the struggle between Confucianism and Legalism, I have proposed a conceptual scheme to compare five crucial aspects of these two schools of thought (Hwang, 1995): value orientations, norms for regulating social behavior, rules for distributing resources, input factors determining the distribution of resources, and the authority who makes decisions (Table 4.1). Confucianism advocates a kind of status ethics. It has differing expectations of scholars and ordinary people. For ordinary people, it is enough to practice the *ren-yi-li* ethical system within the domain of one's family and acquaintances. The guiding principle for their social organization is familism, the social norm for regulating social behavior is *li* (politeness), and the decision-maker who holds the power of distributing resources within the family is the paterfamilias. When allocating resources to others, the first thing to consider is the blood relation with the recipient. Resources are frequently allocated according to the need rule.

Confucianism sets a completely different expectation for scholars. It expects scholars to benefit the world with the *Dao*, and requires them to extend the domain for practicing *rendao* from the individual and family to the greater society; the bigger one's domain for practicing *rendao*, the greater the moral achievement. While the ideal goal of Confucianism is to attain a peaceful, harmonious world,

Table 4.1. *A comparison between five major aspects of Confucianism and Legalism.*

|  | Confucianism | | Legalism |
|  | Ethics for ordinary people | Ethics for scholars |  |
|---|---|---|---|
| 1. Value orientation | Familism | Collectivism | Individualism and collectivism |
| 2. Social norm | Particular *li* (courtesy) | Universal *ren* (benevolence) | Universal law (*fa*) |
| 3. Distributive rule | Need rule | Equality rule | Equity rule |
| 4. Criteria for distribution | Blood relationship | Membership | Contribution |
| 5. Decision-maker | Paterfamilias | Elite (scholar-official) | Ruler |

*Source:* Adapted from Hwang (1995: 26).

what a scholar can really do is to actualize *rendao* in a community or social organization larger than the family. Therefore the value orientation of scholarly social behavior can be termed collectivism. According to the Confucian ethics for scholars, the norm for social acts in such a collectivity should be *ren*, all important resources of the group should be allocated according to the equality rule by morally educated scholars, and every member of the group is entitled to an equal share.

As stated in the previous section, when a Legalist leader is assessing how to allocate rewards and punishments to subordinates, contributions to the accomplishment of organizational goals, rather than blood relationships or group memberships should be considered. Therefore the guiding rule for their social acts comprises both individualism and collectivism. By recognizing the legitimacy of individual interests and by advocating the universality of legal applications, Legalists are individualists. However, Legalists are collectivistic in the sense that they give priority to organizational and national goals rather than to familism and factionism. A delicate combination of parts of both the Confucian and Legalist traditions was created and maintained in the feudalistic society of Imperial China for hundreds of years.

## The Cultural Revolution

After the Communists took over China in 1949, they began to strive to replace Confucianism with the ideology of Marxism. During the Great Leap Forward beginning in 1958, most families were reorganized into self-sufficient communes on the principle of egalitarianism in the hope that people would transfer their loyalty from the family to the state (Merchant, 1975; Robottom, 1969). During the Cultural Revolution from 1966 to 1976, the Communists proposed the slogan: "denounce Confucianism and raise Legalism." People were required to follow the precepts of Marxism, and every act had to be in accordance with the teachings of Chairman Mao Zedong.

The Communists claimed that the nature of these movements was the struggle between Confucianism and Legalism or the struggle between communism and capitalism (Chiou, 1974; Ditter, 1974; MacFarquhar, 1974). But, if these movements are examined with reference to the conceptual scheme in Table 4.1, it can be seen that in fact they are struggles between Confucian ethics for ordinary people and those for scholars. The Communists attempted to replace the Chinese family system with the new organization of communes, where communist cadres played the role of traditional scholar-officials in promoting production by advocating the orthodox ideology of Marxism and allocating all important resources to members of the commune in an equal way (Callis, 1959). Viewed from the perspective of Chinese culture, all these efforts can be said to be attempts to replace the Confucian ethics for ordinary people with those for scholars, or to transform loyalty to family and personal *guanxi* into loyalty to the state and the Party. The Great Leap Forward and the Cultural Revolution proved to be monumental failures: economic productivity declined to an abysmal level, and countless people suffered starvation during these years (Merchant, 1975; Robottom, 1969).

## The struggle between Confucianism and Legalism in Taiwan

When a Chinese state decides to adopt a capitalistic route of economic development and the society gradually transforms from agricultural to industrial/commercial, it is progressing toward a Legalist society as described in Table 4.1. During the process of transformation, it will encounter genuine struggle between Confucianism and Legalism at both the state and firm levels, which may influence the operation of the firm as well as the state as a whole. In an industrial/commercial society of organic solidarity, any conflict or struggle occurring at the societal center may interactively influence the operation of a firm at the periphery (Eisenstadt, 1966). The Taiwanese experience of development is an example. A brief history of Taiwan after the end of World War II is first provided. The lifting of martial law in 1986 is taken as the turning point when Taiwan transformed from a traditional society to a modern one. The nature and influence of the struggles occurring at the societal center and subcenters is discussed.

It is generally agreed that modernization for most Asian countries is essentially a process of exogenous change originating from outside and transmitted to the inside, from the top down, which is different from the endogenous modernization of Christian countries (Bellah, 1970; Eisenstadt, 1966). At the end of the nineteenth century, many Asian intellectuals went abroad to study Western science and technology for production and ways of management. After finishing their study abroad, many of them returned home with the mission of contributing what they had learned abroad to help modernize their home countries.

When an Asian state decides to adopt the capitalistic route of national development, the societal center must make every effort to construct economic and legal systems with a high degree of formal rationality to encourage entrepreneurs to pursue benefit by investing in it and creating organizations to make products to meet the demands of the market. Ideally speaking, both systems should be designed to create a socio-cultural milieu with the characteristics of the Legalistic tradition as described in Table 4.1. In other words, the story of East Asian modernization can be aptly illustrated by an analogy. The capitalistic legal system for economic development is akin to a railroad. The science and technology imported from the West are a locomotive, and the Confucian tradition for achieving performance by diligent work is the fuel driving the engine (Hwang, 1995). The combination of these three factors results in economic development in East Asian countries. The political leaders in power decide to create favorable conditions at the state level, while entrepreneurs make efforts to combine all the subsidiary factors for raising production at the organizational level (Redding, 1988, 1990).

## The Taiwanese experience, 1945–1986

After being liberated from Japan's control in 1945, the Nationalists from China occupied Taiwan and soon held the most important positions in Taiwan's societal center. As an extension of the civil war in China, corruption and incompetence in the Nationalist government resulted in a worsening economy and the Nationalists were bitterly blamed by the local people. The sharp contradiction between the political center and the centrifugal periphery eventually resulted in a large-scale revolt in February 1946, which was suppressed with military force by the Nationalists (Kerr, 1965). After that, the island was controlled by a group of political elites who were mostly from China. They claimed to be the orthodox regime representing the whole of China, took advantage of the Korean War (1950–1953) to obtain aid from the USA, and kept a seat in the United Nations with the assistance of the USA and its allies. Meanwhile, they proclaimed martial law in the name of defending Taiwan against invasion from Communist China, which enabled them to maintain a majority of seats in the people's representative bodies at the societal center without reelections for decades. Only a very few centripetal Taiwanese elites were admitted to the political center or positions in local government. Those centrifugal elites who held a differing ideology were viewed as heterodox and excluded from the societal center.

During this period, the Nationalists had absolute control over the politics of Taiwan, and initiated a revolution from above in the social and economic domains (Gold, 1986). Based on the Principle of the People's Livelihood, they implemented the "375 Rent Reduction Program" and the "Land-to-the-Tiller Program" to reorganize the farm economy structure toward the equalization of landholding and a small-scale farming system (Chen, 1961). Economic investment at that time was aimed at repairing the serious damage caused by the bombing by Allied air forces during World War II and at satisfying the demands of the domestic market. By the end of the 1950s, manufacturing growth for light industrial products was slowing down owing to saturation of the domestic market. The problems of industrial inefficiency, price inflation, and imbalance in external payments become more serious. After a few years of adjustments, the government finally decided to accept advice from a group of US-educated economists and technocrats and took decisive steps in the 1950s to change the overall thrust of policy incentives in favor of export activity (Lin, 1973).

The US Congress had passed the Mutual Security Act in 1951, which was aimed at helping the capitalistic expansion of US private enterprises, and incorporating Allied countries into a new world economic system dominated by the USA. By the end of the 1950s, the USA was suffering from economic depression and eager to find favorable countries where US capital could be invested. It therefore advocated free trade and opened its markets to light-industry foreign products, which had been abandoned by US firms. Meanwhile, Japan, which experienced rapid economic growth for more than ten years after the Korean War, was facing the problem of increasing labor costs and was ready to move its labor-intensive industries to foreign countries where cheaper labor was available. Taiwan soon became Japan's first choice because of its fifty years of colonial experience on Taiwan before World War II.

In 1960, the Taiwanese government announced a Nineteen-Point Reform Program and enacted the Investment Encouragement Law, which provided a basis for the administration to take a series of positive actions toward the realization of outward-oriented growth of the economy. The actions included establishing export-processing zones, providing enterprises with low-interest productive loans, liberalizing restrictions to encourage the import of certain important raw materials, and remitting taxes and duties for export goods (Lin, 1973). These measures enabled Taiwan to achieve rapid economic development. In 1971, Taiwan was expelled from the United Nations, and Chiang Ching-kuo was appointed prime minister the next year. He began to initiate the "Ten Big Construction Projects" and developed capital- and technology-intensive industry. This series of government actions not only enabled Taiwan to survive the oil crises thereafter, but also laid the foundations for the economic miracle of the 1980s (Balassa, 1981; Chen, 1979; Fei, Ranis, and Kuo, 1979; Ho, 1978).

The Nationalist government adopted a series of strategies to intervene in economic activities and foster private business for the sake of national development (Amsden, 1985; Gold, 1986). Its control over the economic sphere has been termed *paternal domination* (Chang, 1991) or *paternalism* (Pye, 1988), and the strategy for economic development has been labeled *state-led outward-looking growth* (Wade, 1988). Though the Nationalists maintained an authoritarian style of domination and insisted on orthodox ideology in politics, they held an open attitude toward economic affairs. They were able to absorb suggestions from economists and technocrats who had been educated in Western economic theories and practices (Pye, 1988), and constructed formal legal systems to transform domestic economic affairs at the opportune moment with a view to the international economic situation. However, because the legal system has long been viewed by the Chinese as an instrument for ruling the people, it is usually constructed in such a way that an administrative officer with power can interpret it flexibly. Operating in such a social and political environment, enterprises in Taiwan have been differentiated into two broad categories. One category is generally large-scale businesses. They are mainly specialized in doing business with governmental sectors and are subject to major influence by government policies. They maintain close relationships with high-ranking officials in the government and can be termed *relation-oriented enterprises*.

The other category of enterprises is composed mostly of small or medium-scale businesses that concentrate on selling their products in the domestic or international markets, which are their major sources of interest. They pay more attention to improving the quality of their products and to developing new markets. They can be termed *market-oriented enterprises*.

This does not mean that a market-oriented enterprise can totally disregard *guanxi* (social relationships). In order to compete with other products in the market, entrepreneurs must maintain not only public relationships with customers, but also specific networks of marketing channels for selling products. But these relationships are established on the basis of rational calculations and equitable exchange, unlike the merchant–politician relationships aimed at apportioning public resources. The rapid expansion of export-oriented industry as well as the economic miracle of Taiwan during the period from the 1960s to the 1980s was made possible mainly by market-oriented enterprises.

### Development of Chinese family businesses

As soon as the Taiwanese government adopted the policy of encouraging private business and the external environment became favorable for investment, numerous entrepreneurs began to establish various types of industrial organization and produce a variety of products to meet the demands of the market. The most typical business organization established in Taiwan was the family business or family enterprise (Hwang, 1990). During the 1970s, when the export-processing industry of Taiwan was in the early stage of rapid development, numerous small-scale family firms were established in suburban areas. Families set up crude plants around or even in their dwellings, bought the necessary mechanical equipment, received orders from large-scale factories nearby, and provided them with products or semiproducts, thus becoming satellite plants to big factories. Such networks of *guanxi* for production enabled small or medium-scale firms to operate without huge amounts of investment, to accept orders beyond their own capacity for production, and to transfer parts of jobs to other firms within their networks, thus reducing capital and management risk to a minimum (Vogel, 1991). Most workers in such plants are family members or relatives. They generally work hard in the name of familism. The profits thus earned are mostly controlled by the head of the family, and the most important resources are allocated according to the need rule. In order to maximize the productivity of the plant and to accumulate wealth for the family, all members of the family must do their best and take only what they need from the profits.

When such family businesses are successful and demand for their products outstrips supply, owner-managers are urged to hire employees from the labor market outside the *guanxi* network. During the era of rapid development of the export-processing industry in Taiwan, it was common for small plants to evolve into medium or large businesses with dozens or hundreds of employees within two or three years. However, the organizational pattern for most medium or small plants is still the family enterprise. Top managers in the organization are usually the owners of the enterprise. They generally prefer a paternalist or autocratic style of management, frequently assign family members to occupy such important positions as financier or accountant, and rarely tell subordinates about the policy of the organization in a definite, clear manner. The delegation of authority to staff is limited, and the division of power and responsibility is usually ambiguous (Negandi, 1973; Redding, 1988, 1990; Silin, 1976).

Managers and subordinates in family enterprises may frequently encounter the struggle between Confucianism and Legalism. On the one hand, employees and staff may ask the owner-managers to set up formal regulations for manpower policies, personnel selection, job design, job evaluation, promotion, and compensation and then to exercise strict discipline in executing these regulations. On the other hand, because strict adherence to regulations restricts the abuse of power, managers and staff in their *guanxi* network may oppose the establishment or the execution of certain regulations when it is in contradiction to their interests. There are also instances where employees object to rules of control that are applied arbitrarily and unilaterally to employees but not to managers, or to distant employees but not to intimates.

Both cultural traditions, of Confucianism and Legalism, emphasize the value of respecting and being obedient to authority. In such a cultural tradition, most employees are used to accepting a paternalistic style of management. In order to make more money to support their families, most are concerned about distributive justice in the organization. They may compare their own income with that of others who are doing similar tasks in the same or a different organization. Once individuals believe that they are overpaid or that their income is fair, they may have higher work morale. People are concerned about distributive justice not merely for utilitarian reasons. As a family business grows larger to include non-family members, organizational distributive justice also experiences a shift from the need rule to the equity rule. If workers believe that they are underpaid or not fairly treated, work morale may decrease, or they may leave for another better job. This is one plausible reason why the industry of Taiwan showed a high turnover rate during the 1970s (Yu, 1977).

### Political capitalism

The political situation of Taiwan faced drastic change when its economy was undergoing successive stages of rapid development during the 1970s. Taiwan was expelled from the United Nations in 1971, and Chiang Ching-kuo was appointed prime minister the next year. In order to consolidate his control over the regime, he assigned many centripetal Taiwanese elites to key positions in the government. The accomplishment of his "Ten Big Construction Projects" enabled Taiwan to maintain its economic progress, but it could not prevent its diplomatic failures. In the 1970s, Taiwan severed diplomatic relations with most major countries and lost its seat in many international organizations. Chiang was elected to the post of president by the National Assembly at the beginning of 1978. But, the USA declared its recognition of the People's Republic of China, and severed diplomatic relations with Taiwan, at the end of that year, destroying Taiwan's people's confidence in their government's claim that it represented the orthodoxy of China. Political opponents began to initiate a series of political movements advocating a new ideology of "Taiwanese consciousness," which enabled them to win more votes in the successive elections of the 1980s.

In 1986, the Democratic Progressive Party, the first opposition party in Taiwan, declared its establishment with the tacit permission of President Chiang Ching-kuo. A variety of social movements mushroomed in the new atmosphere of democracy, and the National Government lifted martial law, which had been enforced for about forty years. President Chiang died in 1988, and was succeeded by Vice-President Lee Teng-hui.

The establishment of the Democratic Progressive Party had important implications for the political modernization of Taiwan. It represented the institutionalization of centrifugal elites who advocated an opposing ideology in the political market to compete with the ruling party for the opportunity of holding the reins of government. But the democratization of politics brought some unexpected consequences to society. In comparison with the "Taiwanese consciousness" advocated by the Democratic Progressives for identification with Taiwan, the "Chinese consciousness" insisted on by the Nationalists for forty years became impractical and vulnerable to attack from political opponents. As soon as Lee became president, he tried, on the one hand, to adjust the Nationalist Party's ideology to cope with political change, but, on the other, he had to preserve national symbols to deal with the conservatives in his party. His pragmatic adjustments led him to a series of political struggles with other Nationalist Party leaders. In order to consolidate his personal power to deal with the challenges from the opposing party, and to expel conservatives from the Nationalist Party, Lee began to foster the power of local forces by strengthening the party's connections with local politicians and entrepreneurs. After the lifting of martial law, numerous local politicians attempted to gain positions in the central representative bodies, which had previously been occupied by the privileged-class immigrants from China. With the tacit permission of the Nationalists, they even tried to win elections by bribery. Many of them originally accumulated their wealth and power by engaging in land speculation, monopolizing public construction projects, or even running illegal businesses. Once they occupied positions of central power, their greed was stimulated.

Although the Democratic Progressives and the Nationalists held different political ideologies, many of their major politicians were not significantly different in their behavioral patterns in running personal businesses, developing *guanxi* networks, and striving for support from local factions. Viewing legislation as an omnipotent tool for winning support from voters, they urged the administration either to reduce a variety of tax rates, or to increase expenditures for various social welfare schemes, and many of them were especially interested in locating public construction projects in their electoral districts. Such large-scale projects were coveted by politicians and businessmen. They colluded with foreign or domestic big businesses to urge the administration to raise the minimum bids for public construction projects so that the domestic firms would receive contracts with gigantic profits. As a consequence, huge amounts of government funds were wasted, the quality of public construction worsened, and government expenditures and national debts increased rapidly.

As described, enterprises in Taiwan can be categorized as relation-oriented or market-oriented. If a nation decides to develop technology-intensive industry, the government must create a stable social environment and construct a legal system for encouraging entrepreneurs to make long-term investments in R&D. In contrast, if the government is unable to create a favorable environment for long-term investment, and a large group of politicians are constantly involved in political struggles, the administration is unable to adhere to legal principles in a strict and unbiased way, and most entrepreneurs will believe that it would be very difficult for their enterprises to survive without special connections with political power. In this situation of political capitalism, it is very unlikely a market-oriented enterprise will make long-term investments or upgrade its technical level.

According to the framework in Table 4.1, the corruption of political capitalism can be interpreted as a consequence of overindulgence in Confucian ethics for ordinary people by some politically influential families. The moral codes of incorruption and immaculation in Confucian ethics for scholars and officials are frequently ignored. They build up the *guanxi* networks of their factions, and utilize the *renqing* rule in pursuit of personal profit at the sacrifice of public interest. In contrast, any endeavor to stop political capitalism or to remedy corruption by appealing to the legal system can be viewed as an effort to advocate fairness (*gongdao*). The dialectical dialogue between elites as expressed in public opinion over a specific case of corruption can be said to be a modern manifestation of the struggle between Confucianism and Legalism.

## Conclusion

Although cultural factors may have an influence on social behavior, the actual motivating factor for an individual social act is the pursuit of personal interest. Hanfei's focus on personal interest corresponds to Max Weber's (1978) viewpoint that social acts are always motivated by one's desire for certain benefits, while cultural ideas are like the controller of a railroad who determines the direction of action. This point can be further illustrated with an analogy by Karl Marx, who said:

> People construct their own history. But they are not constructing it in such a condition that they may have an arbitrary choice. When people are busy in reforming themselves as well as events around, they may appeal to the soul of their ancestors, using their names, slogans, and clothes, putting on their armor which has long been respected, and speaking in terms of their language, to act out new phases of world history (Marx and Engels, 1965: 121).

People in Confucian society, just like human beings in other cultures, are driven by their personal desires to compete with others in striving for various goals to satisfy their needs. The cultural traditions of Confucianism and Legalism are the "names, slogans, clothes, armor, and language" frequently used by Chinese to pursue their personal goals. It remains to be seen how they act out the new phase of their history.

### Notes

1  *Spring and Autumn* is the annals of the state of Lu (722–484 BCE). The chronicle history was written by Confucius who recorded and judged people and historical events in an honest and strict way.
2  Guan Zhong, in Zhai (2005: II, 818–847).
3  Hanfei, *Zhudao* [The way of the ruler], in Watson (1967: 16–20).
4  Duyvendak (1963).
5  Xunzi, in Dubs (1972: 24–47).

6 All quotations from the works of Chinese philosophers have been translated by the author with reference to the translations by Liao (1939–59) and Watson (1967).

7 Liao (1939–1959: II, 275–297); Watson (1967: 96–117).

8 For examples, see Hanfei's works on *Beinei* (Guarding against the interior), in Liao (1939–1959: I, 145–150); *Liufan* (Six contrarieties) in Liao (1939–1959: II, 237–247); and *Wuaichushuozuoshang* (Outer congeries of sayings, the upper left series) in Liao (1939–1959: II, 26–62).

9 Confucius, in Lau (1992: 132–147).

10 Liao (1939–1959: I, 275–277).

11 Liao (1939–1959: I, 46–51); Watson (1967: 30–34).

12 Liao (1939–1959: II, 199–206).

13 Liao (1939–1959: II, 199–206).

14 Liao (1939–1959: I, 30–35); Watson (1967: 16–20).

15 Liao (1939–1959: I, 278–280).

16 Liao (1939–1959: I, 278–280).

17 Liao (1939–1959: I, 278–280).

18 Liao (1939–1959: II, 172–188).

19 Liao (1939–1959: I, 36–46); Watson (1967: 21–29).

20 Liao (1939–1959: I, 229–236).

21 Liao (1939–1959: II, 248–257).

22 Liao (1939–1959: II, 248–257).

23 Liao (1939–1959: II, 275–297); Watson (1967: 96–117).

24 Liao (1939–1959: II, 63–85).

25 Liao (1939–1959: II, 46–50).

26 *Lichi*, in Legge (2003: 61–119).

27 Liao (1939–1959: I, 36–46); Watson (1967: 21–29).

28 Liao (1939–1959: I, 150–155).

29 Liao (1939–1959: I, 156–168).

30 Liao (1939–1959: II, 326–329).

31 Liao (1939–1959: II, 326–329).

32 Liao (1939–1959: II, 326–329).

33 Liao (1939–1959: II, 212–216).

34 Liao (1939–1959: I, 269–274).

35 Liao (1939–1959: I, 269–274).

36 Liao (1939–1959: II, 207–209).

37 Liao (1939–1959: II, 237–247).

38 Liao (1939–1959: I, 46–51); Watson (1967: 30–34).

39 Liao (1939–1959: I, 36–46); Watson (1967: 21–29).

40 Liao (1939–1959: II, 298–310).

41 The dyadic roles in the five cardinal relations are: father and son; husband and wife; sovereign and subject; between brothers; and between friends.

References

Amsden, A. A. 1985. "The state and Taiwan's economic development," in P. B. Evans, D. Rueschemeyer, and T. Skoopol (eds.), *Bringing the state back*, New York: Cambridge University Press, pp. 78–106.

Balassa, B. A. 1981. *The newly industrializing countries in the world economy*. New York: Pergamon.

Befu, H. 1980. "Structural and motivational approaches to social exchange," in K. J. Gergen, M. S. Greengerg, and R. H. Willis (eds.), *Social exchange*, New York: Plenum, pp. 197–214.

Bellah, R. N. 1970. *Tokugawa Religion*. Boston: Beacon.

Berger, P. L. 1988. "An East Asian model," in P. L. Berger and H. M. Hsiao (eds.), *In search of an East Asian development model*, New Brunswick, NJ: Transaction Books, pp. 3–11.

Callis, H. G. 1959. *China, Confucian and Communist*. New York: Holt.

Chang, J. M. 1991. "The relationship between enterprise and state in Taiwan area after World War II: a paternalistic political economic structure of authority," *Sun Yat-Sen Science Quarterly* 6(1): 13–34 (in Chinese).

Chen, C. 1961. *Land reform in Taiwan*. Taipei: China Publishing Co.

Chen, E. K. Y. 1979. *Hyper-growth in Asian economics: a comparative study of Hong Kong, Japan, Korea, Singapore, and Taiwan*. New York: Holmes & Meier.

Cheng, C. K. 1944. "Familism: the foundation of Chinese social organization," *Social Forces* 23: 50–59.

Chiou, C. 1974. *Maoism in action: the Cultural Revolution*. New York: Crane Russak.

Chu, T. T. 1961. *Law and society in traditional China*. Paris: Mouton.

Ditter, L. 1974. *Liu Shao-Ch'I and the Chinese Cultural Revolution: the politics of mass criticism*. Berkeley: University of California Press.

Dubs, H. H. 1972 (trans.). *The works of Hsüntze*. Taipei: Confucius Publishing Company.

Durkheim, E. 1984 [1933]. *The division of labour in society*, trans. W. D. Halls. Houndmills, Hampshire: Macmillan.

Duyvendak, J. J. L. 1963 (trans.). *The book of Lord Shang: a classic of the Chinese school of law*. Chicago: University of Chicago Press.

Eisenstadt, S. N. 1966. *Modernization: protest and change*. Englewood Cliffs, NJ: Prentice Hall.

Fei, J. C. H., Ranis, G., and Kuo, S. W. Y. 1979. *Growth with equity: the Taiwan case*. New York: Oxford University Press.

French, J., and Raven, B. 1959. "The bases of social power," in D. Cartwright (ed.), *Studies in social power*, Ann Arbor: University of Michigan Press, pp. 150–167.

Gold, T. B. 1986. *State and society in the Taiwan miracle.* New York: M.E. Sharpe.

Ho, S. P. S. 1978. *Economics of Taiwan 1960–1970.* New Haven: Yale University Press.

Hsu, F. L. K. 1967. *Under the ancestors' shadow: Kinship, personality and social mobility in village China.* Garden City, NJ: Anchorbooks.

Hwang, K. K. 1987. "Face and favor: the Chinese power game," *American Journal of Sociology* 92(4): 944–974.

1988. *Confucianism and East Asian modernization.* Taipei: Chu-Liu Books (in Chinese).

1990. "Modernization of the Chinese family business," *International Journal of Psychology* 25(5/6): 593–618.

1991. "Dao and the transformative power of Confucianism: a theory of East Asian modernization," in W. M. Tu (ed.), *The triadic chord,* Singapore: Institute of East Asian philosophies, pp. 229–278.

1995. "The struggle between Confucianism and Legalism in Chinese society and productivity: a Taiwan experience," in K. K. Hwang (ed.), *Easternization: socio-cultural impact on productivity,* Tokyo: Asian Productivity Organization, pp. 15–46.

2001. "The deep structure of Confucianism: a social psychological approach," *Asian Philosophy* 11(3): 179–204.

Kerr, G. H. 1965. *Formosa betrayed.* Boston: Houghton Mifflin.

Lang, O. 1946. *Chinese family and society.* New Haven: Yale University Press.

Lau, D. C. 1992 (trans.). *The Analects: Lun Yü.* Hong Kong: Chinese University Press.

Legge, J. 2003 (trans.). *Li Chi: Book of rites, part I.* Whitefish, MT: Kessinger.

Liao, W. K. 1939–59 (trans.). *The complete works of Han Fei Tzu : a classic of Chinese legalism,* 2 vols. London: Arthur Probsthain.

Lin, C. Y. 1973. *Industrialization in Taiwan (1946–1972): trade and import-substitution policies for developing countries.* New York: Praeger.

MacFarquhar, R. 1974. *The origins of the cultural revolution.* New York: Columbia University Press.

Merchant, L. R. 1975. *The turbulent giant: Communist theory and practice in China.* Sydney: Australia and New Zealand Book Co.

Marx, K., and Engels, F. 1965. *Collection of works by Marx and Engels,* trans. Bureau for Translating and Editing Works of Marx, Engels, Lenin, and Stalin of the Chinese Communist Party. Beijing: People's Publisher (in Chinese).

Negandi, A. R. 1973. *Management and economic development: the case of Taiwan.* The Hague: Martinus Nijhoff.

Pye, L. 1988. "The new Asian capitalism: a political portrait," in P. L. Berger and H. M. Hsiao, (eds.), *In search of an East Asian development model*, New Brunswick, NJ: Transaction Books, pp. 81–98.

Redding, S. G. 1988. "The role of entrepreneur in the New Asian Capitalism," in P. L. Berger and H. M. Hsiao (eds.), *In Search of An East Asian Development Model*, New Brunswick, NJ: Transaction Books, pp. 99–111.

1990. *The spirit of Chinese capitalism*. New York: Walter de Gruyter.

Robottom, J. 1969. *China in revolution*. New York: McGraw-Hill.

Shils, E. 1976. *Tradition*. Chicago: University of Chicago Press.

Silin, R. H. 1976. *Leadership and values: the organization of large scale Taiwanese enterprises*. Cambridge, MA: Harvard University Press.

Vogel, E. F. 1991. *The four little dragons: the spread of industrialization in East Asia*. Cambridge, MA: Harvard University Press.

Wade, R. 1988. "State intervention in 'out-looking' development: neoclassical theory and Taiwanese practice," in G. White (ed.), *Developmental states in East Asia*. Houndmills, Hampshire: Macmillan.

Watson, B. 1967 (trans.). *Basic writings of Mo Tzu, Hsün Tzu, and Han Fei Tzu*. New York: Columbia University press.

Weber, M. 1978. *Economy and society*, ed. G. Roth and C. Wittich, trans. E. Fishhoff, 2 vols. Berkeley: University of California Press.

Winch, R. F. 1966. *The modern family*, 2nd edn. New York: Holt.

Yang, C. F. 1988. "Familism and development: an examination of the role of family in contemporary China Mainland, Hong Kong and Taiwan," in D. Sinha and H. S. R. Kao (eds.), *Social value and development: Asian perspectives*, New Delhi: Sage, pp. 93–123.

Yu, H. J. 1977. "An investigation on variables related to turn-over behavior," *Thoughts and Speech* 15(2): 26–32 (in Chinese).

Zhai, J. 2005 (trans.). *Guanxi*, 2 vols. Guilin: Guangxi Normal University Press.

# 5 | Strategic leadership of Sunzi in the Art of war

## HAI-FA SUN, CHAO-CHUAN CHEN, AND SHI-HE ZHANG

UCH PREVIOUS WRITING on Sunzi and his book, the *Art of war*, has focused on strategies and tactics of disguise, deception, and maneuvering for the purpose of winning. In this chapter, however, we study the *Art of war* from a leadership perspective, namely, how, in the view of Sunzi, military commanders exercise strategic situationalism, namely, situation-making (*zhao shi*) to lead an army to victory. Based on the analysis of the *Art of war*, we delve into Sunzi's philosophical views of humaneness, holism, and dialecticism. We then identify the positive and negative attributes of a leader in relation to strategic leadership. Furthermore, we elaborate Sunzi's strategic situationalism into (a) creating positional advantage in the environment, (b) creating organizational advantage within the organization, (c) building morale within the troops, and (d) leveraging and adapting to situations. Finally we discuss theoretical and practical implications of Sunzi's strategic leadership theory in a global environment.

## Historical background and philosophical foundations

The exact period of Sunzi's life is the subject of debate. Giles believed (Garvin, 2003) that Sunzi was a contemporary of Confucius in the Spring and Autumn Period in Chinese history (771–481 BCE) whereas Griffith (1971), who wrote his doctoral dissertation on the *Art of war*, concluded that Sunzi was born a generation after Confucius and that the *Art of war* was written during the chaotic and turbulent period of the Warring States (453–221 BCE) that followed the Spring and Autumn Period. Sunzi is also known as Sun Wu with Sun being the family name. Zi was a honorary title meaning "master." Sunzi and his ancestors obtained their family name by a historical coincidence as their original name was Chen and then Tian. Sunzi's grandfather, under the family name of Tian, was awarded a large piece of land (today's Hui Min County, Shangdong Province, China) under the official title of Sun by the king of the Qi state for his military achievement in a war against the state of Lü. Over time, the family came to be known as Sun instead of Tian. Being born into a family of experts on military and political affairs and living in the state of Qi, which boasted many great military and political philosophers of the Warring States Period, Sunzi was blessed with an invaluable rich inheritance of political and military philosophies and practices. He later came to the state of Wu and presented to the king of Wu his thirteen chapters of the *Art of war*. He became a principal strategist of the Wu state and is believed to have contributed greatly to its ascendance.

Griffith (1971: 30) contended that we can appreciate the originality of Sunzi's thought "only if we are aware of the qualitative difference which distinguished warfare of the fifth and fourth centuries from that of the earlier periods." First, toward the end of the Zhou dynasty, there was the dissolution of a unified kingdom and the loss of control of the central government. With the emergence of the Warring States of multiple lords and kings, there was a deterioration of Confucian moral standards and an increasing reliance on severe punitive laws for maintaining social order. The time called for "a coherent strategic and tactic theory of a practical doctrine governing intelligence, planning, command, operation, and administrative procedures" and Sunzi "was the first man to provide such a theory and such a doctrine" (Griffith, 1971: 25). Second, there was the emergence of large-scale standing armies officered by professionals. In the earlier Ancient China, battles were fought mainly by four-horse chariots, with foot soldiers more or less expendable; armies were drafted by the sovereign kings from noble families for temporary employment in specific battles. The foot soldiers were typically peasants or serfs, hastily assembled and poorly trained, led by officers from different noble families. The Warring States Period, however, witnessed the emergence of large and standing armies formed by the states, composed of conscripted peasants and disciplined and well-trained troops, and commanded by professional officers not from noble families. "These armies were spearheaded by elite or shock troops specially selected for their courage, skill, discipline, and loyalty"; "Staff included numerous specialists: weather forecasters, map makers, commissary officers, and engineers to plan tunneling and mining operations. Others were experts on river crossing, amphibious operations, inundating, attack by fire, and the use of smoke" (Griffith, 1971: 34–35). In summary, the armies of the Chinese Warring States were large organizations with the emergence of professional generals, similar to the development of large business corporations with the emergence of professional managers in the West as described in the scientific management literature. Such organizational characteristics allowed Sunzi to develop a science (or art) of warfare and a theory of leadership and administration, which we will elaborate later in this chapter.

The third significant development of the Warring States Period was the existence of the divergent philosophies that Sunzi was able to draw upon in developing his theory of strategy and leadership. The ultimate objective of the policies of the powerful states was an empire and, to gain competitive advantage in accomplishing that goal, the state kings encouraged scholars of different schools of thought to provide counsel on military and war strategies, which were an integral part of the power politics of the time. The schools of thought that had most impact on Sunzi and his writings in the *Art of war* seem to be primarily Confucianism, Daoism, and Legalism. We refer the reader to Chapters 1 and 2 of this book for Confucianism, Chapter 3 for Daoism, and Chapter 4 for Legalism. Here it suffices to say that Sunzi drew upon Confucianist thoughts on benevolence, righteousness, ritual propriety, and wisdom. These concepts are used in the *Art of war* to define, evaluate, and guide leadership, strategy, and tactics. Among the Daoist ideas that have the greatest impact on Sunzi's strategic leadership theory are the dialectic relationship between the contradictory forces of *yin* and *yang*, and the significance of the five basic natural elements of water, fire, wood, metal, and earth in warfare. The Legalist ideas of law (*fa*), authority (*shi*), and tactics (*shu*) were also key concepts used by Sunzi in discussing leadership strategies and tactics.

## The themes of the *Art of war*

Although many of Sunzi's sayings have been widely popularized in the West as well as in China, they tend to be quoted out of the context of the complete work. Here we attempt first to conduct a content analysis of the book to abstract the themes of each of the thirteen chapters that make up the book. Our analysis is conducted on the original ancient Chinese version of the *Art of war* as edited by Wu, Wu, and

Lin (2001). This edition includes not only the original ancient Chinese text but also a modern Chinese translation and an English translation. Where necessary we consulted other English translations of the *Art of war* by Cleary (2000), Griffith (1971), and Giles (Garvin, 2003). The original ancient Chinese text has a total of 6088 characters. The extent of the text is deceptively small because ancient Chinese texts tend to be concise and loaded with rich information. As an example, we randomly selected 77 ancient Chinese characters in Chapter 2 and found that the equivalent modern Chinese version has 159 characters and the equivalent English version has 134 words.

In Table 5.1 we list the major topics of each chapter together with one or two major sentences for illustration and a count of the number of characters.

The first chapter is an introduction and an overview of the whole book. It captures the essence of Sunzi's military philosophy. It emphasizes the importance of war for the survival of the state and proposes five parameters to determine the outcome of a war, which include the Way (the *Dao*, the moral support of the populace), meteorological and topographical conditions of military operations, the leadership quality of the commanders, and the organization of the army. The opening chapter also defines war as a matter of strategizing rather than direct fighting and contains the famous saying popularized by Mao, namely, "attack when they are unprepared and make a move when they least expect it." It is apparent that Chapter 1 reflects the influence of the Confucian *Dao* of benevolence, the Daoist *Dao* of dialecticism in the strategies, and the legalistic prescriptions of how to run the military organization.

The following ten chapters (Chapters 2–11) are concerned with the objectives and the development and execution of strategies and tactics. In Chapters 2 and 3, "Waging war" and "Attacking by stratagem," Sunzi proposes two overall strategic objectives, namely speedy and complete victories, reflecting his humanist perspective of war as well as the Daoist dialecticism of winning and losing. In Chapter 2, emphasizing the human and economic cost of war, Sunzi proposes that a speedy victory is preferred to a protracted one because protracted wars not only cost more resources and lives but also have logistic and psychological effects on the operation and morale of the troops. One specific proposal that stands out in this chapter is about how to replenish the army by "obtaining military supplies from home

Table 5.1. *Thematic contents of the* Art of war.

| Chapter | Contents and themes | No. of characters |
|---|---|---|
| 1. Assessments | a. The mission of war.<br>b. Five factors: the *Dao* (the ruler's benevolence and the confidence of his people), heaven (weather), earth (terrain), the quality of command, and the rules and regulations of the army.<br>c. Generals to create strategic advantage for gaining victory.<br>*Key sentences*: It is he who masters them (five assessments) that wins and he who does not that loses. Attack when they are unprepared and make the move when they do not expect it. | 336 |
| 2. Waging war | The main objective of a war is quick victory; a prolonged war is disastrous. A wise general replenishes his troops with supplies and captives from the enemy.<br>*Key sentence*: The commander who knows how to conduct a war is the arbiter of the people's fate, the man on whom the nation's security depends. | 342 |
| 3. Attacking by stratagem | a. Taking the enemy whole and intact by using stratagem and diplomacy before attacking.<br>b. Three ways a sovereign can bring disaster to the army.<br>c. Five factors for predicting winning.<br>*Key sentences*: Those skilled in war subdue the enemy without fighting, capture the enemy's cities without assaulting them, and overthrow the enemy's kingdom without protracted operations. The side that has a capable commander who is free of interference from the sovereign will win. | 423 |
| 4. Disposition | a. Strategic generals make themselves invincible and then wait for the enemy's moment of vulnerability.<br>b. Gaining overwhelming advantage over the opponent. | 309 |

Table 5.1. (*cont.*)

| Chapter | Contents and themes | No. of characters |
|---------|---------------------|-------------------|
| | *Key sentence*: The skilled warrior seeks victory by cultivating the Way and strengthening rules and regulations, and in so doing, gains the advantage over the enemy. | |
| 5. Momentum | a. Mixing and reconfiguring orthodox (*zheng*) and extraordinary/surprise (*qi*) methods.<br>b. Gaining momentum by positioning and timing.<br>*Key sentence*: Order and disorder are a matter of organization, courage and cowardice are a matter of momentum, and strength and weakness are a matter of disposition. | 390 |
| 6. Strengths and weaknesses | Concealing own situation to confuse and mislead the enemy. Changing tactics in anticipation of or in reaction to the enemy situation.<br>*Key sentences*: There is no fixed pattern in the use of tactics in war. He who wins modifies his tactics in accordance with the changing enemy situation. | 598 |
| 7. Maneuvering | a. Maneuvering to turn problems into advantage.<br>b. Gaining advantages of morale, strength, and adaptation.<br>*Key sentence*: Those who are skilled in war avoid the enemy when its spirit is high and strike when its spirit drains. | 473 |
| 8. Adaptations | a. Nine variations of tactics.<br>b. Five dangers of a leader: reckless, cowardly, quick-tempered, too delicate a sense of honor, too compassionate.<br>*Key sentence*: Generals who know all possible adaptations to take advantage of the ground know how to use military forces. | 245 |
| 9. Deploying troops | a. Occupying advantageous positions in different situations.<br>b. Assessing the positions of the enemy.<br>c. How to build devoted and deployable troops. | 611 |

**Table 5.1.** (*cont.*)

| Chapter | Contents and themes | No. of characters |
|---------|---------------------|-------------------|
| | *Key sentences*: If soldiers are punished before a personal attachment to the leader is formed, they will not submit. When directives are consistently carried out, there is mutual satisfaction between the leader and the troops (Cleary, 2000: 150). | |
| 10. Terrain | a. Six types of terrain and ways of taking advantage of terrain. b. Six calamities caused by internal factors of the leadership. c. Relationship with the sovereign and the troop. *Key sentence*: Know your enemy and know yourself, victory will not be at risk; know both heaven and earth, and victory will be complete. | 545 |
| 11. Nine grounds | a. Differentiating nine types of ground or situation and ways of dealing with them b. Factors affecting the morale and the psychology of the troop. *Key sentence*: The Way to manage an army is to try to make the strong and the weak achieve a uniform level of courage, just as the proper utilization of terrain lies in making the best use of both high- and low-lying grounds. | 1071 |
| 12. Attacking by fire | a. Five types of fire attack. b. Cautions against launching war. *Key sentence*: The sovereign should not start a war simply out of anger; the commander or general should not fight a battle simply because he is resentful. | 280 |
| 13. Intelligence agents | a. Five types of agent. b. Importance and ways of using intelligence agents. *Key sentence*: Only the enlightened sovereign and wise commander who are capable of using the most intelligent people as agents are destined to accomplish great things. | 465 |

but acquiring life provisions of the army from the enemy territory." Chapter 3 proposes complete victory as another strategic objective, which means taking the enemy in complete and intact units (be they state, army, battalion, or squad) rather than destroying or breaking them. Furthermore, Sunzi advocates winning by strategy instead of direct physical combat and offers the famous saying of "know yourself and know your enemy [and] you will be invincible."

Chapters 4 and 5, on "Disposition" (*xing*) and "Momentum" (*shi*), are about the formational and positional determinants of war outcomes. Victory or defeat depends on the relative position and strength of the opposing parties. Victorious leaders are those who create advantages for their troops or place their troops in the advantageous positions and those who vary strategies and tactics through different configurations of action and non-action, conventional and surprise actions, and offense and defense. Chapter 6 on "Strengths and weaknesses" is about the strategic use of strength and weakness including focusing on one's own strength, avoiding the opponent's strength, and matching one's own strengths with the opponent's weaknesses. Of course, concealing one's own real strengths and weaknesses, confusing the opponent with configuration, and discovering true strengths and weaknesses of the opponent are all part of the strategies and tactics.

Chapter 7 on "Maneuvering" goes into details about gaining advantage over the opponent in morale, positioning, strength, and timing and emphasizes further the importance of attacking the opponent's weakness with one's strength. Chapter 8 on "Adaptations" explores ways of responding to various emergent conditions and warns against uniformity and predictability. "There are routes not to be followed, armies not to be attacked, citadels not to be besieged, territory not to be fought over, and orders of sovereignty not to be obeyed." In decision-making, leaders must consider both favorable and unfavorable factors so as to be fully prepared and positioned to win.

In Chapters 9–11 we see Sunzi's systematic attention to physical and situational factors and his situational perspectives on warfare. In Chapter 9, Sunzi deals with issues of a marching army, and offers advice on how to observe and assess the enemy. In Chapters 10 and 11, Sunzi passes his deep knowledge of various terrains and grounds, their effects on the emotion and morale of the soldiers, and strategies and tactics in dealing with the situations.

The last two chapters, while offering specific effective tactics for fire attacks and using intelligence agents, echo the opening chapter by emphasizing great caution in using destructive tactics such as incendiary attacks. "The enlightened sovereign approaches the question of war with utmost caution and the good commander warns himself against rash action." To Sunzi, rushing into war and failing to win is the opposite of benevolence, as war destroys lives, properties, and resources. Employing intelligence agents is promoted as more benevolent and effective because it obtains more accurate information on the enemy and contributes to strategic formation and implementation. How to employ and reward intelligence agents is therefore an essential part of warfare. He concludes: "only the enlightened sovereign and wise commander who are capable of using the most intelligent people as agents are destined to accomplish great things."

In summary, the *Art of war* opens with an overview of the mission of war and the general parameters for assessing the potential for winning or losing, goes on to the discussion of strategies and tactics for dealing with complex and varying war situations, and ends with a chapter on the importance of intelligence.

## A leadership perspective on the *Art of war*

The *Art of war* has long been known to Westerners as well as to the Chinese as a classic of military strategy. It has also been applied to marketing and interfirm relationships by business and management. Researchers taking a pure perspective of strategy typically study military commanders or business executives in the context of conflict and competition in which rivals maneuver to defeat, overpower, or gain advantage over each other. In this chapter we approach the work from a leadership perspective, one in which we make a closer connection to the context of general organization and management. While conflict and competition is certainly part of the reality of leadership in the business environment, there are other issues that go beyond, such as the relationship between the sovereign and the military leadership and between the commanders and the soldiers, and issues of how to organize, coordinate, control, and motivate the army. While the strategic perspective has the enemy or opponent as the major target, a leadership perspective gives more attention to the leader, the follower, and their interactions with the surrounding environment.

Table 5.2. *Frequency of keywords in the* Art of war.

| Keyword and frequency | Group total |
|---|---|
| *Commander* | 60 |
| General (*jiang*) 49 | |
| Officer (*shi*) 9 | |
| Commander (*shuai*) 2 | |
| *Soldier* | 90 |
| Soldier (*bing*) 71 | |
| Private (*zu*) 19 | |
| *Army* | 69 |
| Army (*jun*) 60 | |
| Division (*shi*) 9 | |
| *Opponent/enemy* | 70 |
| *Situation/environment* | 65 |
| Form (*xing*) 34 | |
| Position (*shi*) 16 | |
| Change (*bian*) 15 | |
| *Victory/defeat* | 103 |
| Victory (*sheng*) 84 | |
| Defeat (*bai*) 13 | |
| Danger (*dai*) 3 | |
| Loss (*fu*) 3 | |

As a first step toward approaching the *Art of war* from a leadership perspective, we conduct a simple content analysis, counting the frequency of keywords referring to factors in military leadership, namely, the commander, the soldier, the army, the enemy, the situation/environment, and the outcome (victory or defeat). We define strategic leadership in the military context as how *commanders* lead the *army/soldiers* to battle against the *enemy* taking advantage of *situational contingencies* in order to win *victories*. As can be seen in Table 5.2, references to victory or defeat are the most frequently made (103 times) with those to soldiers coming next (90). References to the enemy (70), the commander (60), the army (69), and the situation (65) are more or less the same. These simple statistics suggest to us that in military leadership winning victory is the ultimate criterion of success and the enemy is a dominant concern. However, it also suggests that the soldiers and the army are also salient factors. Lastly, the consideration of situation and environment is of equal importance to Sunzi's leadership theory. All these justify our leadership approach to the study of the *Art of war* and suggest that Sunzi's theory of warfare is relevant and applicable not only to strategy but also to leadership for military and non-military organizations.

Based on the analysis of Sunzi's views on warfare and his prescriptions to the focal commander on how to achieve organizational outcomes through strategic maneuver on the key elements of an organized action, we frame Sunzi's philosophy in terms of strategic leadership. While paying attention to ways of organizing, developing, and motivating a highly effective organization we also highlight the importance of factors external to the leader–member relationship including the higher authority, the larger community, and alliances and enemies, and the immanent situational and contextual factors. The term strategic leadership also suggests a system or institutional perspective as opposed to the supervisor–subordinate perspectives taken by theories of leadership such as the situational theory (Hersey and Blanchard, 1974, 1993), the path–goal theory (House, 1971), and the LMX theory (Liden and Graen, 1980).

## Philosophical foundations of Sunzi's strategic leadership

### Humanist foundation

In the context of war and combat, which are inherently destructive and which often legitimize strategies and tactics morally and ethically unacceptable in non-combat situations, Sunzi's humanist orientation is recognized by specialists (Cleary, 2000) but overlooked in the popular literature. Here we present evidence of the Confucian philosophy of benevolence and righteousness in Sunzi's warfare philosophy. Table 5.3 lists sentences from the *Art of war* that illustrate Confucian values of benevolence and righteousness.

Sunzi prescribed humanism in four types of relationship that the leader has: with the community at large, with higher authority, with subordinates, and with the enemy. Humanism refers to a higher purpose and legitimacy of leadership activities and it prescribes basic

Table 5.3. *Examples of the humanist foundation of strategic leadership.*

| Excerpts | Chapter |
| --- | --- |
| *The higher purpose of leadership: service to the community at large* | |
| War is a question of vital importance to the state, a matter of life and death, the road to survival or ruin. (Righteousness) | Assessments |
| The Way means inducing the people to have the same aim as the sovereign so that they will share death and share life, without fear of danger. (Righteousness) | Assessments |
| We know that the leader of the army is in charge of the lives of the people and the safety of the nation. (Righteousness) | Waging war |
| Generals are assistant to the nations. When their assistance is complete, the country is strong. When their assistance is defective, the country is weak. Those whose upper and lower ranks have the same desire are victorious. (Righteousness) | Attacking by stratagem |
| Those who use arms will cultivate the Way and keep the rules. Thus they can govern in such a way as to prevail over the corrupt. (Righteousness) | Disposition |
| Thus one advances without seeking glory, retreats without avoiding blame, only protecting people, to the benefit of the government as well, thus rendering valuable service to the nation. (Righteousness) | Terrain |
| Act when it is beneficial; desist if it is not . . . Therefore an enlightened government is careful about this; a good military leadership is alert to this. This is the way to secure a nation and keep the armed forces whole. (Righteousness) | Attacking by fire |
| *Relationship with higher authority* | |
| The ordinary rule for use of military force is for the military commander to receive the orders from the sovereignty. (Righteousness) | Attacking by stratagem; Adaptations |
| *Relationship with subordinates* | |
| Look upon your soldiers as you do infants, and they willingly go into deep valleys with you; look upon your soldiers as beloved children, and they willingly die with you. (Benevolence) | Terrain |

Table 5.3. (*cont.*)

| Excerpts | Chapter |
|---|---|
| If soldiers are punished before a personal attachment to the leadership is formed, they will not submit, and if they do not submit they are hard to employ. If punishments are not executed after personal attachment has been established with the soldiers, then they cannot be employed. (Benevolence) | Maneuvering |
| *Relationship with the enemy*<br>Generally in war, the best policy is to take the enemy state whole and intact; to destroy it is not. (Benevolence) | Attacking by stratagem |
| The best policy in war is to thwart the enemy's strategy. The second is to disrupt his alliances through diplomatic means. The third is to attack his army in the field, and the worst is to attack walled cities. (Benevolence) | Attacking by stratagem |
| Prisoners of war should be treated kindly and taken into your ranks. (Benevolence) | Waging war |
| Do not intercept an enemy returning home; in surrounding the enemy, leave him an escape route; do not press a cornered enemy. (Benevolence) | Maneuvering |

rules of conduct for the leader in relation to other relevant parties, and set boundaries for strategies and actions in the name of achieving organizational purposes. With regard to higher purpose, Sunzi sees military leadership not merely about winning victories but about serving the nation and the people, about following the Way of benevolence, and winning over support from the people. In leader–member relationships, Sunzi clearly emphasizes hierarchical authority in that the general takes orders from the sovereign and the soldiers from the commander. There are, however, two qualifications to this type of authority. First, he gives the field commander the autonomy to follow the Way of the war rather than the whims of the sovereign and, second, he requires commanders to treat soldiers just as parents treat children. With regard to benevolence to the enemy, Sunzi emphasizes defense, swift and complete victory, and to win over rather than destroy the enemy for the ultimate goal of building a unified empire.

## Holistic and dialectic foundations

While Confucianism prevailed mainly in the social life of traditional Chinese societies, Daoism provided ontological and epistemological bases for the holistic and dialectic views of the Chinese (Nisbett *et al.*, 2001). It is evident that Sunzi's leadership theory is based on his holistic and dialectic approach to the participants, elements, and processes of military organization and operation. The holistic approach is manifested primarily in two ways. The first is the comprehensiveness, that is, the extent to which the conception and the analysis of a given phenomenon cover all possible constituent elements. We are struck with Sunzi's frequent use of numbers to exhaust possible categories. For example, there are five fundamental factors to be compared between warring armies, three ways a sovereign can bring disaster to his army, six fatal problems occurring in an army, five fatal faults for a commander; there are nine varying tactics, five types of fire attack, and five types of spy; and finally there are six types of terrain and nine types of ground. Besides comprehensiveness, holism stresses the interrelationship of constituent elements within and across systems. For instance, terrain is one of the five fundamental factors and terrain itself consists of six types and the effect of terrain on the outcome of a battle must be assessed by combining knowledge of one's own army with that of one's enemy's army. The holistic view therefore seeks to attend to all relevant elements of a phenomenon and its surrounding situation. Applying the holistic view to leadership, it places the leader in a field of social actions that consists of other actors and forces, which may enable and constrain the leader simultaneously, and it is up to the leader to take strategic actions which maximize and leverage enablers but minimize the effect of constraints.

Chinese dialecticism is intricately related to holism because of the Daoist systemic view of the universe: the *Dao* is the Way which gives birth to the dual, *yin* and *yang*. *Yin* and *yang*, in turn, produce the trio of heaven, earth, and humanity, which in turn creates water, fire, metal, wood, and soil, which in turn generate myriad things. Dualism is therefore a fundamental concept of dialecticism. The dichotomous confrontational nature of war lends itself readily to the use of the dualist framework and Sunzi uses it abundantly. The theme of self versus enemy, especially the importance of knowing self and knowing the enemy, runs through the whole book. The two warring sides are assessed in terms of size (few vs. many) and strength (strong vs. weak); strategies and tactics are characterized in terms of orthodox (*zheng*) vs. unorthodox (*chi*), attack vs. defense, advance vs. retreat, and fullness vs. emptiness; outcomes are assessed in terms of gains vs. losses and victories vs. defeats, etc. Dualism and coexistence, however, do not mean a stable, static, or balanced relation between the opposing forces. Rather they are in constant flux and change, which can be subtle and gradual in some situations but radical and dramatic in others. So when conditions are ripe the weak can become strong or in a given situation the weak entity can occupy a strong position (of course through stratagem) and vice versa (of course because of poor or no strategy). Strategies and tactics in dealing with the enemy can all boil down to creating and leveraging one's own strength and invulnerability while creating and increasing the enemy's vulnerability by creating situational, psychological, and operational advantages. Due to this dynamic feature, dialecticism encourages holistic thinking so as to be in touch with the full reality, and at the same time it motivates activism and proactivity to influence and leverage a situation rather than allowing oneself to be overwhelmed by it or merely reacting to it.

## Sunzi's strategic leadership

Sunzi's adherence to the holistic approach to warfare makes his leadership theory fundamentally situational. Of the five determinants of a victory in war, three are external factors (the socio-political environment, the weather, and the terrain) and two are internal to the organization (the quality of the leader and the condition of the army). Sunzi devotes two full chapters to physical terrain (Chapter 10) and regions (Chapter 11) and one full chapter explicitly to varying tactics according to situational contingencies (Chapter 8). In other chapters about strategies, there are clear themes of using unorthodoxy and surprise, and of varying tactics according to circumstances. Sunzi's situational approach to leadership is also reflected in the importance he places on situational psychological factors relative to individual ones. He argues that "one who is skilled in directing war always tries to turn the situation to his advantage rather than make excessive demands on his subordinates" (Chapter 5), which suggests that success depends more on how the troops are strategically and situationally deployed by the leader than on the quality or psychological state of the individual soldiers *per se*. Furthermore, Sunzi sees followers' cohesion and morale as largely a function of situation rather than a purely chronic condition of the army. He predicts that troops will have greater morale when they are at the beginning of a campaign, when they find themselves deep in the enemy's territory, when they are rested, and when they have no way to back out (Chapter 11). He concludes that "an army under such conditions will be vigilant without admonishment, will carry out their duties without compulsion, will be devoted without constraint, will observe discipline even though they are not under close surveillance" (Chapter 11: 103). However, Sunzi's strategic situationalism of leadership is closer to the notion of strategic choice (Child, 1995) than the notion of situational determinism in the organizational behavior literature (Davis-Blake and Pfeffer, 1989). Despite, or indeed because of, his situational views of individual psychology and organizational effectiveness, Sunzi believes strongly that success lies in the ability of the leader on the one hand to comprehend and appreciate the power of a situation and, on the other, to rise above the situation by creating, leveraging, and adapting to the existing and emergent environment. This is what we call strategic situationalism. We depict the strategic situationalism model in Figure 5.1, in which the first component describes attributes of the leader, which enable strategic leadership activities to affect the situation and the followers, which in turn lead to success.

**Figure 5.1.** Sunzi's model of strategic situationalism.
(Solid lines refer to causal relationships on which Sunzi focused; dotted lines are possible but obscure causal relationships.)

## Individual attributes of the strategic leader

The *Art of war* contains many descriptions of the attributes of an ideal leader. In describing an ideal sovereign the most common terms Sunzi uses are humaneness (benevolence and righteousness) and enlightenedness. In describing an ideal general, Sunzi lists five attributes: wisdom, trustworthiness, benevolence, courage, and firmness (Chapter 1: 5). While benevolence is the most important virtue of the Confucian *Dao* of government, wisdom appears to be the most important attribute of the strategic leader for Sunzi's *Dao* of war. It is a much broader concept than intelligence as it refers to the acquisition of knowledge and skills through accumulation and the ability to fulfill one's responsibility. In fact, wisdom may arguably be the overarching attribute for Sunzi, as it is capable of incorporating courage, firmness or even benevolence and trustworthiness. In describing the wisdom of the general, Sunzi refers to understanding the broader political mission of war, seeing the *Dao* of *yin* and *yang* (seeing danger inherent in advantages, but advantage in dangers), having foreknowledge of the enemy and the battleground situation, recognizing emergent changes of the situation, and having the skill to use unorthodox strategies, to leverage situations (e.g. different kinds of region), to deploy troops according to the situation, and to win the troops' loyalty and compliance through soft and hard means. In superior–subordinate relations, trustworthiness, for Sunzi, seems to refer primarily to loyalty to the superior whereas, in contrast, benevolence is directed downward toward the subordinates. Courage may be the ideal attribute that is most special to military organization and combat situations, but to a large extent so is firmness. However, firmness may be more universal to all organizations as it counterbalances benevolence, for Sunzi believes that benevolence without firmness creates loyalty but not deployability.

Sunzi also lists five fatal flaws of a strategic leader that can bring calamity to the leader and the troops (Chapter 8). "Those who are ready to die can be killed; those who are intent on living can be captured; those who are quick to anger can be shamed; those who are puritanical can be disgraced; those who love people can be troubled" (Cleary, 2000: 135). These are vulnerabilities of the leader that can be strategically exploited by the enemy in combat situations. Although these have been typically viewed as character or trait flaws (e.g. Griffith, 1971), they can also be viewed as cognitive and emotional errors committed in response to extremely turbulent and volatile situations. Regardless of whether they are chronic traits or situationally induced characteristics, they are flaws. Notice that except for fear of death and quick temper, three qualities could be viewed as positive attributes of courage, honor, and benevolence if they exist in moderation or are counter-balanced by other attributes. When a leader is wedded to an otherwise good value or a course of action to the exclusion of other values and options, the otherwise good attribute becomes a flaw. Courage without wisdom and benevolence without firm discipline are examples. So it is singlemindedness that is fatal because the leader is unable to adapt to the complex and changing situation or more vulnerable to strategic maneuvering by more skillful opponents. In pointing out these flaws, Sunzi in effect is holding a holistic and situational view of positive leadership characteristics. Furthermore, because the singleminded overzealous leader is typically guided by emotion rather than by knowledge of the objective situations and the sound reasoning of strategic thinking, Sunzi points to the importance of emotional stability and balance for strategic thinking and strategic operation. He repeatedly warns against launching wars and battles as a result of the emotion of the sovereign and the general. Emotions, he warns, can be reversed but perished states and lost lives cannot be brought back.

## Strategic situationalism

Key to Sunzi's leadership theory is the Chinese concept of situation (*shi*), situation-making (*zhao shi*), and situational adaptation (*yin shi*). The Chinese term *shi* (close to the English pronunciation of shrrr) has been translated into English as force, position, power, or momentum. In the *Art of war*, Sunzi devoted one chapter (Chapter 5) to the topic of *shi*. The purpose of strategies and tactics regarding *shi* is to create a positive position (*you shi*) relative to an opponent, i.e. relative advantage, and the more overwhelming the advantage, the greater the likelihood of swift and complete victory. Sunzi devoted another chapter (Chapter 4) to a closely related concept, *xing*, which means formation, shape, or configuration. For example, the word for terrain in Chinese is *di xing* (topography). In modern Chinese, *xing* and *shi* when used together (*xing shi*) mean a situation of any kind and any scope, but in the *Art of war,* however, strategic situational advantage is further divided into subtypes of advantage: positional (terrain), organizational, and morale/spirit (*qi shi*).

## Creating positional advantage

The most potent advantage according to Sunzi lies in placing the organization in an advantageous position *vis-à-vis* other organizations in a given field of operation. This involves creating a strategically favorable environment for the organization. In the most basic sense of the term, Sunzi refers to the positional advantage of terrain (*di shi*). "When torrential water moves boulders, it is because of its momentum [*shi*] . . . Logs and rocks remain immobile when they are on level ground but fall forward when on a steep slope. The strategic advantage of troops skillfully commanded in battle may be compared to the momentum of round boulders rolling down from mountain heights." Sunzi emphasizes that it is far more effective for commanders to create situations (*zhao shi*) in which troops are advantageously positioned and ready than to demand bravery and heroism when faced with adversity. Strategic leadership should therefore pay more attention to creating favorable situations than accepting and working within given situations. The former requires strategic thinking, foreknowledge, and proactivity. Sunzi prescribes many proactive behaviors for creating a preponderance of positional advantage relative to opponents, ranging through full preparation, arriving early, employing more troops, and providing better logistics, etc. However, positional advantage seems to start with or boil down to advantage in knowing, especially in having information, as can be seen in the great importance of "knowing yourself and knowing your enemy." It is no wonder the book starts with war parameter assessment, which requires information on warring parties and ends with the importance of using secret agents for information advantage. Lord (2000: 304) observed that because Sunzi believed in "the manipulability of the strategic environment," he is remarkably different from Western military strategists such as Clausewitz. While Clausewitz emphasizes the chance and uncertainty of warfare and highlights the importance of intuition and the will of the leader, Sunzi places high priority on intelligence about the actual conditions of the battle, and affords it a strategically decisive role. Sunzi's emphasis on deception in warfare will also be better understood from this information-oriented strategic approach.

## Creating organizational advantage

One of the five parameters of winning is the organization of the army, by which Sunzi refers to the unity of command, the consistent enforcement of rules and regulations, clear rewards and punishments, and the coordination of different parts of the army. Sunzi starts the chapter on momentum by stating that whether commanding many or few troops, a large or small army, it is a matter of organization, of instituting layers of control, and of communication. As an aside, it is amazing to discover how so many of Sunzi's ideas on the science of war are reflected in the Western science of management, especially in the essential managerial functions of planning, organizing, commanding, and controlling as proposed by Henri Fayol (1916), who wrote his book about two thousand years after the *Art of war*. According to Griffith, the *Art of war* was translated into French in Paris in 1772. One wonders if Fayol had read and reflected on Sunzi. Sunzi proposes constant variations of orthodox and unorthodox formations in deploying troops. The conventional formations are generally used to engage the opponent while the surprise tactics are employed to win victories. Yet, unconventional and deceptive tactics such as feigning confusion, weakness, and retreat rely heavily on the order, strength, and unity that lie in the organizational advantages.

There seems to be a paradox in Sunzi's insistence on a rather rigid structure of unity of command and organizational discipline on one hand but flexibility, innovation, and variation of actions on the other. Sunzi's answer to the paradox lies in the leader's strategic discretion (Hambrick and Finkelstein, 1987) as well as the leader's ability to create and leverage situational and psychological advantages. Sunzi insists on non-interference from the sovereign on matters of military operation and on the autonomy and discretion of the commander. While acknowledging that the commander receives his mandate from the sovereign, after the commander sets out, "there are commands of the sovereign he should not obey" just as there are situations in which "there are roads he should not take, armies he should not attack, walled cities he should not assault, territories he should not contest for" (Chapter 8: 69). He warns of three ways that a sovereign could bring disaster to the army: arbitrarily ordering the army to advance or retreat when in fact it should not, interfering with the administration of the army, and interfering with the commander's strategies and tactics (Chapter 3).

Clearly, Sunzi believes that although the mandate is set from the top (which itself is subject to the criteria of righteousness and bene-volence) subordinates should be fully empowered to execute the mandate without interference from above especially when the higher authority has no full knowledge of the situation in the field. Sunzi also believes in following the Way of war (*zhan dao*), namely, following the rationality of acting according to the objective contin-gent requirement of the war rather than the subjective wishes of the sovereign or the general. "Thus, if the Way of war guarantees you victory, it is right for you to insist on fighting even if the sovereign has said not to. Where the Way of war does not allow victory, it is right for you to refuse to fight even if the sovereign says you must. Therefore, a commander who decides to advance without any thought of winning personal fame and to withdraw without fear of punishment and whose only concern is to protect his people and serve his sovereign is an invaluable asset to the state" (Chapter 10: 93).

## Creating morale advantage (*qi shi*)

Morale advantage refers to a psychological advantage, the degree of superiority of a troop over its enemy in terms of a conviction of morality and efficacy and a determination to win victory. With such momentum of spirit and energy the army will be like the cascading of pent-up water thundering through a steep gorge. How then is such morale momentum created? First, the legitimacy of command, for example, that of the sovereign over the general, the army, and the populace in general, originates from the Way, namely, righteousness and benevolence of those invested with authority as displayed in Table 5.3. Sunzi sees the psychological identification and attachment of the rank and file with the leader and the organization as essential. "If troops are punished before their loyalty is secured they will be disobedient. If not obedient, it is difficulty to employ them" (Chapter 9: 85). Second, benevolence must be coupled with discipline through training and deployment. Officers should be benevolent but strict with the soldiers, gain their loyalty, and have a harmonious rela-tionship with them (Chapter 9). Such hard–soft tactics, of course, reflect the Daoist way of thinking and are consistent with the pater-nalistic model. It should be noted, as we did earlier, that in Sunzi's strategic situationalism, morale is not merely a function of internal subjective qualities of the organizational members. Organizational and positional advantages outside the person are other ways of inducing psychological advantage.

### Leveraging and adaptation

While situation-making stresses creating favorable positional, organizational, and psychological situations, taking advantage and adapting to existing situations is also part of strategic situationalism, and this is closest to the contingency approach of leadership in the West (Fiedler, 1977; Hersey and Blanchard, 1974). In Chinese, leveraging and adaptation are called *yin shi*, literally meaning "following the situation." Change of operations and tactics in response to emergent situations is a major component of strategic leadership. The emergent situations may present opportunities to be leveraged and constraints to be adapted to. Like Laozi, the master of Daoism, Sunzi likens the leader's ability to change to a property of water. Sunzi asserts that as water changes its course in accordance with the contours of the terrain so do commanders change their tactics in accordance to the situation. "There is no fixed pattern in the use of tactics in war just as there is not constant course in the flow of water" (Chapter 6: 57). The variation and change of tactics are based on understanding all aspects of the situation: the location, the time, the state and condition of one's own army versus those of the opponent's. The key is to understand fully the emergent and the potential favorable and unfavorable factors. It is in the context of adaptation and change that Sunzi identifies those five fatal flaws of the commander (Chapter 9). These flaws orient the commander to staying on a wrong course because of adherence to some predetermined doctrine, high authority, or emotion.

### Theoretical and practical implications

The *Art of war* by Sunzi has been very influential in Chinese political and military history and there is evidence that it has influenced the thinking and practice of political and military leaders in modern China (e.g. Mao's guerrilla war), Japan, and the West (e.g. Cleary, 2000; Griffith, 1971; Lord, 2000). Maxims of competitive strategies and tactics directly and indirectly attributed to the *Art of war* permeate speeches by Chinese and Western business executives. Instead of digging into that body of literature, we present our thoughts on the theoretical and practical implications of the *Art of war* in a global context.

First and foremost, we are struck by Sunzi's non-relational approach to leadership. Admittedly one can see a reflection of the Confucian dyadic model of interpersonal role relationships such as that between the sovereign and the minister and between the parent and the child. Yet, Sunzi is mostly concerned with the whole organization: its legitimacy, its systems of operation and administration, the collective followership, or the unity and morale of the organizational members. His unit of analysis and his target of leadership actions are more often than not at the collective rather than the individual or the dyadic levels. His collectivity also tends to be at the highest collectivity level, that is, the overall organization rather than its individual divisions and subdivisions. Such an approach speaks to the Western literature on strategic leadership (Boal and Hooijberg, 2001; Finkelstein and Hambrick, 1996) and contributes to it by emphasizing the creation of external and internal winning environments. The system and situational approach to leadership complements dyadic models of leader–member relationships (Graen and Uhl-Bien, 1995). Leadership in the global context calls not only for cross-cultural relationship-building but also for attention to issues of external and internal environments, system-level adaptation, and collective identification.

Second, Sunzi's theory of situationalism provides interesting critiques on the person–situation debate in the organizational behavior literature and on cross-cultural research on cognition. The person–situation debate centers around whether it is individuals' stable internal characteristics or the external situation that determine people's behavior (Davis-Blake and Pfeffer, 1989; Ross and Nisbett, 1991; Salancik and Pfeffer, 1978). Dispositionalists believe that the impact of individual characteristics is more significant whereas situationalists believe in the power of the situation. Cross-cultural comparative research on cognition and behavior shows that the Chinese are more holistic in that they see more situational causal factors, whereas Westerners are more analytic and agential as they are more likely to see individual actors as causal agents of events (Nisbett *et al.*, 2001). Both these bodies of literature might suggest that Chinese leaders, relative to their Western counterparts, believe more in the power of situation than in that of individuals, so that Chinese leadership is expected to be less agential, less assertive, or less proactive with regards to situation or environment. This, however, is not what we observe in Sunzi's leadership philosophy as manifested in the *Art of war*. What we observe is that while Sunzi does believe in the causal power of the situation he nevertheless also believes in great leaders being masters of situation-making, situation manipulation, and situation leveraging. Sunzi's theory of strategic situationalism fits well with the Daoist way of contradictory thinking but in our view has great significance for leadership research and practice as organizations become more complex, dynamic, and global. Leadership researchers could conduct research to test empirically such seemingly contradictory propositions. More importantly, researchers can theorize cognitive and behavioral factors that orient leaders to be both holistic in cognition and agential in action in exercising strategic leadership.

The third point of both theoretical and practical importance is Sunzi's concept of wisdom and the importance of information. We pointed out that the Chinese concept of wisdom or enlightenment bears some resemblance to the concept of intelligence in Western psychology and leadership (Kirkpatrick and Locke, 1991). But there may be important differences. First, the Western concept of intelligence is a personality trait that is largely hereditary and non-malleable whereas the Chinese concept of wisdom is acquired through continuous study and practice. Second, the Chinese concept of wisdom is also broader than managerial wisdom as conceived by Boal and Hooijberg (2001) or job-related knowledge (Kirkpatrick and Locke, 1991). Most likely the Chinese concept of wisdom is multidimensional and, in Sunzi's conceptions, it could be a meta-characteristic of what leadership is about. More conceptual work is needed to refine and specify wisdom and establish its validity in leadership research. Wisdom could very well be the key leader characteristic that accounts for or moderates strategic situationalism.

Another point relating to wisdom is about strategic information-seeking. Lord (2000: 304) credited Sunzi for "anticipating the information-oriented strategic approach of the contemporary revolution in military affairs" and, we want to add, in the affairs of business and management as well. It can be further argued that if information-seeking becomes the norm, information quality in terms of completeness, relevance, and accuracy and information management may be important factors that affect the effectiveness of strategic situationalism.

Lastly, issues of ethics are becoming more salient as companies are facing greater global as well as domestic competition. Sunzi's infamous quote that "war is a game of deception" (Chapter 1: 9) needs to be considered in its historical context as well as in the context of war being ridden with conflict and violence. Sunzi's aversion to aggression and destruction for the sake of vengeance and his appeal to justice and benevolence reflected the Confucian philosophy of benevolence and humaneness. However, his deception tactics were severely condemned by Xunzi, a Confucianist contemporary of Sunzi, on the grounds of morality and ethicality. It is obvious that Sunzi's deceptive tactics are almost always directed toward the enemy but in Chapter 11 he also entertained situations in which the officer needs to be inscrutable and to keep the soldiers ignorant of the military plan and the battle situation, all in the name of maintaining the unity and morale of the army. The question arises of whether, and, if so, to what extent and on what bases, organizations and leaders may use deception or information asymmetry in their transactions with their opponents or their employees. Where should the benchmark of moral and ethical standards in military, political, and business conflicts be set, and should there be different ethical standards for domestic and international conflicts? In summary, future researchers must seriously consider the incorporation of ethics into their model of strategic leadership and must address the ethical challenges raised in Sunzi's *Art of war.*

## References

Boal, K. B., and Hooijberg, R. 2001. "Strategic leadership research: moving on," *Leadership Quarterly* 11(4): 515–549.

Child, J. 1995. *Strategic choice: the perspective and its contemporary relevance.* Cambridge: Judge Institute of Management Studies.

Cleary, T. 2000. *The art of war.* Boston: Shambhala.

Davis-Blake, A., and Pfeffer, J. 1989. "Just a mirage: the search for dispositional effects in organizational research," *Academy of Management Review* 14(3): 385–400.

Fayol, H. 1916. *Industrial and general administration.* Paris: Dunod.

Fiedler, F. E. 1967. *A theory of leadership effectiveness.* New York: McGraw-Hill.

Finkelstein, S., and Hambrick, D. C. 1996. *Strategic leadership: top executives and their effects on organizations.* St. Paul, MN: West.

Garvin, D. 2003. *Sun tzu: the art of war.* New York: Barnes and Noble.

Graen, G. B., and Uhl-Bien, M. 1995. "Relationship-based approach to leadership: development of leader–member exchange (LMX) theory of leadership over 25 years: applying a multi-level multi-domain perspective," *Leadership Quarterly* 6(2): 219–247.

Griffith, S. B. 1971. *Sunzi: the art of war.* Oxford: Oxford University Press.

Hambrick, D. C., and Finkelstein, S. 1987. "Managerial discretion: a bridge between polar views of organizations," *Research in Organizational Behavior* 9: 369–406.

House, R. J. 1971. "A path–goal theory of leader effectiveness," *Administrative Science Quarterly* 16: 321–338.

Hersey, P., and Blanchard, K. H. 1974. "So you want to know your leadership style?" *Training and Development Journal* 35 (February): 1–15.

1993. *Management of organizational behavior: utilizing Human Resources,* 6th edn. Englewood Cliffs, NJ: Prentice Hall.

Kirkpatrick, S. A., and Locke, E. A. 1991. "Leadership: do traits matter?" *Academy of Management Executive* 5 (May): 48–60.

Liden, R., and Graen, G. 1980. "Generalizability of the vertical dyad linkage model of leadership," *Academy of Management Journal* 23: 451–465.

Lord, C. 2000. "A note on Sunzi," *Comparative Strategy* 19: 301–307.

Nisbett, R., Peng, K., Choi, I., and Norenzayan, A. 2001. "Culture and systems of thought: holistic versus analytic cognition," *Psychological Review* 108: 291–310.

Ross, L., and Nisbett, R. 1991. *The person and the situation: perspectives of social psychology.* New York: McGraw-Hill.

Salancik, G. R., and Pfeffer, J. 1978. "A social information processing approach to job attitudes and task design," *Administrative Science Quarterly* 23: 224–253.

Wu, R. S., Wu, X. L., and Lin, W. S. 2001. *Sunzi: the art of war; Sun bin: the art of war.* Beijing: Foreign Languages Press.

Yukl, G. 1998. *Leadership in organizations,* 4th edn. Englewood Cliffs, NJ: Prentice Hall.

# Modern Chinese leadership theories and practices

# 6 | Paternalistic leadership in Chinese organizations: research progress and future research directions

JIING-LIH FARH, JIAN LIANG, LI-FANG CHOU, AND BOR-SHIUAN CHENG

P ATERNALISTIC LEADERSHIP (PL) is an indigenous Chinese leadership style that is rooted in China's patriarchal tradition and has been found to be prevalent in overseas Chinese family businesses. Farh and Cheng (2000) proposed a model of PL that has three components: authoritarianism, benevolence, and moral leadership. Since then, a series of empirical studies have been conducted by Cheng and his colleagues to examine the validity of Farh and Cheng's PL model using a variety of samples from Taiwan and mainland China. In this chapter, we review this body of research and identify promising areas for future research.

## Introduction

In the second half of the twentieth century, entrepreneurship among overseas Chinese exploded not only in Chinese-dominated communities such as Hong Kong, Singapore, and Taiwan, but also in Southeast Asian countries, such as Indonesia, Malaysia, Thailand, and the Philippines, where the Chinese are in the minority (Weidenbaum, 1996). Scholars who were intrigued by this phenomenon embarked on a series of studies of the practices of overseas Chinese businesses. They discovered a distinct management/leadership style called paternalism, widely practiced among the owners/managers of overseas Chinese family businesses (e.g. Cheng, 1995c; Redding, 1990; Silin, 1976; Westwood, 1997). Paternalism, which is rooted in the traditional Chinese family structure, has crossed the boundary of families and generalized to the workplace. Like the father in a Chinese family, the superior in a company is expected to provide guidance, protection, nurture, and care to the subordinate; like a dutiful son, the subordinate, in return, is normally required to be loyal and deferent to the superior (Aycan, 2006). Paternalism has become a salient feature that characterizes the vertical interactions within Chinese organizations.

Based on an extensive review of this body of literature, Farh and Cheng (2000) proposed a model of paternalistic leadership (PL), in which PL was defined as a type of leadership that combines strong and clear authority with concern, considerateness, and elements of moral leadership. Since then, a series of empirical studies have been conducted on PL to examine the effects of its dimensions in a variety of organizational settings across Taiwan and mainland China. Most of these studies have been published in Chinese books and journals. The accumulated empirical findings and the need for cross-cultural scholarly exchange make an integrative review timely and necessary. The purpose of this chapter is to take stock of progress in this body of literature and offer suggestions to guide future research.

## Paternalistic leadership: its meaning and cultural origin

Silin (1976) was among the first to note the paternalistic management style of overseas Chinese owners/managers. In the 1960s, when Taiwan's economy was just beginning to take off, Silin conducted an anthropological study of the management practices at a large private enterprise in Taiwan. He found that the leadership concepts and behavioral styles of Taiwanese business owners/managers were markedly different from those in the United States. He summarized these differences into several categories of management style, including didactic leadership, moral leadership, centralized authority, maintaining social distance with subordinates, keeping intentions ill-defined, and implementing control tactics. Building on Silin's (1976) and others' works, Redding (1990) identified paternalism as a key element of "Chinese capitalism" after in-depth interviews with seventy-two owner/managers of overseas Chinese family businesses. Following the work of Silin (1976) and Redding (1990), Westwood (1997) proposed a model of "paternalistic headship" for Chinese family businesses. Westwood's model described nine stylistic elements of headship: didactic leadership, non-specific intentions, reputation-building, protection of dominance, political manipulation, patronage and nepotism, conflict diffusion, aloofness and social distance, and dialogue ideal, which exist in the general structural characteristics of centralization, low formalization, harmony-building, and personalism. Using a psychological approach, Cheng

(1995a, 1995b, 1995c) examined indigenous leadership behaviors in a variety of organizations in Taiwan, including family businesses, high-tech companies, schools, and the army, and found that PL was widespread in his samples.

Based on a thorough review of the extant research, Farh and Cheng (2000) proposed their three-dimensional model of PL, the dimensions being authoritarianism, benevolence, and moral leadership. Authoritarianism refers to a leader's behavior of asserting strong authority and control over subordinates and demanding unquestioned obedience from subordinates. Benevolence implies that a leader demonstrates individualized, holistic concern for subordinates' personal and familial well-being. Moral leadership is broadly depicted as a leader's behavior that demonstrates superior moral character and integrity in (a) not acting selfishly (especially refraining from abusing authority for personal gain) and (b) leading by example. Farh and Cheng's (2000) model clearly identified the basic content domain of PL, which facilitates subsequent empirical studies on PL.

In creating a context (Chinese) specific model, Farh and Cheng (2000) devoted a great deal of attention to the social and cultural forces underpinning PL. Authoritarian leadership could be traced to the cultural traditions of Confucianism and Legalism. Under the influence of Confucianism, the father–son relationship is considered paramount and supersedes all other social relations. By virtue of his role, a father has legitimate authority over his children and all other family members. Meanwhile, the Legalist doctrine, which was prevalent in dynastic China, called for the emperor to distrust his ministers and maintain absolute power and control over them through political manipulation. The confluence of these two traditions leads to Politicized Confucianism, which legitimizes the superior's absolute power and authority over his inferiors. This tradition later generalizes to all forms of hierarchical organizations in Chinese societies in which a leader has the right to maintain strong authority over subordinates, and the subordinates are obligated to obey.

Benevolent leadership also originates in Confucianism, which emphasizes mutuality in social relations – a benevolent ruler with his loyal ministers, a kind father with his filial sons, a righteous husband with his submissive wife, a gentle elder brother with his obedient younger brother, and a kind elder with the deferent junior. Relational harmony is maintained when each party performs his/her roles dutifully.

For example, a father should be kind to his children, and the children should show respect and filial piety to their father. Confucian ethics also stress the importance of reciprocity (*bao*) in social relations. Benevolence on the part of the superiors should generate indebtedness on the part of the inferiors, who should try to reciprocate in earnest. This reciprocity may take the form of genuine gratitude, personal loyalty, or obedience to and compliance with the superior's requests, even beyond what is normally required in the subordinate role (Yang, 1957). When this relationship generalizes to the workplace, mutual obligations based on duty fulfillment emerge. They entail protection of the follower by the leader and loyalty toward the leader by the followers.

Finally, Confucius believed that, both in the realm of family and in government, the use of moral principles, moral examples, and moral persuasion should be emphasized. Chinese society has a long history of selecting and evaluating leaders on moral grounds. Law and punishment are inherently ineffective because they can only regulate overt behaviors, not inner thoughts. The most effective form of governance is thus leading by virtue and moral example. In China where the tradition of the rule of law was never firmly established in its long history, the citizens were always at the mercy of the ruler. As a result, the moral excellence of the ruler is essential for guarding against abuses of authority and protecting the citizens. Therefore, in Chinese organizations, moral leadership is not only rooted in Confucian ethics, but also desired by subordinates for their own safety against potential abuses of authority by the superior.

## Effects of paternalistic leadership on subordinate outcomes

Farh and Cheng's (2000) model further identified the typical subordinate responses to authoritarianism, benevolence, and moral leadership (see Figure 6.1). Specifically, the leader's authoritarian behavior is expected to evoke the psychological responses of dependence and compliance on the part of subordinates, whereas the leader's benevolence is expected to be matched by the subordinate's gratitude and obligation to pay back, and the leader's morality is expected to lead to the subordinate's respect for and identification with the leader. These subordinate role responses are rooted in traditional Chinese culture, which emphasizes dependence on and submission to authority on

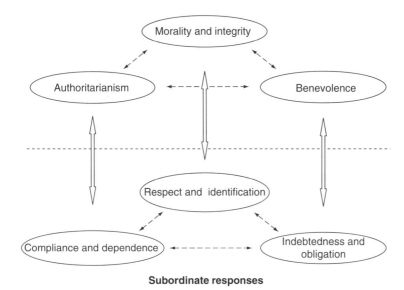

Figure 6.1. Farh and Cheng's model of paternalistic leadership.
*Source:* Adapted from Farh and Cheng (2000).

the part of the follower in a hierarchical relationship, obligations to repay favors given by others, and the importance of accepting moral teachings.

Implicit in the cultural logic of Farh and Cheng's (2000) model is the complementarity of leader and subordinate roles. Authoritarian leadership cannot work unless subordinates have been socialized to respect the vertical hierarchy and have a dependent mind-set (Pye, 1981; Redding, 1990). The leader's benevolence cannot be sustained if it does not engender feelings of indebtedness and a willingness to reciprocate in subordinates. Moral leadership works only if subordinates identify with their leader's moral superiority and are willing to imitate it. When both leaders and subordinates play their respective culturally prescribed roles, relational harmony prevails. But when one party abandons its role while the other still expects compliance with cultural roles, this will lead to strain, disharmony, and, at worst, a breakdown of the relationship.

Based on the above framework, a series of empirical studies were conducted to examine the model's validity. These efforts first focused on the development of a research instrument to measure the three dimensions of the PL model, then examined the effects of the PL dimensions on the subordinate's psychological responses (defined as compliance without dissent, gratitude and repayment, and identification and imitation), and finally explored the impact of PL dimensions on a variety of subordinate outcomes such as workplace emotion, job performance, job attitudes, and organizational citizenship behavior (OCB).

### The development of a PL scale

Cheng, Chou, and Farh (2000) constructed a forty-two-item Paternalistic Leadership Scale (PLS) that has three subscales (authoritarianism, benevolence, and morality) corresponding to the three dimensions of PL. The construct domains of the PLS were derived primarily from the earlier ideographical works by Cheng (1995a, 1995b, 1995c). The domain of authoritarian leadership includes *powerfully subduing*, referring to insisting on complete obedience from followers; *authority and control*, referring to having a final say on all key decisions in the workplace; *intention hiding*, referring to keeping distance from followers; *rigorousness*, referring to imposing strict discipline on followers, and *doctrine*, referring to instructing followers to achieve high performance. The domain of benevolent leadership contains *individualized care*, and *understanding and forgiving*. The domain of moral leadership includes *integrity and fulfilling one's obligations, never taking advantage of others*, and the *selfless paragon*. Using two independent samples from Taiwan (a private conglomerate and a set of primary schools), Cheng, Chou, and Farh (2000) found that the items of the PLS loaded highly on their intended dimensions, the three dimensions of PL were statistically distinct, and each subscale had high internal consistency. The construct validity of the PLS was thus preliminarily established.

Six empirical studies have used the PLS to examine the effects of PL dimensions on subordinate psychological responses and outcomes (Cheng, Huang, and Chou, 2002; Cheng *et al.*, 2003; Cheng *et al.*, 2004; Cheng, Shieh, and Chou, 2002; Farh *et al.*, 2006; Wu, Hsu, and Cheng, 2002). Two of these studies were conducted in mainland China and five in Taiwan, drawing on samples from a variety of organizations, including private businesses, high-tech firms, and primary schools.

### Main effects of authoritarian leadership

Inconsistent with the prediction by Farh and Cheng (2000), research using the PLS did not find a consistent positive correlation between authoritarian leadership and the subordinate's psychological response of compliance. Cheng *et al.* (2004) found that compliance was uncorrelated with authoritarian leadership ($r = -.06$, n.s.), but significantly correlated with moral leadership ($r = .41$, $p < .01$) and benevolent leadership ($r = .42$, $p < .01$). Farh *et al.* (2006) found that while compliance was significantly correlated with authoritarian leadership ($r = .21$, $p < .01$), it was correlated even more strongly with benevolent leadership ($r = .34$, $p < .01$) and equally strongly with moral leadership ($r = .24$, $p < .01$). Using structural equation modeling, Farh *et al.* (2006) further showed that fear of the leader mediated the effect of authoritarian leadership on compliance, and compliance was linked with benevolent and moral leadership through the subordinate's gratitude and repayment, and identification with the leader. These findings, taken together, do not show that compliance is an immediate psychological response to authoritarian leadership; instead, fear of the leader seems to be a more direct, psychological response to authoritarianism. These findings also suggest that compliance may be considered as a more distal outcome of PL, affected by all three psychological responses of gratitude and repayment, identification with the leader, and fear of the leader.

In terms of subordinate outcomes, authoritarian leadership was found to be negatively correlated with commitment to the team, satisfaction with the leader, job performance, intention to stay (Cheng, Huang, and Chou, 2002), OCB, loyalty to and trust in the supervisor (Cheng, Shieh, and Chou, 2002), and organizational commitment (Farh *et al.*, 2006), and positively correlated with angry feelings (Wu, Hsu, and Cheng, 2002). These findings suggest that the exercise of authoritarian leadership in modern Chinese organizations is unappreciated by the followers and accompanied by a host of negative outcomes.

### Main effects of benevolent leadership
In support of Farh and Cheng's (2000) model, benevolence was found to be strongly positively correlated with gratitude and repayment (Cheng *et al.*, 2004; Farh *et al.*, 2006). While gratitude and repayment were also correlated with moral leadership, their correlation with benevolent leadership was stronger ($r = .65$ vs. .48 in Cheng *et al.*, 2004; $r = .49$ vs. .18 in Farh *et al.*, 2006). This relationship was not moderated by situational factors, such as subordinate dependence on the leader for resources or the subordinate's orientation to tradition

(Farh *et al.*, 2006). This is not surprising given the centrality of the norm of reciprocity (*bao*) in Chinese societies (Yang, 1957). While some traditional values (e.g. respect for authority, male domination) have been eroded by societal modernization, the reciprocity value endures (Cheng and Farh, 2001; Yang, 1998). As expected, benevolent leadership also had positive effects on work attitudes and performance including satisfaction with the leader, loyalty to the leader, commitment to the organization, job performance, and OCB (Cheng, Huang, and Chou, 2002; Cheng, Shieh, and Chou, 2002; Cheng *et al.*, 2003; Cheng *et al.*, 2004; Farh *et al.*, 2006).

### Main effects of moral leadership
Consistent with the prediction of Farh and Cheng's (2000) model, moral leadership was strongly associated with the subordinate's psychological response of identification with the leader (Cheng *et al.*, 2004; Farh *et al.*, 2006). When all three PL dimensions were entered into the regression equation simultaneously to predict identification with the leader, moral leadership had the largest beta weight (Farh *et al.*, 2006). Similar to benevolence, moral leadership was found to be consistently positively correlated with subordinate outcomes such as satisfaction with the leader, loyalty to the leader, commitment to the organization/team, job performance, and OCB (Cheng, Huang, and Chou, 2002; Cheng, Shieh, and Chou, 2002; Cheng *et al.*, 2003; Cheng *et al.*, 2004; Farh *et al.*, 2006). In the above analyses, moral leadership was often found to have the largest effect on subordinate outcomes (Cheng *et al.*, 2003; Farh *et al.* 2006), and, as pointed out earlier, its positive effect on compliance was even stronger than the effect of authoritarianism (Cheng *et al.*, 2004; Farh *et al.*, 2006). These findings point to the significance of the leader's morality in leader–subordinate relationships in contemporary Chinese organizations.

### Interactive effects of the three dimensions
Since each of the three dimensions of PL captures a key aspect of paternalistic leadership, a logical research question follows: do they mutually reinforce each other in producing interactive effects that go beyond their individual main effects? Although Farh and Cheng (2000) were mute on the three-way interactions, they did point out that high authoritarianism in conjunction with high benevolence represents an ideal type of leadership widely accepted in traditional

Chinese culture. Given the importance of moral leadership, it is conceivable that the leader's morality may further reinforce the effects of high authoritarianism–high benevolence leadership to produce a highly effective leader.

Several studies have explored the interactive effects of the three PL dimensions, using hierarchical multiple regression analysis. While none of these studies found the three-way interaction, the two-way interaction between authoritarianism and benevolence was sometimes observed in attitudinal outcomes. For example, Cheng, Huang, and Chou (2002) found a significant interaction between authoritarian and benevolent leadership on satisfaction with the leader in work teams in Taiwan. Similar interactions were observed for identification, compliance, and repayment and gratitude in Cheng *et al.* (2004). These two-way interactions, when plotted, reveal that when a leader has high benevolence, authoritarian leadership has either a slightly positive effect or no effect on the subordinates' attitudes; when a leader has low benevolence, authoritarianism has a negative effect on the subordinates' attitudes. This pattern of interaction offers some support for the proposition that an "ideal" leader in Chinese organizations is simultaneously benevolent and "strict" (in the sense of applying harsh discipline) toward subordinates.

In addition, an interaction between morality and authoritarianism on attitudinal outcomes was sometimes observed (Cheng *et al.*, 2003; Cheng *et al.*, 2004). This observation shows that when a leader was perceived as having high morality, authoritarianism had a negative effect on the subordinates' attitudes; when the leader's morality was perceived as low, authoritarianism had a positive effect on the subordinates' attitudes. This interactive effect is difficult to interpret, and we shall not elaborate here. In sum, we found very limited evidence about the interactive effects of PL dimensions on subordinate outcomes in existing studies. The most promising finding appears to be the interaction between authoritarianism and benevolence. Since this interactive effect has not been found reliably across studies (Farh *et al.*, 2006), there may be some contextual factors that condition its effect. Future research should examine this issue further before any firm conclusions are drawn.

### Comparison with transformational leadership

Because PL is an indigenous leadership model, it is important to determine whether its dimensions could account for unique variance in subordinate outcomes beyond that predicted by well-established Western leadership theories. In two of these studies (Cheng, Shieh, and Chou, 2002; Cheng *et al.*, 2004), transformational and transactional leadership were included along with PL to examine this question empirically. Results showed that PL did account for unique variances in subordinates' outcomes after controlling for transformational and transactional leadership. The strongest evidence was presented in Cheng, Shieh, and Chou (2002) in which the teacher's OCB was regressed on the principal's transformational and transactional leadership along with PL dimensions and demographic control variables. Results showed that benevolent and moral leadership emerged as the only leadership variables that had significant positive effects on the teacher's OCB. These results suggest that PL can explain unique variances in subordinate outcomes that go beyond those explained by Western leadership models.

### Summary and discussion

Empirical research thus far has shown that Farh and Cheng's (2000) model is a viable framework to conceptualize PL in Chinese contexts. When operationalized by PLS, the three dimensions of PL are conceptually and empirically distinct. They also account for a significant amount of variance in subordinates' psychological responses and attitudinal and behavioral outcomes beyond those explained by Western leadership theories. While these findings are encouraging, this stream of research does have major limitations that need to be overcome in future research.

Theoretically speaking, the content domain of each PL dimension was derived inductively from the management style of owners/managers of Chinese family businesses in the 1960s to 1980s. Some of the behaviors observed are now outdated due to the pace of modernization throughout the Greater China region. Inclusion of outdated behaviors in the content domain of PL makes the model less relevant to the modern context. This is particularly serious for the dimension of authoritarian leadership. The strong negative overtone of some of the behaviors illustrating authoritarian leadership causes it to be negatively correlated with benevolent and moral leadership. Clearly, there is a need to revisit the content domain of each PL dimension and to develop a second-generation research instrument for PL that is better suited to the twenty-first century.

There are also methodological limitations in this body of literature that need to be overcome in future research. First, in five of the seven studies, the data were collected from a single source, subordinate surveys, which render the research findings vulnerable to common method bias. Second, all of the seven studies employed a cross-sectional research design, which makes it difficult to draw firm conclusions about the causal relationships between PL and subordinate psychological responses or outcomes. Finally, even though the seven studies were conducted in divergent contexts (e.g. private firms, work teams, primary schools), all of them examined PL and its effects at the dyadic level. This limits our ability to draw conclusions about the possible effects of PL on outcomes at the level of the organization or the work unit.

## Situational moderators of paternalistic leadership

Since Farh and Cheng's (2000) model of PL is embedded in a set of social/cultural/organizational conditions, the effects of PL on subordinate outcomes are not expected to be uniform across all situations. Hall and Rosenthal (1991: 447) pointed out that "If we want to know how well we are doing in the biological, psychological, and social sciences, an index that will serve us well is how far we have advanced in our understanding of the moderator variables of our field." Therefore, to advance our knowledge of *when* PL makes a difference in the workplace, we should examine situational factors as moderators in PL research. Two situational factors have been studied in the PL literature: subordinate traditionality and subordinate dependence on the leader for resources.

### Subordinate traditionality

The construct of Chinese traditionality was conceived by Yang in the 1980s and defined as "the typical pattern of more or less related motivational, evaluative, attitudinal and temperamental traits that is most frequently observed in people in traditional Chinese society and can still be found in people in contemporary Chinese societies such as Taiwan, Hong Kong, and mainland China" (Yang, 2003: 265). Farh, Earley, and Lin (1997) first introduced this construct into organizational science. They selected five items to measure the degree to which an individual endorses the hierarchical role relationships specified by

Chinese traditional culture. Social order in traditional Chinese societies is founded on five fundamental relationships (*wu-lun*) of Confucianism: emperor–subject, father–son, husband–wife, elder–younger, and friend–friend. Four of these five cardinal relationships are hierarchical in nature. Individual loyalty and obedience to the authorities are viewed as the prerequisites of social harmony (Bond and Hwang, 1987).

Nowadays, Chinese people differ greatly in their degrees of modernization, education, wealth, and values. Societal modernization has weakened the foundation of respect for authority in contemporary Chinese societies to varying degrees. Therefore, the Chinese differ in their identification with traditional values such as respect for authority. Unquestioned obedience to authority may not be considered as a "taken for granted" value by all Chinese, especially for the younger generations with higher education (Cheng and Farh, 2001). Empirical studies have already shown the variance of traditionality within Chinese societies and its regulating effect on people's working attitudes and behaviors (e.g. Farh, Earley, and Lin, 1997; Farh, Hackett, and Liang, 2007; Hui, Lee, and Rousseau, 2004).

Our general prediction here is that individuals who identify with traditional Chinese cultural values (e.g. submission to authority) are more likely to respond positively to PL than are those who do not. Two of three studies examining the moderating role of individual traditionality found general support for this proposition. For example, Cheng *et al.* (2004) reported that in terms of the three psychological responses to PL (identification, compliance, and gratitude), authoritarian leadership had no effects on subordinates with low traditionality, but had positive effects on those with high traditionality. Farh *et al.* (2006) found that authoritarianism did not lower satisfaction with the leader for those who endorsed traditional Chinese values, but it had a strong negative effect for those who did not. Cheng *et al.* (2003), however, failed to find the moderating effect of traditionality in a sample from the Chinese mainland. In summary, there is good evidence that subordinates' responses to authoritarianism are contingent on their individual values for traditionality, but the findings have not been entirely consistent across studies.

### Subordinate dependence on the leader for resources
Besides traditionality, the dependence of subordinates on their supervisors for resources may also affect subordinates' responses to PL

dimensions. There are two different ways of conceptualizing subordinate dependence in the literature. On the one hand, subordinate dependence may be construed from a psychological approach, which describes the extent to which an employee wishes the leader to facilitate the paths towards individual, group, and/or organizational goals (e.g. Kerr and Jermier, 1978). An alternative view is to construe it as resource-based dependence imposed by the organizational structure (e.g. French and Raven, 1960). This reflects the degree of the managers' dominance over subordinates in the workplace. We use this second view of dependence. Redding (1990) suggested that the strong dependence of subordinates on their supervisor is a salient characteristic of paternalism in overseas Chinese family businesses. This structurally imposed dependence is a useful angle for understanding the boundary conditions of PL effects. The logic behind this hypothesized effect is straightforward. Subordinates are less likely to respond to paternalistic leadership when they are resource-independent than when they are resource-dependent.

Farh *et al.* (2006) studied the moderating effects of subordinates' dependence on the leader for resources on the relationship between the PL dimensions and subordinates' outcomes. Consistent with their general predictions, they found that (i) authoritarianism was more strongly associated with fear of the leader when the subordinates' resource dependence was high than when it was low; and (ii) benevolence had a stronger, positive effect on subordinates' identification, compliance, and organizational commitment when subordinates' resource dependence was high than when it was low. These findings, taken together, suggest that when subordinates depend heavily on their leaders for resources, authoritarian and benevolent leadership tend to have stronger effects on subordinates. Interestingly, Farh *et al.* (2006) reported a "reverse" moderating effect for moral leadership. That is, the leader's morality had a stronger positive effect on the subordinates' identification, compliance, and commitment when subordinates' dependence was low than when it was high. The leader's morality actually had a more potent effect when subordinates did not depend on their leaders for resources. If these results can be replicated in future research, they suggest that the three dimensions of PL involve different psychological mechanisms in influencing workers' attitudes and behaviors. Future research should examine this issue further.

## Summary and discussion

The above research shows that PL works more positively or less negatively when subordinates endorse traditional values and when subordinates heavily depend on their leaders for resources. These findings provide support for the general proposition that the PL model is deeply embedded in its Chinese context, and its effects on subordinates are conditioned by a set of situational factors. Future research should examine more systematically how situational factors, ranging from subordinates' values and personalities to the leader's characteristics, to task and organizational characteristics, may amplify or neutralize the effects of PL on subordinates' and work-unit outcomes.

## A configurational approach to paternalistic leadership

Most leadership theories (e.g. Fiedler, 1967; House, 1971) have taken a reductionistic approach to examining the leadership phenomenon (Meyer, Tsui, and Hinnings, 1993). They presume the relationships between leadership and outcomes are deterministic and focus on a limited number of variables. An alternative approach would be to treat leadership as a multidimensional phenomenon and analyze leaders' relations to their contexts and outcomes as configurational problems (Meyer, Tsui, and Hinnings, 1993). As we have discussed, PL is a complex concept, existing in a specific socio-cultural context, embracing conflicting elements (e.g. domineering coupled with individualized care), and working through divergent psychological mechanisms. This complexity calls for a holistic approach to studying PL. In this section, we explore a configurational approach to PL with an attempt to answer the following questions. What are the different types of PL leader that exist in Chinese organizations? Which types of PL leader do Chinese employees prefer? To which types of PL leader do Chinese followers respond favorably?

According to Meyer, Tsui, and Hinnings (1993), configuration refers to any multidimensional constellation of conceptually distinct characteristics that commonly occur together. Configurations can be represented in typologies developed conceptually from theories or captured in taxonomies through empirical research. Configuration has occasionally been used in earlier leadership research. For example, Smith and Foti (1998) analyzed leader emergence from a configurational perspective. They measured leaders with three dispositional variables (dominance, self-efficacy, and intelligence) and then used a median split to derive eight multivariable patterns to explain the emergence of leaders. Lord and Maher (1991) suggested that followers tend to classify leadership perceptions in different cognitive categories, and they communicate information about their leadership perceptions through those shared names (category labels). Thus, a typology of PL leaders, together with some revision of the conceptual dimensions, seems to be useful for stimulating future research.

### Eight types of paternalistic leaders

Following Smith and Foti (1998) and Lord and Maher (1991), we propose a typology of paternalistic leaders based on the level of absolute values (High versus Low) on each of the three core dimensions of PL (Authoritarianism, Benevolence, and moral Character or moral leadership). As we dichotomize the three dimensions, they together produce eight types of PL leader. We use capital letter "A" to represent high authoritarianism, lower-case letter "a" for low authoritarianism; "B" for high benevolence, "b" for low benevolence; and "C" for high moral character, and "c" for low moral character. We briefly describe the eight types.

> *Type 1. Authentic PL leaders* (ABC). These leaders are characterized by high authoritarianism, high benevolence, and high moral character. We label them as authentic as they are closest to the ideal type of PL leaders as conceptualized by Farh and Cheng (2000). These leaders motivate subordinates through all three types of psychological mechanism (i.e., fear, gratitude and repayment, and identification and respect) simultaneously.
>
> *Type 2. Godfather PL leaders* (ABc). These leaders exhibit high authoritarian and benevolent behaviors toward subordinates but with low moral character. We label them as godfathers because they are self-serving leaders who lead through creating fear and gratitude and repayment in the minds of their followers.
>
> *Type 3. Disciplinarian PL leaders* (AbC). This group of leaders has high authoritarianism and moral character but low benevolence. We label them as disciplinarian leaders because they tend to be strict, uphold high performance standards, and pay little attention to subordinates' personal needs.

*Type 4. Dictatorial PL leaders* (Abc). This group of leaders combines high authoritarianism with low benevolence and low moral
character. In the eyes of followers, these leaders give scant attention to their needs. They do not identify with or respect these
leaders, because of the leaders' perceived low moral character.
These leaders are tyrants who rule primarily by ruthless use of
positional authority.

*Type 5. Selfless benefactor PL leaders* (aBC). These leaders act
benevolently toward subordinates while upholding high personal
moral standards and exercising little authoritarianism. They lead
by winning subordinates' respect and gratitude and rarely resort
to positional authority.

*Type 6. Indulgent PL leaders* (aBc). These leaders are highly
benevolent toward subordinates but have low authoritarianism
and moral character. They influence followers primarily through
acting nicely, thereby creating gratitude and indebtedness on the
part of followers.

*Type 7. Ideological PL leaders* (abC). These leaders exhibit both
low authoritarianism and low benevolence but high personal
moral character. They are labeled as ideological because they
influence subordinates primarily through their personal beliefs
and moral excellence.

*Type 8.* Laissez-faire *PL leaders* (abc). This group of leaders has low
levels for all three dimensions of PL. We think that this group
of leaders exists rarely in contemporary Chinese organizations
because they will not be able to meet the basic requirements of
leadership. They are included here merely as a residual category
for comparison purposes.

## Employee preferences for the eight types of paternalistic leader

To find out which PL type matches the ideal leadership type as
perceived by employees, Niu (2006) created eight scenarios depicting
the eight types of paternalistic leader. In all, 265 employees from
various private organizations in Taiwan read through each of the eight
scenarios in random order and then selected one type of PL leader
that they considered to be closest to their ideal leader. Two sample
scenarios are presented below.

Mr. Chen is a supervisor who cares about his subordinates. He would like to
show consideration and provide a hand when his followers have troubles in

their work or lives. He is serious at work and never shows his intentions frankly. He has harsh words if his followers fail to meet his requirements. He is also very strict about himself. He conducts his personal life in an ethical manner and sets an example of how to do things in the right way for his followers. (Authentic PL leader, ABC)

Mr. Chen is a supervisor who is inconsiderate towards his followers. He refuses to provide a hand when the followers have troubles in their work or lives, because he would see these as their own personal issues. He has a casual attitude towards his followers. He does not have high expectations for them and refuses to criticize them even when they cannot meet his requirements. In addition, he may take advantage of his followers, or promote his private interests under the guise of serving the public. Sometimes, he may say one thing and do another, seize the honor and shift the blame. (*Laissez-faire* PL leader, abc)

Table 6.1 (see the columns headed "Ideal leader choice) shows the distribution of the respondent's choice of ideal leaders among the eight types of PL leader. Several interesting findings emerge from the data. First, only four types of leader received a significant number of votes as ideal leaders. The most popular one was Type 5 Selfless benefactor (aBC) (48.3%), followed by Type 1 Authentic (ABC) (26.0%), Type 7 Ideological (abC) (18.1%), and Type 3 Disciplinarian (AbC) (5.7%). The remaining four types, i.e. Type 2 Godfather (ABc), Type 4 Dictatorial (Abc), Type 6 Indulgent (aBc), and Type 8 *Laissez-faire* (abc), combined received only 2.0% of the votes. Second, as a whole, what distinguishes ideal leaders from non-ideal leaders is the moral character of the leader. Only PL types with high moral character received votes as ideal leaders. None of the PL types with low moral character received a significant number of votes. Finally, Type 1 Authentic (ABC) emerged as the second most popular type as it received 26.0% of the total votes. This indicates that Authentic PL is a viable form of PL according to Taiwanese employees in private firms.

### Distribution of the eight types of paternalistic leader in organizations

To examine the actual distribution of leaders across the eight PL types and subordinate responses to each type, we reanalyzed the data from two samples reported in Cheng, Chou, and Farh (2000). The school sample included 501 teachers describing the leadership style of their principals in 175 schools, while the firm sample included

Table 6.1. *Distributions of ideal leader choices and actual leaders across the eight types of paternalistic leader.*

| Paternalistic leader type | Ideal leader choice | | School principals | | Distribution of actual leaders — Managers in a private conglomerate | |
|---|---|---|---|---|---|---|
| | Frequency | % | Frequency | % | Frequency | % |
| 1  Authentic (ABC) | 69 | 26.0 | 32 | 6.4 | 87 | 18.0 |
| 2  Godfather (ABc) | 2 | 0.8 | 1 | 0.2 | 6 | 1.2 |
| 3  Disciplinarian (AbC) | 15 | 5.7 | 28 | 6.0 | 40 | 8.3 |
| 4  Dictatorial (Abc) | 2 | 0.8 | 20 | 3.4 | 27 | 6.0 |
| 5  Selfless benefactor (aBC) | 128 | 48.3 | 325 | 64.9 | 237 | 49.1 |
| 6  Indulgent (aBc) | 1 | 0.4 | 29 | 5.8 | 4 | 0.8 |
| 7  Ideological (abC) | 48 | 18.1 | 50 | 10.0 | 63 | 13.0 |
| 8  *Laissez-faire* (abc) | 0 | 0.0 | 16 | 3.2 | 19 | 3.9 |
| Total | 265 | 100 | 501 | 100 | 483 | 100 |

*Note:*
Paternalistic leader types are coded: A = high authoritarian; a = low authoritarian; B = high benevolence; b = low benevolence; C = high moral character; c = low moral character.

*Sources:* Sample for ideal leader choice distribution from Niu (2006); samples for actual leader distribution from Cheng, Chou, and Farh (2000).

483 employees rating some 250 managers in a private conglomerate. Both groups of respondents completed the PLS on their direct supervisors and gave their attitudinal responses to their leaders (i.e. satisfaction with the leader and trust in the leader). The two samples, one drawn from a private conglomerate and one from public primary schools, provide a good opportunity to see the actual distribution of the eight types of PL leader in two different organizational contexts.

Since the PLS employs a six-point Likert scale for rating leadership behavior (1 = strongly disagree; 2 = disagree; 3 = slightly disagree; 4 = slightly agree; 5 = agree; 6 = strongly agree), we use the mid-point of the absolute scale (3.5) as the cutoff to determine whether a leader was high or low on each PL dimension. Admittedly, this dichotomization is crude. Nevertheless, it indicated a rough distribution of leadership across the eight PL types in the two samples. The results are also listed in Table 6.1 (see the columns headed "Distribution of actual leaders"). The results show that the distribution of actual leaders in the private conglomerate across the eight PL types was similar to the ideal leader distribution found in Niu's (2006) study. Indeed, the chi-square test reveals that the two distributions were not significantly different (chi-square = 2.28, $p > .05$). For example, in Niu's (2006) study Type 5 Selfless benefactor (aBC) was the most frequently chosen ideal leader (48.3%), which was followed by Type 1 Authentic (ABC) (26.0%). In the conglomerate sample, the largest group of leaders was also Type 5 Selfless benefactor (49.1%), followed by Type 1 Authentic (18.0%). The distribution of actual leaders in the school sample (i.e. principals) followed a somewhat different pattern. The chi-square test comparing the distributions of actual leaders for the school sample to those for the firm sample was statistically significant (chi-square = 8.46, $p < .05$), as was the test comparing the school sample to Niu's (2006) ideal leader distributions (chi-square = 16.06, $p < .05$). The results in Table 6.1 show that about two-thirds of the principals were classified as Type 5 Selfless benefactor (aBC) (64.9%) with Type 7 Ideological as a distant second (abC) (10.0%). Only 6.4% of the principals were classified as Type 1 Authentic (ABC). These findings show that organizational context has a strong influence on the emergence of different types of paternalistic leadership. Authoritarian leadership is more prevalent in private firms than in public primary schools.

We further examined the effects of PL types on the followers' satisfaction with, and trust in, the leader in both the private firm and school samples. In the school sample, satisfaction in the supervisor was measured by nine items using the six-point Likert scale ($\alpha = .97$; a sample item was "I am satisfied with the effort the principal has made for the school"), whereas in the firm sample, satisfaction in the supervisor was measured by a single item that indicates the extent to which the respondents were satisfied with their direct supervisor on a hundred-point scale (ranging from 0 to 100). In both samples, trust in the leader was measured using seven items ($\alpha = .92$ and .93 for school-teachers and firm employees, respectively; a sample item is "my supervisor and I share our ideas, feelings and expectations with each other"). Our general expectation was that Type 5 Selfless benefactor (abc) and Type 1 Authentic (ABC) leaders would be viewed as more satisfactory and trustworthy than would the other types. Type 5 Selfless benefactor leaders were similar to servant leaders (Spears, 1998), who lead by being good role models, caring about followers' well-being, and exercising restraint in using formal authority. Type 1 Authentic leaders fit our definition of PL tightly. The congruence between Chinese cultural values and leadership behavior argues for its acceptance and perceived effectiveness (cf. House, Wright, and Aditya, 1997). Because we had only a few cases in the four PL types involving low moral leadership, we collapsed them into one group, treating them as a residual group for comparison. We first conducted a one-way ANOVA to see if followers' satisfaction and trust in the leader varied significantly across PL types. We then performed paired *t*-tests to identify between-group differences. The results are shown in Table 6.2.

Table 6.2. *Means of trust in supervisor and satisfaction with supervision across paternalistic leader types.*

| | School sample | | Conglomerate sample | |
|---|---|---|---|---|
| Paternalistic leader type | Trust in supervisor | Supervisory satisfaction | Trust in supervisor | Supervisory satisfaction |
| Type 1 Authentic (ABC) | $4.61^a$ | $4.40^a$ | $4.51^a$ | $80.18^{bc}$ |
| Type 3 Disciplinarian (AbC) | $3.60^b$ | $3.16^b$ | $3.74^b$ | $63.38^a$ |
| Type 5 Selfless benefactor (aBC) | $4.90^a$ | $4.92^c$ | $4.79^c$ | $81.94^b$ |
| Type 7 Ideological (abC) | $3.95^b$ | $3.94^{ad}$ | $4.16^d$ | $75.11^c$ |
| Residual group including Type 2 (ABc), Type 4 (Abc), Type 6 (aBc), and Type 8 (abc) | $3.95^b$ | $3.85^d$ | $3.11^e$ | $51.29^d$ |
| F value | $46.03^{**}$ | $53.47^{**}$ | $90.64^{**}$ | $56.26^{**}$ |

*Note:*
Within each column, two means having different superscripts were significantly different at $p < .05$; two means sharing a common superscript were not significantly different.
$^{**}P < .01$.

Satisfaction with, and trust in, the leader differed significantly across the five PL types. In both the school and the firm samples, trust and satisfaction were highest for Type 5 Selfless benefactor, followed by Type 1 Authentic, then Type 7 Ideological, and finally Type 3 Disciplinarian. Moreover, the residual group where PL types with low moral character were collapsed also had low levels of trust and satisfaction. In the firm sample, the residual group had the lowest satisfaction and trust ratings among all groups. In the school sample, the residual group had ratings lower than Type 5 Selfless benefactor and Type 1 Authentic groups but it had ratings somewhat higher than Type 3 Disciplinarian and about the same level as Type 7 Ideological leaders.

**Summary and Discussion**
From Farh and Cheng's (2000) conceptual framework of PL, we may classify leaders in Chinese organizations into eight types. From the distributions of ideal leaders and actual leaders in the private firm and public school samples, we found four major types of PL in Chinese organizations in Taiwan, including Type 5 (Selfless benefactor), Type 1 (Authentic), Type 3 (Disciplinarian), and Type 7 (Ideological). Note that all four types of PL leaders have high perceived moral character, but differ from each other in the extent to which they exhibit authoritarianism and benevolence. In selecting ideal leaders, employees eschewed PL types with low moral character, regardless of the leader's benevolence and authoritarianism. In actual leader distribution, less than 15 percent of the leaders were perceived as having low moral character in both the school and the firm samples. In terms of followers' trust and satisfaction with the leader, leaders with low moral character received significantly lower ratings than their counterparts with high moral character (especially in the firm sample). These results suggest that moral character is a necessary condition for emerging leaders in Chinese organizations. This is understandable. In a culture with high power distance and high particularism, such as China, followers tend to depend on the leaders far more so than in egalitarian, universalistic societies such as the USA. Without self-imposed moral restraints by the leader, authoritarian and benevolent leadership styles could easily slip into manipulative tactics that serve only the goals of the leader at the expense of the followers.

Another interesting finding that emerged from the above analysis is that employee responses to the leader's authoritarianism vary depending on the organizational context. Note that there is a much higher percentage of Type 1 Authentic leaders (ABC) in the private firm than in public schools (6.4% vs. 18.0%), and the satisfaction level for Type 1 Authentic leaders (ABC) relative to Type 5 Selfless leaders (aBC) was considerably lower in public schools than in the private firm. These findings suggest that, in private firms, employees are more receptive to authoritarianism by their managers, whereas, in public schools, teachers are much less willing to accept a principal's authoritarianism. We speculate that the differential attitude toward authoritarianism may be due to the different nature of authority in the two organizational contexts. Unlike private firms where authority is derived from private ownership and fully delegated to the management, both principals and teachers are public servants hired by the government education ministry through taxpayer revenues. The authority of the principal is thus circumscribed by the regulations set by governmental agencies and the professional and autonomous status of the teachers. In such a context, authoritarianism by principals is more likely to be seen as illegitimate and resented by the teachers. These findings point out that the authoritarian dimension of PL is highly contingent on situational factors. In addition to the subordinates' authority orientation (i.e. traditionality) and their resource dependence on the leader, the organizational context also plays an important role in affecting how followers respond to their leaders.

## Future research directions

Thus far, we have reviewed research findings based on Farh and Cheng's (2000) PL model. In this section, we point out several areas for future research. We begin by suggesting refinements in the measurement of PL and then by calling for a multilevel approach to PL and extending this research to other cultural contexts.

### *Revising the construct domains of PL*

In the paper in which the PL model was originally introduced, the specific behaviors identified for each PL dimension were based on case studies of the management styles of owners/managers of overseas

Chinese family businesses from the 1960s to the 1980s. The specific behaviors were thus "illustrative, not exhaustive" (Farh and Cheng, 2000: 97). With rapid societal modernization, family businesses no longer play such a dominant role in the Chinese economy, and there has also been an accompanying change in social values. These changes call for a re-examination of the construct domain of PL to render it compatible with the contemporary period. We view the continuing update of the construct domain as a natural part of the construct validation process (Schwab, 1980). As Hanisch, Hulin, and Roznowski pointed out, "it takes time to conceptualize important constructs, refine them, and accurately assess them" (1998: 464). Table 6.3 summarizes a few proposed changes of construct domains for the three PL dimensions, along with their original illustrative behaviors as described by Farh and Cheng (2000). Although we propose to update part of the construct domain of the PL dimensions, the overall definition of each PL dimension remains the same as in the original model.

**Authoritarian leadership**
In Farh and Cheng's (2000) model, authoritarianism describes leader behaviors that assert absolute authority and control over subordinates and demand unquestioned obedience of them. It is used to capture the leadership characteristics in a socio-political context in which authoritarianism was widely practiced and viewed as legitimate at all levels of the society. But with increased prosperity, higher educational levels, and democratization in Chinese societies, the younger generations have different expectations concerning their employment relationships. They care more about their self-advancement than about obligations to firms and are much less willing to accept the hierarchical structure of bureaucracy (Liu, 2003). Meanwhile, competitive pressure also forces Chinese businesses everywhere to demand more contributions from their employees. Nowadays, employees are frequently required to be responsible for the business results achieved, rather than to follow a narrow set of guidelines or seek permission for variance (Hempel and Chang, 2002). Therefore, the construct domain of authoritarian leadership needs revision.

The original set of authoritarian behaviors (column 1 of Table 6.3) includes asserting authority and control, building a lofty image, acting in a didactic style, and underestimating subordinate competence. Several of these behaviors are so outdated that they tend to be rejected

Table 6.3. *Revised construct domain of paternalistic leadership dimensions.*

| Original domain (Farh and Cheng, 2000) | Revised domain |
|---|---|
| *Authoritarian leadership* | |

| Original domain (Farh and Cheng, 2000) | Revised domain |
|---|---|
| Authority and control | Authority and control |
| • Unwilling to delegate | • Expect obedience |
| • Top-down communication | • Insist on making final |
| • Information secrecy | decisions on key issues |
| • Tight control | • Guard key information tightly |
| Image-building | • Tight control |
| • Act in a dignified manner | Reputation-building |
| • Exhibit high self-confidence | • Act in a dignified manner |
| • Information manipulation | • Exhibit high self-confidence |
| Didactic behaviour | Strict discipline |
| • Insist on high performance standards | • Insist on high performance standards |
| • Reprimand subordinates for poor performance | • Do not tolerate low performance |
| • Provide guidance and instructions for improvements | • Do not compromise on core company values |
| Underestimation of subordinate competence | • Apply strict discipline |
| • Ignore subordinate suggestions | |
| • Belittle subordinate contributions | |

| | *Benevolent leadership* |
|---|---|
| Individualized care | Individualized care in non-work domain |
| • Treat employees as family members | • Treat employees as family members |
| • Provide job security | • Assist during personal crises |
| • Assist during personal crises | • Show holistic concern |
| • Show holistic concern | • Avoid embarrassing subordinates in public |
| • Avoid embarrassing subordinates in public | |
| • Leave room even in extreme cases | |

Table 6.3. (*cont.*)

| Original domain (Farh and Cheng, 2000) | Revised domain |
|---|---|
| | Individualized care in work domain |
| | • Concern about career development |
| | • Provide feedback, coaching, and mentoring |
| | • Provide job security |
| | • Allow chances for correcting mistakes |

| *Moral leadership* | |
|---|---|

| Unselfishness | Unselfishness |
|---|---|
| • Reject egocentric impulses for a higher moral good | • Do not abuse authority for personal gain |
| • Put collective interests ahead of personal interests | • Do not mix personal interests with business interests |
| • Adhere personally to rules of proper and virtuous behavior | • Put collective interests ahead of personal interests |
| Lead by example | Job devotion |
| • Act as an exemplar in work and personal conduct | • Competent for the job |
| • Demonstrate financial and commercial success | • Lead by example |
| | • Treat people fairly |
| | • Act responsibly |
| | Personal integrity |
| | • Honesty; keeping promises; self-discipline; kindness |

categorically by most subordinates today. Including such behaviors in the domain of authoritarian leadership will not only provoke negative reactions by subordinates, but also undermine the legitimacy of the leader's authority. Thus, we propose to delete two behaviors that have negative implications – "ignore subordinate suggestions" and "belittle subordinate contributions" – and reword several others to soften their negative implications. For example, "unwilling to delegate" and "top-down communication" are replaced by "insist on making final decisions on key issues"; "information secrecy" is changed into "guard key information tightly"; "reprimand subordinates for poor performance" is changed into "do not tolerate low performance." In addition, we propose to add a couple of behaviors (i.e. "expect obedience" and "apply strict discipline") that are central to the definition of authoritarianism. Four other core behaviors ("tight control," "act in a dignified manner," "exhibit high self-confidence," and "insist on high performance standards") are retained without modification.

### Benevolent leadership

Leader benevolence refers to behavior that demonstrates individualized, holistic concern for a subordinate's well-being (Farh and Cheng, 2000). The original domain of benevolence includes six behaviors, five of which focus on the supervisor's concern for employees in the non-work domain and only one in the work domain. To correct this imbalance, we propose to partition the domain of benevolence into "individualized care in the non-work domain" and "individualized care in the work domain". Among the original six behaviors, four are under the non-work domain, one is in the work domain ("provide job security"), and one is dropped due to the ambiguity of its meaning ("leave room even in extreme cases"). We propose to add a few supportive behaviors in the work domain, including "concern about career advancement"; "provide constructive feedback, coaching, and mentoring"; and "allow chances for correcting mistakes."

### Moral leadership

In the original model, only two behaviors were listed under moral leadership: (i) avoiding acting selfishly; and (ii) leading by example. To make moral leadership more relevant for a broad range of managers, we propose to broaden its construct domain. Using an open-ended questionnaire, Farh and Liang (2005) surveyed over 300 PRC managers/employees from a variety of organizations about key behaviors/ attributes of the moral leaders they had encountered. More than 600 moral behaviors or attributes were collected. The ensuing content analysis identified six clusters of moral leader behaviors. Besides unselfishness and leading by example, they also found "job devotion" and "personal integrity" to be key elements of moral leadership. "Job devotion" refers to being competent for the job, leading by example, treating people fairly, and acting responsibly. "Personal integrity" includes honesty, keeping promises, self-discipline, and kindness. We propose to include these behaviors/attributes in the domain of moral leadership.

With the proposed revision of the construct domains of PL dimensions, the immediate need is to develop a new scale for measuring PL. This is an essential task for the future development of PL research.

## A multilevel approach to PL

Empirical research on PL following Farh and Cheng (2000) has taken an individual approach, which focused on the influence of leaders (typically lower-level managers) on their individual subordinates. This is in sharp contrast with earlier ideographical/anthropological research by Silin (1976), Redding (1990), and Westwood (1997), which typically focused on the paternalistic management style of CEOs and their influence on the entire organization. Since organizations are complex systems that involve interlocking processes operating at multiple levels, a complete account of PL's effects in organizations calls for a multilevel approach. In Figure 6.2, we outline a multilevel model of PL.

At the upper level of the organization, PL refers to the overall management style and practices used by the CEO and the top management team. They can be viewed as types of "ambient stimuli" that pervade the work unit and are shared among unit members (Chen and Kanfer, 2006; Hackman, 1992). PL manifests itself in management practices (such as a centralized organization structure, top-down decision-making style, and treating employees as family members) and results in a paternalistic climate in the workplace. The paternalistic management practices and accompanying climate influence work-unit outcomes, with their specific effects contingent upon situational factors such as the ownership structure of the firm, the environment in which the firm operates, and the technology employed by the firm. As Farh and Cheng (2000) suggest, the paternalistic management style is expected to generate more positive outcomes in family-owned businesses operating in a simple task environment using stable technology.

At the lower level of the organization, PL refers to paternalistic leader behaviors exhibited by middle- or lower-level managers toward

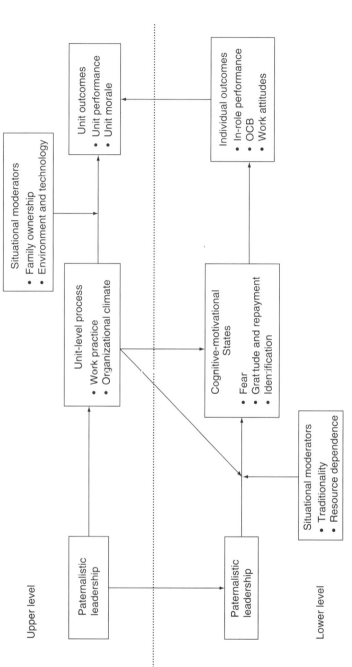

**Figure 6.2.** A multilevel model of paternalistic leadership.

their subordinates. PL impacts follower outcomes (in-role performance, OCB, and work attitudes) through followers' cognitive-motivational states (fear, gratitude, and identification). As we noted in the previous section, this mediated relationship has been substantiated by prior research. There is also considerable evidence that traditionality and resource dependence among followers moderates the relationship between PL and subordinates' psychological responses or states.

The upper-level and lower-level leadership processes interact in three ways in the multilevel model. First, there is a top-down influence flowing from upper-level leaders to lower-level leaders. By virtue of their high-status position in the hierarchy and their ability to control resources, high-level managers are natural role models for low-level managers (Antonakis and Atwater, 2002; Bandura, 1996). This role modeling effect is likely to be especially strong when the leadership/ management style of upper-level managers is perceived as effective by lower-level managers.

Second, the paternalistic management style of upper-level managers and the organizational climate will impact the followers' cognitive-motivational states directly beyond the influence of the low-level managers' PL. In a society with high power distance and collectivism, the paternalistic management practices/climate will not only shape subordinates' cognitive-motivational states, but also may serve as a situational enhancer for the lower-level PL effects. As Schneider (2000) has pointed out, the organizational climate could signal the management's expectations to employees and help them to determine which behavior is appropriate in a given work environment. Employees in a work unit where the paternalistic climate has been established are more likely to be receptive to their direct supervisor's PL. Thus, we expect a synergy between low-level managers' PL and a paternalistic climate in the work unit. Besides the top-down effects, there is a bottom-up effect in the model as well. Outcomes at the individual level in aggregate will influence outcomes at the unit level.

In summary, this multilevel approach to PL corroborates the recommendation to examine the impact of leadership behaviors from both the perspective of individual employees' idiosyncratic experiences, and the shared view of work-unit members' overall experience (e.g. Dansereau and Yammarino, 1998; Liao and Chuang, 2007). We propose not only differential mechanisms for upper-level and lower-level PL, but also their cross-level interaction effects. Future research on PL should take into account the full complexity of the leadership phenomenon in organizations and investigate PL using a multilevel approach.

## Beyond the Chinese family business context

Existing research suggests that Farh and Cheng's (2000) model of PL can generalize to different organizations in Chinese contexts. Note that empirical tests of PL were conducted on the basis of diverse samples, rather than simply family-owned Chinese firms (e.g. public schools in Taiwan, state-owned firms and foreign investment ventures in mainland China). Beyond the Chinese contexts, paternalism has been argued to be a salient characteristic in many Asian countries, such as Japan and Korea (Redding, Norman, and Schlander, 1994), India (Sinha, 1990), and Turkey (Aycan, 2006). In these Asian countries, as in China, family-based hierarchy extends to society at large. For example, Sinha (1990) proposed a nurturant–task-oriented model for India in which an ideal leader is both nurturant and task-oriented. According to this model, the supervisor would offer benevolent support for subordinates provided that the subordinates respect and obey the supervisor, work hard, and are highly productive. These findings suggest that the PL model could transcend Chinese cultural contexts and generalize to other Asian contexts. Future research should empirically test the generalizability of the PL model beyond the Chinese contexts.

## Comparison with other leadership theories

Future research should also compare the PL model against other established theories of leadership. For example, both the leader–member exchange theory (LMX) and the PL model assume that there is a personalistic relationship between a leader and a follower. The two models differ in that LMX theory is predicated on social exchange theory, whereas the PL model is based on hierarchical role relationships rooted in traditional Chinese families and culture. Which of the two models does a better job in accounting for the leader–follower dynamics in contemporary Chinese society? Similar research is needed to compare the PL model with the transformational and transactional leadership theories. Through such research, we could gain a clearer picture of the unique contribution of the PL model to the leadership literature.

## Conclusion

In this chapter, we have reviewed the empirical research on Farh and Cheng's (2000) model of PL and identified several fruitful areas for future research. Most theories of leadership in organizational behavior originated in the USA and Western Europe and are hypothesized to be universally applicable to non-Western contexts. Departing from this tradition, we proposed a Chinese culture-specific leadership theory, built on China's patriarchal family tradition. The PL model provides a new perspective on leadership in the Chinese context by focusing on three dimensions of leadership (authoritarianism, benevolence, and moral leadership) that have been ignored in the Western leadership literature. Subsequent empirical research by Cheng and his associates has shown that the PL model could account for a substantial amount of variance in subordinate outcomes in Chinese contexts. Our review further shows that the PL model could be further expanded to allow for a configurational and a multilevel approach to investigating leadership. Future research should update the construct domains of PL dimensions to keep it more applicable to the modern context and test its generalizability beyond the Chinese cultural context.

*References*

Antonakis, J., and Atwater, L. 2002. "Leader distance: a review and a proposed theory," *Leadership Quarterly* 13: 673–704.

Aycan, Z. 2006. "Paternalism: towards conceptual refinement and operationalization," in K. S. Yang, K. K. Hwang, and U. Kim (eds.), *Scientific advances in indigenous psychologies: empirical, philosophical, and cultural contributions*, Cambridge: Cambridge University Press, pp. 445–466.

Bandura, R. 1986. *Social foundations of thought and action: a social cognitive theory*. Englewood Cliffs, NJ: Prentice Hall.

Bond, M. H., and Hwang, K. K. 1987. "The social psychology of Chinese people," in M. H. Bond (ed.), *The psychology of Chinese people*, New York: Oxford University Press.

Chen, G., and Kanfer, R. 2006. "Toward a system theory of motivated behavior in work teams," *Research in Organizational Behavior* 27: 223–267.

Cheng, B. S. 1995a. *Authoritarian values and executive leadership: the case of Taiwanese family enterprises*. Report prepared for Taiwan's National Science Council. Taiwan: National Taiwan University (in Chinese).

1995b. "*Chaxuegeju* and Chinese organizational behavior," *Indigenous Psychological Research in Chinese Societies* 3: 142–219 (in Chinese).

1995c. "Paternalistic authority and leadership: a case study of a Taiwanese CEO," *Bulletin of the Institute of Ethnology Academic Sinica* 79: 119–73 (in Chinese).

Cheng, B. S., Chou L. F., and Farh, J. L. 2000. "A triad model of paternalistic leadership: the constructs and measurement," *Indigenous Psychological Research in Chinese Societies* 14: 3–64 (in Chinese).

Cheng, B. S., Chou, L. F., Huang, M. P., Farh. J. L., and Peng, S. 2003. "A triad model of paternalistic leadership: evidence from business organization in Mainland China," *Indigenous Psychological Research in Chinese Societies* 20: 209–252 (in Chinese).

Cheng, B. S., Chou, L. F., Huang, M. P., Wu, T. Y., and Farh, J. L. 2004. "Paternalistic leadership and subordinate reverence: establishing a leadership model in Chinese organizations," *Asian Journal of Social Psychology* 7: 89–117.

Cheng, B. S., and Farh, J. L. 2001. "Social orientation in Chinese societies: a comparison of employees from Taiwan and Chinese mainland," *Chinese Journal of Psychology* 43: 207–221 (in Chinese).

Cheng, B. S., Huang, M. P., and Chou, L. F. 2002. "Paternalistic leadership and its effectiveness: evidence from Chinese organizational teams," *Journal of Psychology in Chinese Societies* 3: 85–112 (in Chinese).

Cheng, B. S., Shieh, P. Y., and Chou, L. F. 2002. "The principal's leadership, leader–member exchange quality, and the teacher's extra-role behavior: the effects of transformational and paternalistic leadership," *Indigenous Psychological Research in Chinese Societies* 17: 105–161 (in Chinese).

Dansereau, F., and Yammarino, F. J. 1998. *Leadership. The multiple-level approaches: classical and new wave*. Amsterdam: Elsevier Science/JAI Press.

Farh, J. L., and Cheng, B. S. 2000. "A cultural analysis of paternalistic leadership in Chinese organizations," in J. T. Li, A. S. Tsui, and E. Weldon (eds.), *Management and organizations in the Chinese context*, London: Macmillan, pp. 94–127.

Farh, J. L., Cheng, B. S., Chou, L. F., and Chu, X. P. 2006. "Authority and benevolence: employees' responses to paternalistic leadership in

China," in A. S. Tsui, Y. Bian, and L. Cheng (eds.), *China's domestic private firms: multidisciplinary perspectives on management and performance*, New York: M. E. Sharpe, pp. 230–260.

Farh, J. L., Earley, P. C., and Lin, S. C. 1997. "Impetus for action: a cultural analysis of justice and organizational citizenship behavior in Chinese society," *Administrative Science Quarterly* 42: 421–444.

Farh, J. L., Hackett, R., and Liang, J. 2007 "Individual-level cultural values as moderators of perceived organizational support—employee outcomes relationships in China: comparing the effects of power distance and traditionality," *Academy of Management Journal* 50: 715–729.

Farh, J. L., and Liang, J. 2005. "Moral leadership in the Chinese context: an exploratory study," Working Paper, Hong Kong University of Science and Technology.

Fiedler, F. E. 1967. *A theory of leadership effectiveness*. New York: McGraw-Hill.

French, R.P., and Raven, B. 1960. "The bases of social power," in D. Cartwright and A. F. Zander (eds.), *Group dynamics: research and theory*, New York: Harper & Row, pp. 607–623.

Hackman, J. R. 1992. "Group influences on individuals in organizations," in M. D. Dunnette and L. M. Hough (eds.), *Handbook of industrial and organizational psychology*, Palo Alto, CA: Consulting Psychologists Press, Vol. III, pp. 199–267.

Hall, J. A., and Rosenthal, R. 1991. "Testing for moderator variables in meta-analysis: issues and methods," *Communication Monographs* 59: 437–448.

Hanisch, K. A., Hulin, C. L., and Roznowski, M. 1998. "The importance of individuals' repertoires of behaviors: the scientific appropriateness of studying multiple behaviors and general attitudes," *Journal of Organizational Behavior* 19: 463–480.

Hempel, P. S., and Chang, C. D. 2002. "Reconciling traditional Chinese management with high-tech Taiwan," *Human Resource Management Journal* 12: 77–95.

House, R. J. 1971. "A path–goal theory of leader effectiveness," *Administrative Science Quarterly* 16: 321–339.

House, R. J., Wright, N. S., and Aditya, R. N. 1997. "Cross-cultural research on organizational leadership: a critical analysis and a proposed theory," in P. C. Earley and M. Erez (eds.), *New perspectives on international industrial/organizational psychology*, San Francisco, CA: Jossey Bass, pp. 535–625.

Hui, C., Lee, C., and Rousseau, D. M. 2004. "Employment relationships in China: do workers relate to the organization or to people?" *Organization Science* 15: 232–240.

Kerr, S., and Jermier, J. M. 1978. "Substitutes for leadership: their meaning and measurement," *Organizational Behavior and Human Performance* 22: 375–403.

Liao, H., and Chuang, A. 2007 "Transforming custom service employees and climates: a multi-level multi-source examination of the role of transformational leadership in building service relationships," *Journal of Applied Psychology* 92: 1006–1019.

Liu, S. 2003. "Culture within culture: unity and diversity of two generations of employees in state-owned enterprises," *Human Relations* 56: 387–417.

Lord, R. G., and Maher, K. J. 1991. *Leadership and information processing: linking perceptions and performance*. Boston: Unwin Hyman.

Meyer, A. D., Tsui, A. S., and Hinnings, C. R. 1993. "Configurational approaches to organizational analysis," *Academy of Management Journal* 36: 1175–1195.

Niu, C. P. 2006. *"Paternalistic leadership and its effectiveness: a scenario-based analysis,"* unpublished MPhil thesis, National Taiwan University.

Pye, L. W. 1981. *Dynamics of Chinese politics*. Cambridge, MA: Oelgeschlager, Gunn and Hain.

Redding, S. G. 1990. *The spirit of Chinese capitalism*. New York: Walter de Gruyter.

Redding, S. G., Norman, A., and Schlander, A. 1994. "The nature of individual attachment to theory: a review of East Asian variations," in H. C. Triandis, M. D. Dunnett, and L. M. Hough (eds.), *Handbook of industrial and organizational psychology*, Palo Alto, CA: Consulting Psychological Press, vol. IV, pp. 674–688.

Schneider, B. 2000. "The psychological life of organizations," in N. M. Ashkanasy, C. P. M. Wilderom, and M. F. Peterson (eds.), *Handbook of organizational culture and climate*, Thousand Oaks, CA: Sage, pp. 11–23.

Schwab, D. P. 1980. "Construct validity in organizational behavior," *Research in Organizational Behavior* 2: 3–43.

Silin, R. H. 1976. *Leadership and value: the organization of large-scale Taiwan enterprises*. Cambridge, MA: Harvard University Press.

Sinha, J. B. P. 1990. *Work culture in Indian context*. New Delhi: Sage.

Smith, J. A., and Foti, R. J. 1998. "A pattern approach to the study of leader emergence," *Leadership Quarterly* 9:147–161.

Spears, L. C. 1998. *Insights on leadership: service, stewardship, spirit and servant leadership*. New York: Wiley.

Weidenbaum, M. 1996. "The Chinese family business enterprise," *California Management Review* 38: 141–156.

Westwood, R. I. 1997. "Harmony and patriarchy: the cultural basis for 'paternalistic headship' among the overseas Chinese," *Organization Studies* 18: 445–480.

Wu, T. Y., Hsu, W. L., and Cheng, B. S. 2002. "Expressing or suppressing anger: subordinates' anger responses to supervisors' authoritarian behaviors in a Taiwan enterprise," *Indigenous Psychological Research in Chinese Societies* 18: 3–49 (in Chinese).

Yang, K. S. 1998. "Chinese responses to modernization: a psychological analysis," *Asian Journal of Social Psychology* 1: 75–97.

    2003. "Methodological and theoretical issues on psychological traditionality and modernity research in an Asian society: in response to Kwang-Kuo Hwang and beyond," *Asian Journal of Social Psychology* 6: 263–285.

Yang, L. S. 1957. "The concept of *pao* as a basis for social relations in China," in J. K. Fairbank (ed.), *Chinese thought and institutions*, Chicago: University of Chicago Press, pp. 291–309.

# 7 | The leadership theories and practices of Mao Zedong and Deng Xiaoping

## XIN-AN LU AND JIE LU

N O ONE in the history of the People's Republic of China (PRC) could replace Mao Zedong (or Mao Tse-tung) and Deng Xiaoping, the former mainly remembered as the founding father of the Republic, and the latter, as the architect of China's economic reforms. Studies of Chinese leadership theory and practice cannot afford to ignore these two figures. Investigation of the distinct leadership theories and practices of these two individuals will enrich the understanding of leadership from a global perspective.

This chapter gives brief biographies of Mao Zedong and Deng Xiaoping, explains their major leadership theories, philosophies, and practices, and compares their distinct leadership styles and personalities. In synopsis, Mao in his leadership philosophy believed in "seeking truth from facts," the "analytical dialectics of contradiction," and "serving the people." Mao's leadership practice is largely one of the "mass line" and "democratic centralism." Deng, however, believed in reformism and pragmatism in his leadership philosophy. To fulfill his pragmatic reforms, Deng practiced experimentalism and gradualism as his instrumentality. Despite the important similarities in their thoughts on leadership, Mao and Deng seemed to contrast sharply in their leadership methods and styles. Mao was more idealistic and holistic, and a visionary on nationalism; Deng, in contrast, was more realistic, details-oriented, and a visionary on economic development. It is hoped that these introductions to Mao and Deng will contribute to a broader understanding of leadership theory and practice from a global perspective.

## Mao Zedong's leadership theory and practice

### A biography of Mao Zedong (1893–1976)

Born in the village of Shaoshan, Hunan province in south-east central China, the son of a farmer, Mao was the leader and leading theorist of the Chinese revolution. He founded the People's Republic of China (PRC) in 1949 and served as the chairman of the Chinese Communist Party (CCP) and president of the Republic until his death (with the exception of the period 1959–1968 when Liu Shaoqi was the president of the Republic).

Mao graduated from the First Provincial Normal School in Chang-sha (capital of Hunan Province) in 1918 and worked as a librarian at Beijing University, where he read copiously and was influenced by such pioneer Communists as Li Dazhao and Chen Duxiu, who took leading parts in the May Fourth Movement (1919). Mao became a Marxist and a founding member of the CCP in 1921. He organized (1920s) peasant and industrial unions sponsored by the Kuomintang (or the Nationalist Party) and directed (1926) the Kuomintang's Peasant Movement Training Institute. Following the Kuomintang–Communist split (1927), the failure of Mao's "Autumn Harvest Uprising" resulted in his ouster from the central committee of the Communist Party.

From 1928 to 1931, Mao, with the help of Zhu De and later of Lin Biao, moved from cities to the countryside and established rural revolutionary bases and the Red Army. He was elected chairman of the newly established Soviet Republic of China in Jiangxi province in 1931. Five encirclement and annihilation campaigns by Chiang Kai-shek against the Communist Party eventually forced the latter into the Long March (6000 miles/9656 km) from Jiangxi to Yan'an in northern China for its survival. When Japan invaded China in 1937, the CCP concentrated its forces against Japan's invasion. Though some may claim that there were other forces resisting the Japanese invasion of China, Mao provided the leadership, in theory and in practice, for the Communist Party that was the mainstay of resistance to the Japanese invasion. Mao lost at least five of his family members and other relatives for the causes of the Chinese revolution and the anti-Japan war (Han, 1987). In 1945, China won the war against the Japanese, and the Kuomintang and the CCP began to engage in a civil war for control of China. The CCP drove Chiang Kai-shek's Kuomintang to Taiwan from mainland China in 1949 and established the PRC.

Mao initially followed the Soviet model of economic development and social change until the Sino-USSR split in 1958. In the same year, Mao launched the Great Leap Forward in an attempt to rejuvenate China's economy after the USSR's withdrawal of its aid to China.

Mao lost much of his influence on account of the catastrophic failure of the Great Leap Forward movement (Li, 1994). In an attempt to redress the effects of the aforesaid movement, Mao launched the Great Proletarian Cultural Revolution (1966–1976), which turned into a "holocaust" (Naím, 2005). Mao's death from a prolonged illness in 1976 brought a prompt end to the Cultural Revolution because of the nation's strong reaction against the "cult of personality" and the excessive collectivism and egalitarianism that had emerged during the Cultural Revolution. A prolific political, military, philosophical, social, and economic essayist, Mao was also a significant minor poet. His major works are collected in the five volumes of the *Selected works of Mao Zedong*. (For more detailed biographical descriptions of Mao, see Li, 1994; Pye, 1976; and Shan, 2005).

## *"Seek truth from facts"* (shi-shi-qiu-shi)

Mao Zedong once inscribed a four-character slogan, "Seek truth from facts," for the Central Party School in Yan'an (for many years the central base of Mao's Chinese Revolution) as the fundamental principle for tackling the problems confronting the Chinese Communist Party. This principle became the fundamental thought in Mao's leadership philosophy, the faithful execution of which contributed to his great successes during the Chinese Revolutionary War (1921–1937), the Anti-Japan War (1937–1945), and the Chinese Civil War with Chiang Kai-shek (1945–1949). Mao did not dogmatically adopt Marxism-Leninism, but "sinified" them to suit the actual conditions in China (Knight, 2005; Shan, 2005). Mao's "sinification" of Marxism according to Chinese conditions crystallized into what became known as the "Thoughts of Mao Zedong", perceived by scholars (e.g. Gorman, 1982) as Mao's great contribution to orthodox Marxism.

The essence of "seeking truth from facts" is expounded at length in Mao's famous essay "On practice," published in July 1937, later included in volume I of the *Selected works of Mao Zedong* (Mao, 1954a). "Facts," Mao explained, are the totality of things existing in the external world; "truth" represents the inherent laws, regularities, and interconnections in the objective reality; and "seek" means to investigate. Any job must proceed from the actual conditions inside and outside the country, the province, and the county, exhorted Mao. Guidelines for actions must derive from intrinsic laws (rather than from pre-conceived dogmas) and interdependences among objective realities. "Seeking truth from facts," according to Mao, is not only a philosophical principle, but, more importantly, should also guide the execution of practical affairs.

Mao contended that humankind's social practice alone is the criterion of the truth of their knowledge of the external world. "In reality, man's knowledge becomes verified only when, in the process of social practice . . . he achieves the anticipated results" (Mao, 1954a: 283). It is not subjective views and feelings, but objective outcomes in social practice, that are the ultimate criteria for judging the "truth" of any knowledge or theory. Mao positioned "practice" as the primary and basic standpoint in the dialectical materialist theory of knowledge (Mao, 1954a: 282–285).

Mao thus distinguished between perception and reason. "Perception only solves the problem of phenomena; reason alone solves the problem of essence" (Mao 1954a: 286). The resolution of both these problems cannot, even in the slightest degree, be separated from practice. The sole method of "knowing a thing" is by coming into contact with it, or by living and practicing in its environment. This is the path to knowledge which every person actually travels (Mao, 1954a: 286–289). "There can be no knowledge apart from practice" (Mao, 1954a: 288).

Mao defined the emergence and growth of knowledge as a spiraling process. First, knowledge must develop from a perception of phenomena to a rational theory of a thing's essence. Second, knowledge in the form of rational theory needs to be applied to (revolutionary) practice. Third, the validity of rational knowledge must be tested by being redirected at the practice of changing the world, "must be again applied in the practice of production, in the practice of revolutionary class struggle and revolutionary national struggle, as well as in the practice of scientific experimentation" (Mao, 1954a: 293). In short, "[k]nowledge starts with practice, reaches the theoretical plane via practice, and then has to return to practice" (Mao, 1954a: 292). If found defective in the test by practice, rational knowledge must be revised and retested. The spiraling process of knowledge acquisition thus goes on endlessly with the emergence and change of new conditions. The spirit of Mao's "seeking truth from facts" may be encapsulated in his oft-quoted slogan, "No investigation, no right to speak," which insists that leaders have no right to instruct or command if they made no efforts to get to the bottom of situations and facts.

Mao's practice of his "seeking truth from facts" before 1949 seems to contrast with that after 1949. During the Chinese Revolutionary War (1921–1937), the Anti-Japan War (1937–1945), and the Chinese Civil War with Chiang Kai-shek (1945–1949), Mao did faithfully practice his leadership philosophy of "seeking truth from facts." In 1927, for instance, Chiang Kai-shek's attempts to purge the Communists almost destroyed them. Mao decided that unique Chinese conditions (with the bulk of the Chinese population being peasants and the bulk of China being rural) necessitated an adaptation of the orthodox Marxist notion that the Communist revolution must proceed from major cities with the leadership of the urban working class. Mao believed that the CCP could only succeed at that time by "encircling the cities from the countryside." Mao's unorthodox strategy emerged from following his principle of "seeking truth from facts," the facts of actual Chinese conditions. He had acquired an intimate understanding of the Chinese countryside through his background of growing up in rural China and his painstaking in-depth investigation of rural China (see, for instance, his article of March 1927, "Report on an investigation of the peasant movement in Hunan," in Mao, 1954a). Mao did not overlook the important fact that the peasantry then accounted for the bulk of the Chinese population.

Mao successfully consolidated the power of the CCP by soliciting and depending on the vast Chinese peasant class by means of the implementation of land reforms and the imposition of stringent discipline in the Red Army (Knight, 2005; Shan, 2005). Mao's bold modification of orthodox Marxism worked brilliantly. The leadership philosophy of "seeking truth from facts" was also plentifully reflected in his leadership practice of the "mass line," as will be explained later in this chapter.

Concerning Mao's post-1949 practice of his own leadership philosophy of "seeking truth from facts," there exists controversy. Some believe that he was sincerely practicing his leadership philosophy; it was because of "technical miscalculations and insufficiently informed lieutenants" (Wilson, 1977: 8) that Mao failed to achieve planned results in the Great Leap Forward (1958–1959) and the Cultural Revolution (1966–1976). Other scholars (e.g. Li, 1994; Shan, 2005) contend, however, that the post-1949 Mao was unduly influenced by overambitious utopianism and power struggles within the CCP; Mao did not faithfully practice his own leadership philosophy of "seeking truth from facts," the results of which were the disasters of the Great Leap Forward and the Great Proletarian Cultural Revolution.

## The analytical dialectics of contradiction

A second prominent principle in Mao's leadership philosophy may be the analytical dialectics of contradiction. Understanding this principle helps to illuminate Mao's "pattern of rule" (a term of Oksenberg, 1977) as will be elaborated later in this section. Mao explicated the essence of this leadership philosophy in his renowned essay "On contradiction," published in August 1937 (Mao, 1954a).

"The law of contradiction in things, that is, the law of the unity of opposites, is the most basic law in materialistic dialectics," said Mao (1954b: 13). He contended that this law represents a great revolution in the history of human knowledge, in the form of dialectical materialism as opposed to the metaphysical world outlook (Mao, 1954b: 13–18). According to dialectical materialism, contradiction is ubiquitous in the processes of objectively existing things and of subjective thought and permeates the development of every thing from beginning to end; contradiction is universal and absolute.

To reinforce the concept of the universality of contradiction, Mao argued that no aspect of a thing can exist and be understood by itself. The very existence of a thing presupposes its opposite aspect. Mao invited the reader to juxtapose offense and defense, advance and retreat, victory and defeat as contradictory phenomena in war (Mao, 1954b: 20). In all these instances, "[w]ithout the one, the other cannot exist" (Mao, 1954b: 20). Therefore, investigation of any thing requires attention to the "two sides" of every contradiction within that thing.

Furthermore, Mao recommended, to understand the development of a thing, leaders must pay attention to the internal and external contradictions of that thing. It is, nevertheless, the internal contradictions of a thing that largely determine the nature of its development. Mao argued that external causes are the condition of change and internal causes form the basis of change, and that "social development is chiefly due not to external but internal causes" (Mao, 1954b: 16). Although the interdependence of contradictory aspects is present in all things, Mao averred, the particularity of a contradiction commands special attention. Only so can distinction be achieved regarding the qualitative difference between one form of motion and another form of motion. The particularity of a contradiction constitutes the basis for the immense variety of things in the world. Qualitatively different contradictions can only be resolved by qualitatively different methods (Mao, 1954b: 22–35). It may be added here that the emphasis on the particularity of the contradictions (i.e., the unique nature within a thing) goes hand in hand with the principle of seeking truth from facts (i.e., the totality of the particular reality of a thing).

Concerning the particularity of contradiction, Mao suggested that the principal contradiction needs to be singled out for analysis (Mao, 1954b: 35–42). During the development of a complex thing, there are many contradictions. However, it is "necessarily the principal contradiction whose existence and development determines or influences the existence and development of other contradictions" (Mao, 1954b: 35). One example Mao offered was that in rural China, there were many pairs of forces in contradiction, but the contradiction between the landless peasants and the landowners formed the principal one. The other contradictions, such as that between the kulaks and the poor peasants and the conflict amidst poor peasants and so on, are all determined or influenced by the principal contradiction between the landless peasants and the landowners (Mao, 1954b: 35). Mao contended that at every stage in the development of a process, "whatever happens, there is only one principal contradiction that plays the leading role" (Mao, 1954b: 37). The behavioral guideline from this, Mao taught, is that in studying any complex process in which there are two or more contradictions, every effort must be made to find the principal contradiction. Once this principal contradiction is pinpointed and grasped, all problems can be readily solved (Mao, 1954b: 42). Mao used an analogy for illustration: "Once the head-rope of the fishing net is pulled up, all its meshes open" (*gang-ju-mu-zhang*).

The struggle between the two contradictory elements contained in a thing, Mao argued, will lead to a dialectical process of development. In the motion of all things, there are two states, "the form of relative rest and the form of conspicuous change" (Mao, 1954b: 48). In the first state of motion, a thing is undergoing only quantitative and not qualitative change, resulting in an outward appearance of stability or being at rest. The second state of motion arrives when the quantitative change of a thing in the first state has reached a critical point, giving rise to the dissolution of the thing as an entity. As a result, a qualitative change occurs, hence the appearance of conspicuous change or revolution (Mao, 1954b: 48).

The dialectical process of the development of things dictates that things are constantly transforming themselves from the first to the second state of motion. However, it is through the second stage that the contradiction is resolved. The understanding of this process, Mao emphasized, will make it clear that a class-based society cannot avoid revolutions and revolutionary wars, because without them, it would be impossible to achieve any leap in social development and overthrow the reactionary ruling classes, and therefore impossible for the people to win political power (Mao 1954b: 43–49).

Mao's leadership philosophy of the dialectics of contradiction was reflected aplenty in his leadership practice. During China's revolutionary period (1921–1949), Mao's theory of contradictions reflected, justified, and served his advocacy of the revolutionary transformation of China. After the establishment of the PRC, class struggle remained a prominent theme in all major mass movements launched by Mao, including the "Three-Anti," and "Five-Anti" campaigns[1] in the early 1950s and the Great Proletarian Cultural Revolution from 1966 to 1976. Mao believed that in any class society, times of relative equilibrium are but necessary preparation for times of open antagonism and revolution when the contradiction between the two principal classes reaches the critical point (Li, 1994). Oksenberg (1977: 88) defined Mao's "pattern of rule" as "the alternation between a period of social ferment, mass mobilization, unleashed advance and conflict on the one hand, and a period of consolidation, institutionalization, planned advance and reconciliation on the other." Oksenberg (1977) offered the following illustrations.

The initial period of harmony and the economic rehabilitation of the PRC was followed by the "Three-Anti," and "Five-Anti" campaigns in urban China and the acceleration and completion of land reforms in rural China in 1950–1952. The period from mid-1952 through mid-1955 was characterized by another time of relative equilibrium involving consolidation and institution-building. This was followed by the 1955–1956 collectivization campaign in agriculture, the nationalization of industrial and commercial enterprises, and the severe *su-fan-yun-dong* (rectification movement) in government organs. After another period of relative quietude (1956–1957), the upsurge of the Great Leap Forward of 1958–1960 ensued. Pockets of relative stability were also interspersed within the turmoil of the Cultural Revolution. The observation of Oksenberg (1977) is corroborated by Li's (1994) narration of Mao's life. The motivation behind Mao's method of dialectical development is interpreted by some scholars as his aim of accomplishing the communist utopia (e.g. Chen and Yang, 1992; Yu, 1995), but by others as his desire to consolidate personal power by expurgating opposition (e.g. Li, 1994).

## *"Serve the people"*

"Serve the people" may be a third principle in Mao's leadership philosophy. Even in his childhood, Mao wished to do something great for the oppressed Chinese people. The basic motivation behind Mao's revolutionary efforts was to liberate the Chinese people, the bulk of whom are peasants. He realized that, in order to liberate the Chinese people, the Chinese peasantry must be liberated (Yu, 1995). Orthodox Marxism, however, espouses the Communist party's dependence on the class of workers residing in major urban areas (instead of the peasantry in rural areas) as the revolutionary backbone. To help persuade the young CCP to revise orthodox Marxism to fit it with Chinese reality, Mao wrote "Report on an investigation of the peasant movement in Hunan" (Mao, 1954a) and "On practice" (Mao, 1954a). Although these works proposed the principle of "seeking truth from facts" to help field the pressure from the Soviet Union's orthodox Marxism (see, for instance, Gorman, 1982), Mao's primary motivation and concern was the success of the Chinese revolution and the liberation of the Chinese people.

On September 8, 1944, in memory of Chang Si-de, a soldier in the Guards Regiment of the Central Committee of the Chinese Communist Party who died on active duty, Mao wrote "Serve the people." Citing the Ancient Chinese historian Sima Qian, Mao said that although death befalls all men alike, it may be weightier than Mount Tai or lighter than a feather, and that to die for the people is weightier than Mount Tai. He went on to say that the Chinese people were suffering; it was the Party's duty to save them; the Party must have the interests of the people and the sufferings of the great majority at heart, and when the death is for the people, it is a worthy one.

In his writing of March 1957 (Mao, 1957), Mao criticized cadres whose spirit to serve the people had declined. He emphasized that "Communism is about struggling to serve and benefit the people, for 10 thousand years, whole-heartedly, not half-heartedly, not even with 2/3 of your heart. Those sagging in their spirit to serve the people should be re-invigorated through rectification" (Mao, 1957: 400). Mao continued by asserting that to serve the people well, the cadres must commingle with and keep in close contact with the masses, and must be open and receptive to criticism from the masses (Mao, 1957: 401). Evidently, although Mao did not couch his thoughts in terms of democracy, his leadership philosophy of "serving the people" is quintessentially democratic, and congruent with his mass line, as will be explained later in the chapter.

A prominent motivation (at least ostensibly so as a slogan) for Mao to initiate the Cultural Revolution was to rid China of any privileged class so as to achieve equality for the masses (particularly the peasantry). Millions of "educated youths" in the cities and even high governmental officials were sent to rural China to understand, to appreciate, and "to learn from the peasants." During this time, privileged individuals (e.g. those privileged in education or wealth) may have suffered from criticism and persecution; it was the common people, the impoverished, and the underprivileged that were gloried (Li, 1994). To practice his own principle of "serving the people," Mao sent his son to the Korean War, where he was killed in action (Li, 1994).

## Origin of Mao's leadership philosophy

Knight (2005) argues that the Thoughts of Mao Zedong are clearly and exclusively influenced by a limited number of texts of the New Philosophy, which was Marxism as rendered by Soviet philosophers and by Chinese philosophers converted to the New Philosophy (especially Ai Siqi,[2] Qu Qiubai,[3] and Li Da[4]). Li's narration attests that Mao was an avid reader of two main subjects, Marxism and Chinese history (Li, 1994: 440). The most heavily annotated philosophical texts by Mao include Mark Mitin's *A dialectical and historical materialism* (1936) and M. Shirokov, A. Aizenberg *et al.*'s *A course on dialectical materialism* (see also Mao, 1988). There exists close intertextual congruence between Mao's elaboration of Marxism and the "relatively closed body of texts" (Knight, 2005: 195).[5] Mao used the above two texts as sources for his two most famous essays on philosophy – "On contradiction" and "On practice," which were part of his more extensive "Lecture notes on dialectical materialism" (Knight, 2005). When Mao was most actively engaged in the study of Marxist philosophy (i.e. during his Yan'an years), he was "severely handicapped by a shortage of books, even of the works of Marx and Lenin. Little in the way of a library had survived the Long March" (Bisson, 1973: 37). But this handicap did not seem to curtail Mao's ardent reading of Marxist philosophy; he would consume the several new books brought to him by a visitor "in three or four nights of intensive reading, during which he seemed oblivious to everything else" (Snow, 1972: 111).

Although there exists controversy on the extent and manner of influence, Mao's inspiration from the New Philosophy is evident.[6] This evidence is supported by his naming the central agency for dissemination of Marxist philosophy during his Yan'an years the Yan'an New Philosophy Association. This association was instrumental in consolidating and systematizing Mao's sinification of Marxism under the rubric of the Thoughts of Mao Zedong, to be identified in 1945 as the CCP's "guiding theory" (Knight, 2005).

Chinese history and traditional Chinese philosophy were other influences on Mao's leadership philosophy; various sources (e.g. Li, 1994; Metzger, 1977; Wu, 1983) attest that Mao was an enthusiastic reader of Chinese history and classical Chinese works. Numerous works (e.g. Andrew and Rapp, 2000; Salisbury, 1992) make comparative studies of Mao and emperors in Chinese history. According to Tang, a prominent proposition of traditional Chinese philosophy is "the integration of knowledge and practice" (Tang, 1991: 161). The value of knowledge must be reflected in and tested by practical action. This is remarkably similar to Mao's "seeking truth from facts." A reflection of the central tenet of Confucianism, *ren*, or benevolence, is easily discernible in Mao's "serve the people." Chai and Chai argue that Mao in his writings borrowed two elements of Confucianism in particular: "first, the idea that knowledge must lead to action and that action must be based on knowledge, and, second, the ideal of the commonwealth" (Chai and Chai, 2001: 35–36).

"Serve the people" as an attribute of Mao's leadership philosophy is also influenced by a particular classical Chinese work, Laozi's *Dao de jing*, or *The bible of virtue* (Wagner, 2003). Chapter 7 of this work recommends that the sage should place himself after the people and ignore his own desires and thus be complete and content (Wagner, 2003: 140–141). Chapter 49 of *Dao de jing* exhorts that the saint should not have a heart of his own, but have the heart of the people, and the needs of other people as his own. As the saint's mind is the world's mind, people all over the world give him their ears and eyes (Wagner, 2003: 280–286). Chapter 66 admonishes that one must follow and serve the people in order to lead and master them (Wagner, 2003: 347–349). Chapter 81 teaches that the saint does not serve himself; the more he gives, the more he has. Nature flourishes at the expense of no one; so the sage benefits all men and contends with none (Wagner, 2003: 384–387). Thus, "serving the people" is often given as a central precept in *Dao de jing*.

The influence of Chinese history and classical Chinese philosophy on Mao remains verifiable despite Mao's public dissociation of his ideology from China's past, especially during the Cultural Revolution. However, also verifiable is the occasional discrepancy between Mao's public statements and his private practices (see, for instance, Li [1994] on Mao's personal sentiments toward the United States and his public statements about this same nation; and Deng [1984: 276–296], on Mao's deviation from the Thoughts of Mao Zedong in his post-1949 leadership practice).

Furthermore, according to Dow (1977), it is important to note the congruence between the two major influences on Mao's philosophy, Marxism and Confucianism. Dow enumerated four areas of congruence between Confucianism and Marxian dialectical materialism: (1) the Marxian assertion of matter as the primary source of knowledge and the Confucian principle of the investigation of things as the main means of knowledge acquisition; (2) the Marxian universal law on quality and quantity and the Confucian conception of *li-zhi* (principle–matter); (3) regarding laws of dialectics, the Marxian stress on polarity and struggle and the Confucian stress on the complementarity of opposites; and (4) the unity of theory (knowledge) in both Marxism and Confucianism. Dow's arguments show there is clear coherence among the original influences on Mao's leadership philosophy.

## Mao's leadership style and methodology

Mao's leadership style was largely derived from his leadership philosophy. His belief in "seeking truth from facts" and "serving the people" led to his "mass line." His belief in the dialectics of contradiction led to his "democratic centralism."

Experience has proved, Mao claimed, that whenever the practice of the Party proves correct, it comes from the masses, and goes back for implementation by the masses themselves. Mao termed this as "from the masses, to the masses," meaning that the discrete, inchoate ideas from the masses must first be collected, studied, and synthesized, after which, the "processed" ideas must be propagated and explained to the masses for their willing execution of the ideas. The dialectical cycles of "from the masses, to the masses" will make the Party's leadership more correct, more vital, and more enriched. Mao called this the Marxist epistemology (Mao, 1975).[7]

Some may find peculiar congruence between Mao's mass line and Abraham Lincoln's take on the popular opinion. Lincoln was credited with saying, "Without the opinion of the public, you can do nothing; with the opinion of the public, you can do nothing." What this means, in Maoist terms, would be an opposition to both "command-ism" and "tail-ism" (Mao, 1975). On the one hand, leaders must study and understand the opinions of the masses. On the other hand, leaders must not follow those opinions mechanically or slavishly. The voice of the masses must be not only heeded, but also refined and educated before the masses can effectively practice "their own" voice. According to Li (1994), Mao was clear-sighted about the power of the masses. Both in the pre- and post-liberation eras of his career, he deftly framed his ambitions in a way to win almost spellbound support from the general populace.

The mass line, according to Wilson (1977), was a major contribution by Mao. It helped to de-bureaucratize the Party. Russians had shown that the injustices of capitalism could be rectified by the installation of a vast new bureaucracy, but they failed to address the injustices which, in turn, were created by the new bureaucracy. Wilson (1977) affirmed that Mao was the only major leader to tackle this thorny problem, which he did with his mass line.

Mao's second leadership style or methodology, "democratic centralism," conforms closely with his mass line. The "democratic" part of the concept represents listening to the masses while the "centralism" part represents refinement of the public voice, as explained previously.

## Mao's charismatic leadership and personality

Mao's imprint on China and the world, by all standards, cannot be ignored. He belongs in the company of the few great political figures of the last century. He ruled a quarter of the world's population for a quarter-century with unparalleled intensity (Pye, 1976). Scholars everywhere were and are fascinated by the question, "What enabled Mao to accomplish the seemingly unachievable?"

Many explanations from historical, political, economic, cultural, and social perspectives have been offered (Wilson, 1977). For instance, one possible explanation of Mao's appeal lies less in the man and more in the nature of Chinese society, which means that the populace does seem inclined to treat its leaders as imperial figures and even demi-gods. However, millions of non-Chinese, old and young, who shared no affinity to Mao's rural background and varied social and personal background were also inspired in their own political lives by Mao's words and example (Pye, 1976).

Pye attributes Mao's appeal and greatness to the man's extraordinary ability "to understand, evoke, and direct human emotions and the innumerable ways in which he has used his own persona to command the sentiments and passions of others" (Pye, 1976: 6). Wilson (1977) supports this claim in that elements in many massive movements authored by Mao could hardly be explained in rational terms. Dittmer (1974) recognizes Mao's personality as conforming to Harold Lasswell's definition of the "dramatizing character" whose skill resides in commanding the immediate affective response in others. This dramatizing personality and emotional charisma worked for Mao. Because of the frustrations of impotence and oppression for years in the first half of the last century, the Chinese were responsive to calls for dramatic and revolutionary actions (Pye, 1976).

Thus, Mao's charisma may be partly attributed to his acute understanding of his audience, especially the Chinese peasants who accounted for 80 percent of the Chinese population. According to Snow (1944), as early as the 1920s, Mao began to understand how to channel the emotions of China's peasants toward his revolutionary causes. He saw firsthand that they felt immense anger against their landlords, and he used this to great effect in framing revolutionary goals from the peasants' perspective (e.g. the slogans of "Down with the landlords!" and "Equal distribution of land!"). Edgar Snow (1944), in his famous *Red Star over China,* showed how acutely Mao perceived the sentiments of all groups which he could unite in the revolutionary cause. For instance, Mao discerned Muslims' disenchantment with the Kuomintang general Ma Hung-kuei and his soldiers, whose maltreatment of the Muslims left the latter with a deep and justified distrust of the former. In order to unite the Muslims despite the historical background of racial hatred between the majority group of Han and the minority group of Muslims, Mao allowed and encouraged the establishment of "Mohammedan communities" by the Muslims, which went on to become "village Soviets" (Snow, 1944: 349–355).

Mao's charisma reached the level of a cult during the Cultural Revolution when literally every hand in the nation possessed a red book of Chairman Mao's quotations and a figurine of Mao, sacred objects never to be blasphemed. Mao's omnipresence in the nation (certainly including his portrait on the Tian-an-men rostrum) further enhanced his charisma, indeed even transforming the man into a deity.

Mao's stature in history was clinched by his revolutionary victories, his founding of the PRC and the liberation of the nation from centuries of various types of oppression. Even those post-1949 disasters of Mao could not eclipse this man's grandeur. Mao's leadership philosophy and practice, aided by his poetic charisma, lie at the root of his greatness.

## Deng Xiaoping's leadership theory and practice

### A *biography of Deng Xiaoping (1904–1997)*

Deng Xiaoping was a prominent leader of the CCP, and after 1978 the dominant figure in Chinese politics. Born in Guang-an county of Sichuan province in south-western China, he studied in France on a "work-study" program from 1920 to 1925. He joined the Communist party during this time. In 1926, he studied in Moscow for a short time and went back to China to join the Chinese revolution the following year. He became associated with Mao Zedong at this time. In 1934–1935, he participated in the renowned Long March. He was elected a member of the CCP's Central Committee, became the first secretary of the East China section, then of the South-west China section, and then of the CCP Central Committee from 1949. After 1952, he successively served as the vice-premier of the Government Administration Council, secretary-general of the Central Committee, vice-premier of the State Council, member of the Political Bureau of the Central Committee in 1955, member of the Standing Committee of the Political Bureau, and secretary-general of the CCP Central Committee in 1956. He was divested of all his posts when the Cultural Revolution began, reinstated into the position of vice-premier of the State Council in 1973, and again divested of all his positions after the "Tian-an-men incident" of 1976. In 1977, he was again reinstated in his former positions in the Communist party, the government, and the military.

He presided over the Third Plenum of the Eleventh CCP Central Committee in 1978 and established the key policy of focusing on economic development and opening to the outside world. From 1982, he introduced a series of new thoughts on the reform of the system of the party and government leadership. In 1981, the Sixth Plenum of the Eleventh CCP Central Committee passed a "Resolution on certain questions in the history of our party since the founding of the People's Republic of China," drafted under his direction. This important document helped to clarify and frame the nation's understanding of the holocaust of the Cultural Revolution. He was elected chairman of the CCP Central Military Commission in the same year. In 1984, he introduced the idea of "one country, two systems" as a method of addressing the issue of the return of Hong Kong. His ideas and pragmatic reforms enabled him to be included in *Time* twice, in 1978 and 1985, as Man of the Year. In 1985, he introduced the idea that socialism is not in contradiction to a market economy. In 1992, he toured numerous cities in southern China and offered the famous "talks from tours of the South." He published three volumes of the *Selected works of Deng Xiaoping* in 1983, 1989, and 1993 respectively. Deng Xiaoping was, and is widely considered to be, the architect of China's reforms since the late 1970s. (For more detailed biographies of Deng Xiaoping, see Li, 1994; Stewart, 2001; and Yang, 2005.)

## Deng's reformism

Deng Xiaoping is mostly known as the chief architect of China's reforms. Conventional reference to these reforms is exclusively restricted to post-Mao times. However, Deng's interaction with Mao was one of half a century. Deng's collaboration with and differences from Mao existed long before Mao's death. And Deng's reformist wishes can be traced to the early years of the new PRC.

During Mao's revolutionary wars, Deng had been a stalwart supporter of Mao and the Thoughts of Mao Zedong. During the early 1930s, leftist forces within the CCP opposed Mao's policies for the

Soviet areas in Jiangxi province and tried to oust Mao from his leadership position. Deng's support of Mao caused Deng to lose the position of party secretary of Huichang county, and then of director of propaganda of Jiangxi province. Deng was at that time labeled "the ringleader of the Maoist camp" (Liu, 2001). Mao never forgot Deng's support in those difficult times, which perhaps led to Mao's reinstatement of Deng twice in the central government. Despite their differences after 1949, Mao always believed that Deng was a genuine Marxist (Li, 1994).

Both Mao and Deng worked hard for a strong, independent China. Both believed in Marxism, "seeking truth from the facts," and "serving the people" (see, for instance, Chen and Yang, 1992; Liu, 2001; Yu, 1995; a more elaborate comparative discussion of Mao and Deng follows later in this chapter). However, after 1949 their different methods for achieving the common end led to deep-seated discord and eventually to Deng's broad post-Mao reforms. The failure of Mao's utopian and large-scale movements for a strong China led to Deng's search for better methods. Deng's speeches as early as the 1950s (specific ones of which are introduced later in the chapter) manifested a strong propensity for practicality and gradualism. Deng's ideas were not heeded when Mao was too bright a shining star in China's political sky. As Deng is remembered largely because of his reformism via effective leadership methodology, not because of the thoughts he shared with Mao, this chapter focuses on introducing Deng's reformism and pragmatic, gradualist leadership methodology.

Following Mao's death and the end of the Cultural Revolution, Deng's comprehensive reforms gradually came to full bloom. Deng believed that a strong China cannot come from constant mass struggles for ideological purity and rectification, which as proved in practice had led to disasters. A strong China must first come from economic prosperity, which is indispensable for national independence and strength. In 1978, when Deng took power, he launched a "Movement of Ideological Liberation," a movement of "seeking truth from facts," to take the nation out of the mentality and trauma of the Cultural Revolution, and to prepare the nation for the host of reforms soon to be introduced. Liou (1999) believes that the first lesson for China's post-Mao economic development is Deng's reformism, the cautious execution of which helped to reduce the risks and uncertainties associated with any new reform policy.

To facilitate successful implementation of his reform, Deng decided, first of all, to bring about the nation's recovery from the decade of stagnation and destruction of the Cultural Revolution. He established the key policy of economic development and opening to the outside world at the Third Plenum of the Eleventh CCP Central Committee in 1978. Different from Mao's people's commune system, Deng's policy allowed farmers to manage their own piece of land and to directly benefit from their own labor according to a system of distributed responsibility, thus greatly arousing the enthusiasm of rural China. Scientific management methods were adopted to improve the efficiency of state-owned enterprises and to allow the emergence of private enterprises. Luo (2005) believes that Deng's challenge to what had been mistakenly perceived as genuine Maoist thoughts opened up people's minds, instilled confidence, and facilitated a broad-based economic recovery.

In addition to bringing about the recovery of China's domestic economy, Deng set a new vision by addressing China's relationship with the outside world differently from Mao's epoch. During the Cultural Revolution and for many years before that, China largely isolated itself from the Western world. Yet to build China's economy, Deng decided that China could not afford to ignore developments in science and management that were happening in the Western world. In many of his speeches, Deng emphasized the importance and the benefits of opening to and learning from the outside world. In his speech, "Use the intellectual resources of other countries and open wider to the outside world" (Deng, 1994), for instance, he addressed China's earnest need to attract foreign experts and resources to develop its own major projects, and the need to be flexible to facilitate the import of foreign resources. Deng perceived that opening to the outside world to exploit international opportunities for a strong China was "a matter of strategic importance" (Deng, 1994: 43).

Third, Deng's reforms aimed to improve the efficiency of the government and administration. For a long time in the history of the CCP, party leaders had enjoyed lifelong tenure, with promotion largely determined by seniority. These traditional practices had led to inveterate inertia and lethargy in the government (Luo, 2005). As early as in his speech of 1961, "Promote large numbers of young technicians" (Deng, 1992: 267–268), Deng emphasized the importance of "professional and technical competence" as the main criterion for promotion. "No Party members will be promoted if they are not qualified professionally and technically," and that cadres must be hired in their own field of expertise (Deng, 1992: 268). In his speech, "Questions concerning cadres of the party in power" (Deng, 1992: 297–302), he addressed the need for cadres to be de-posted and demoted for fear of strain by an unnecessarily large number of cadres and for fear of the formation of cliques. He recommended cadre transfer of 5 percent yearly to prevent the formation of cliques that might hamper governmental efficiency (Deng, 1992: 298). He emphasized the importance of systematic and careful evaluation of cadres.

In his speech, "On reform of the political structure" (Deng, 1994: 178–181), Deng advocated the abolition of lifelong tenure of government functionaries and encouraged senior leaders to retire. For the purpose of greater equity and efficiency, he introduced civil service examinations to replace seniority as the criterion for cadre hire and promotion. Deng thus emphasized the importance of an efficient, able, and vital government. He said, "Only with a vigorous leadership that has eliminated bureaucratism, raised efficiency and mobilized the grass-roots units and the rank and file can we have real hope of success in our modernization drive" (Deng, 1994: 181).

Although the success of Deng's reformism is too obvious for the world to ignore, some scholars also draw attention to the negative side of, or challenges to, his reforms. Harding (1997), for instance, believes that Deng's policy had too much emphasis on economic development thereby producing serious inflation and potential political unrest. Officials in the CCP with a Maoist mentality challenged Deng's reformism as a deviation from time-honored socialism, widening the gap between the rich and the poor. Those wishing for more political freedom claimed Deng's reforms were inadequate and contributed little to political change (Harding, 1997).

## Deng's pragmatism

"Black or white, a cat is nice as long as it catches the mice" is perhaps the best-known statement by Deng Xiaoping (Li, 1994: 607). This remark encapsulates Deng's pragmatism. He was a man focused on results rather than means, on practicality rather than ostentation (Li, 1994).

In contrasting Mao's and Deng's eras, Bergmann (1993) characterized Deng's leadership as reform-oriented and pragmatic. The conflict between Deng and Mao during the early years of the PRC largely stemmed from their different methodologies for strengthening China. Deng emphasized the pragmatic end of economic development, for the purpose of which flexible and expedient means could be employed. Mao, on the other hand, focused on ideological purity and revolutionary spirit as the foundation for meaningful national development.

Deng's pragmatism was easily discernible in the early socialist construction period after the establishment of the PRC. In his speech, "Our chief task ahead is building up the country" (Deng, 1992: 242–249), he criticized an economy of waste and central planning that ignored unique local conditions, and admonished against state compensation for unaccounted losses. In terms of projects for urban development, he chose practicality and frugality over grandiose pretense. He said that the daily needs of the general people must be met first and the matter of esthetic grandeur should be considered later when the nation became rich enough. He admonished, "Some comrades stress the need of attractiveness, which is good . . . However, it should not be over-emphasized at the expense of economy and practicality, or without regard to what is actually possible. It is all right if something is not very attractive. We can take care of that in future, when we are rich enough, but for now we should concentrate on economy and practicality . . . Our country is poor, but people are trying to make it appear very rich" (Deng, 1992: 248).

In his speech, "Restore agricultural production" (Deng, 1992: 292–296), he reminded people of the efficacy of pragmatism in the CCP's defeat of Chiang Kai-shek during China's civil war. The form of the method, he said, is not as important as whether the method will work with the given conditions of different rural areas. "We should not stick to a fixed mode of relations of production but adopt whatever mode . . . can help mobilize the masses' initiative," he affirmed (Deng, 1992: 293). Incidentally, it was in this speech that Deng used for the first time his famous remark advocating pragmatism by quoting his long-time comrade Liu Bocheng, "It does not matter if it is a yellow cat or a black cat, as long as it catches mice" (Deng, 1992: 293).[8]

Barnett believes that Deng, along with important leaders such as Liu Shaoqi, Zhou Enlai and Chen Yun, made three attempts (1956–57, 1961–62, 1974–75) "to move China in a more pragmatic direction" (Barnett, 1986: 39). These leaders were concerned that Mao's large-scale mass movements were the single-minded method to achieve national strength. They believed that conditions in many parts of China were not ripe for the accomplishment of ambitious goals by precipitous methods, and that realistic, pragmatic, and flexible methods suitable for local conditions should be used instead. According to Barnett, "Pragmatism was, in fact, Deng's hallmark," and it was pragmatism that led the radicals to charge Deng as a "rightist" during the Cultural Revolution, resulting in his deposition from power twice (Barnett, 1986: 40).

It was perhaps Deng's pragmatism that helped emancipate people's minds from Maoist conventionalities and obdurate ideologies (e.g. "whatever Mao says is correct"), thereby expediting the success of his reform programs (Stewart, 2001). For achieving the pragmatic aims of economic success and national strength for China (which were also Mao's principal aims), he was open to various methods and foreign assistance. He told the nation that a market economy would not be in contradiction to socialism since a market economy would help China's efforts in economic development; and that capitalist management methods would be good because they could also help China's economic aspirations. In foreign policies, he endorsed a balanced approach to all countries (fearing none and following none) so that China could free itself from complex world politics, benefit from its contacts with all neighbors in the international community, and concentrate on its own economic development (Luo, 2005b). To help resolve the issues of Hong Kong and Macao and unify them with the mainland part of China, Deng proposed the "one country, two systems (socialism and capitalism)" theory, focusing less on ideological "isms" and more on practical results. This pragmatic proposal proved effective as seen in the successful return of Hong Kong and Macao to China. However, some scholars (e.g. Ostrov, 2005) contend that Deng's pragmatism was not without weaknesses. Its exclusive focus on economic progress, Ostrov (2005) avers, created a void because of the lack of a national system of spiritual belief (which Maoism had been able to achieve). The absence of a national belief system contributed to the general populace's search for new beliefs, as manifested in the resurgence of new religions in China (Ostrov, 2005).

## Deng's leadership style

In sharp contrast to Mao, who was inclined toward handling affairs under the guidance of elaborate theories and great ideals, Deng

Xiaoping was much more experimental and incremental. With a focus on pragmatic results, Deng was willing to experiment with various and expedient methods, characterized by a process of trial, error, and correction. In his effort for greater and surer success, he adopted a gradual and incremental methodology in his experimentalism. This section will cite Deng's writings and speeches to illustrate his leadership style of experimentalism and cautious gradualism.

Deng Xiaoping was accredited with several famous quotations. One is, "Let's cross the river by feeling for the stepping stones." This well-known saying epitomizes Deng's experimentalism. Deng's reforms and opening to the outside world in the post-Mao years were a great experiment, something completely new for a nation accustomed to Maoist movements. Deng adopted a method of trial, error, and correction in many of his reform endeavors. As seen in many of his speeches, some cited below, he would experiment with a new method or strategy in particular locales before broad adoption of that method or strategy. As affirmed by Pye (1986) and Solinger (1981), Deng's leadership of post-Mao development, though sharing the theoretical root of Mao's "seeking truth from facts," was evidently pragmatic and experimental. It could be argued, by the way, that Deng's political wisdom may be seen here. The reassertion of an important Maoist principle theoretically justifies his economic reforms with orthodox CCP ideology, thereby helping to gain more support from Maoists for the reforms.

Deng experimented with reforms in many areas unfamiliar to a nation governed with the Maoist mentality. The prominent ones included a practical focus on economic development, theoretical reconciliation between socialism and the market economy, establishment of the "special economic zones" that introduced capitalist management, "one country, two systems (socialism and capitalism)" to facilitate the return of Hong Kong, Macao, and hopefully also Taiwan, and abolition of the traditional lifelong tenure of Party functionaries.

In his speech, "Our chief task ahead is building up the country" (Deng, 1992: 242–249), in contrast to Mao's continuous revolution of class struggle, Deng emphasized a gradual rather than grandiose approach to building up the country. Mao inured the nation to a mentality of precipitous methods and massive "great leaps" to catch up quickly with Western superpowers. Everything in the Maoist era needed to be new and grand, but Deng advised against this. He said in the speech that not every enterprise had to be new and colossal. "[W]e should not allow [form] to degenerate into formalism, wasting state funds for the sake of form or stressing the importance of form at the expense of our work," exhorted Deng (1992: 245). In a discussion of how to build Xi'an (a city in central China) in the early years of the PRC, Deng emphasized the economic practicality of different projects such as the location and size of theatres and hotels. In contrast to an indiscriminate focus on grand ostentation, he directed everyone's attention to "solving the problems of concern to the masses that can be solved with a small amount of money or even without spending any money" (Deng, 1992: 248). This incrementalist style and practice persisted into Deng's later reforms.

In his speech, "Restore agricultural production" (Deng, 1992: 292–296), he mentioned a few rural people's communes across the country that were unwilling to relinquish their commune ownership. He advised a gradual approach: if the people there were "unwilling to break them up, let them remain as they are" (Deng, 1992: 293). In the same speech, he said that the entire country in the past was frequently placed under a single plan without adequate consideration of the different conditions and particular circumstances of different areas, and that unsuccessful past experiences should caution against forcing everyone to do the same thing on an exaggerated scale. He was wary of the practice of launching a nationwide movement for each and every undertaking.

In his speech, "Emancipate the mind, seek truth from facts and unite as one in looking to the future" (Deng, 1984: 151–165), he discussed the fact that China lacked trained professionals for legislative work. Therefore, he suggested, "[L]egal provisions will have to be less than perfect to start with, then be gradually improved upon. Some laws and statutes can be tried out in particular localities and later enacted nationally after the experience has been evaluated and improvements have been made" (Deng, 1984: 158). In the same speech, Deng encouraged some regions and people to get rich first to serve as an "impressive example to their 'neighbors'" (Deng, 1984: 164). This practice clearly would not conform to the traditional socialist mentality of equality and egalitarianism in the early years of the PRC. Pye (1986) summarizes Deng's reform method as "gradualist experimentalism."

Deng's gradualist or incrementalist approach was manifest throughout his career. He knew very well how to fuse socialist and political traditions with economic and administrative reforms. Chen, Jefferson, and Singh (1992) characterize Deng's reforms as incremental and practical, with the positive effect of reducing risks. Yang (2005) believes that Deng's reform strategy, starkly contrasting with that of Mikhail Gorbachev of the former Soviet Union, focused on liberal economic reform while adhering to traditional political thoughts and even discouraging political reforms. This approach by Deng perhaps helped him to win support from both conservative and liberal elements in the nation, facilitating stable yet impressive successes in his reforms. Zheng (1999) agrees with Yang and believes that the CCP's crackdown on the dissidents' pro-democracy efforts in 1989 was largely motivated by Deng's belief in incrementalism and pragmatism rather than in revolutionary cataclysm. Zheng argues that Deng's incrementalism has enabled China to "accommodate drastic socioeconomic changes" and yet maintain the ability "to prevent socioeconomic chaos from occurring, chaos that has troubled many former communist states and Third World countries" (Zheng, 1999: 1157).

## Summary and conclusion

### *A comparison of Mao and Deng*

Were Mao and Deng, the most prominent leaders in modern China, the same or different in their leadership philosophy and practice? This question is of great import to scholars of Chinese leadership philosophy. It can be argued that Mao and Deng have both essential commonalities and conspicuous differences between them. Their similarities tend to belong to the realm of their fundamental thoughts; their differences are predominantly in their leadership styles and methodology.

Deng's interactions with Mao covered half a century, and both were among the early founders and leaders of the CCP. Biographical studies of Deng (e.g. Evans, 1997; Liu, 2001; Stewart, 2001; Yu, 1995) reveal that Deng's thoughts emanated from Marxism and the Thoughts of Mao Zedong. Because of his efforts to disseminate Marxism during his "work-study" years in France by mimeographing Marxist works and propaganda flyers, Deng was nicknamed "Dr. Mimeography" (Evans, 1997). Deng's main job during Mao's revolutionary wars seemed to be "political commissar," advocating Marxism and Mao Zedong thoughts (see, for instance, Liu, 2001).

According to Chen and Yang, all activities by Deng were based on the fundamental Maoist thought of "seeking truth from facts" (Chen and Yang, 1992: 74–79). To the extent he differed from Mao, Deng emphasized "historical materialism" and introduced "ideological emancipation" as a necessary step in order to heed historical conditions (particularly China's conditions in the immediate post-Mao years, when disillusionment with Mao's radical mass movements was widespread). Some scholars (e.g. Chen and Yang, 1992; Yu, 1995) argue that Deng's pragmatism represents a deeper and more faithful practice of "seeking truth from facts," with attention not only to facts in the abstract but, more importantly, to facts and social conditions in historical context.

Despite the aforesaid important commonalities between Mao and Deng, the differences between the two in leadership style and methodology are also significant. Dernberger (1999) believes that the fundamental economic institutions and policies, as well as the resulting economic developments, during Mao's era (1949–1975) readily contrast with those in Deng's era (1978–1995). In a comparison, Mao seemed to be more idealistic and holistic, and a visionary on nationalism; Deng seemed to be more realistic and details-minded, and a visionary on economic development.

Many of Mao's mass movements were motivated by idealistic goals he had for the nation. Through the Great Leap Forward, he wanted China to catch up with the United Kingdom in ten years and with the United States in fifteen years. Through the campaign of "learning from Dazhai" (a village Mao set as a national paragon for agricultural development), he wanted every Chinese village to be soon transformed into a new socialist village of social harmony and materialistic abundance. Through the Great Proletarian Cultural Revolution, he wanted the nation to be turned completely into a pure socialist country, with classless equality and freedom from power differentiation. (For more details on Mao's utopianism and idealism, see, for instance, Li, 1994.)

Mao's writings display a philosophical endeavor to grasp the whole world in its totality. His dialectical analysis of contradictions, for instance, stipulates comprehensive understanding of the opposing sides of all the major contradictions in any given thing. His mapping of the entire world into three blocs (the First, the Second, and the Third Worlds) again represents an effort to comprehend the very whole in its entirety. Mao's inclination toward nationwide movements may be another indication of his holistic approach to national affairs. If something is to be done, it must be done holistically with nation-wide perfection.

Mao was a visionary on nationalism. He struggled for decades finally to be able to proudly proclaim on October 1, 1949, "Chinese people have stood up!" Mao was able to redress an imbalance in decision-making in the international arena that had previously been dominated by the West, and introduced China as a solid weight on the scale of international affairs (Wilson, 1977). Schwartz asserted that in Mao's writings, there is an "overwhelming preoccupation with the preservation and enhancement of China as a political-social entity in a world of other societal entities known as nation-states" (Schwartz, 1977: 16) and that Mao refused to identify and conform "Chineseness" with universal cultural, ethical, and social values. Mao visited only one foreign country in his lifetime, the Soviet Union. Describing that sole experience of a foreign visit, he referred to his call to Josef Stalin for assistance as "grabbing meat from the tiger's mouth." Even in his dealings with the Soviet Union, Mao made valiant efforts to assert and achieve China's independence from the "big brother," first from the pressure of the Soviet model of orthodox Marxism in the early revolutionary years, and then under extremely dire national conditions when the Soviet Union withdrew all its economic support from China after the severance of the Sino-Soviet tie (Li, 1994).

Compared with Mao, Deng was more realistic and details-oriented, and more of a visionary on economic construction. Deng's reforms were initiated with the realistic understanding that China was still at the initial stage of socialism, and that people must be motivated not by remote communist visions, but by more immediate individual interests. With this understanding, he designed the "distributed responsibility system" where the individual is more immediately rewarded or penalized with respect to his/her own achievements. This model was in clear contrast to Mao's system of the people's commune where collectivity and egalitarianism was favored. Deng's realistic and details-oriented inclinations were also discerned in his early speeches before his era of reform. As indicated by the analyses of his early speeches presented previously in this chapter, Deng chose realistic and practical results over grand impressions. To help accomplish such results, he depended on cautious and careful analysis of the conditions of different locales, even different locales within the same city (see, for instance, his speech "Our chief task ahead is building up the country," Deng, 1992: 242–249).

Deng rarely launched any experimental endeavor as a nationwide campaign. His approach was to test the idea initially in selected areas. His realism inclined him to accept the practice that some regions and individuals in the nation could get rich first, despite his strong belief in socialism which emphasizes egalitarianism (see, for instance, Deng, 1984: 164).

In his "Remarks on successive drafts of the 'Resolution on certain questions in the history of our party since the founding of the People's Republic of China'"during March 1980 – June 1981 (Deng, 1984: 276–296), Deng obviously gave meticulous attention to historical details rather than follow contemporary feelings to ingratiate popular sentiments. Thanks to his realistic and details-oriented analyses, the resolution represented a balanced reflection on Mao. Deng's appeal largely comes from his careful attention to detailed and specific conditions in the nation and realistic and practical execution of policies congruent with those conditions (Stewart, 2001). Thus, if Mao depended on grand, holistic idealism, Deng depended on details-guided realism.

In the minds of both China and Western nations, Deng is remembered largely as a reformer, a visionary reformer who liberated and rejuvenated the Chinese economy. The bulk of his speeches focused on pragmatic methods that could help China's economic development: pinpointed responsibility to motivate the individual; the importance of the professional, of science and technology, of scientific management knowledge, and of attracting foreign capital; and the efficiency of the government. His "white cat, black cat" statement may also have been engendered by his preoccupation with economic results. It was not until the late 1980s when the nation clamored for broader democracy that Deng seriously addressed ideological strife between different "isms." Before that, his mind was on economic development. His pragmatic and details-oriented methods for economic development clinched the memory of Deng as an economic visionary.

This comparative study of Mao and Deng may be summarized by saying that Mao was revolutionary in both vision and practice, while Deng was revolutionary in vision but pragmatic and incremental in practice and methodology. Scholars may acquire new insights on the nature of effective leadership by studying commonalities between

Mao and Deng in fundamental thought on the one hand, while noting failure of Mao's post-1949 radical and revolutionary methods in comparison with the success of Deng's pragmatic and incremental methods on the other.

## Conclusion

Mao Zedong successfully completed China's political revolution and political modernization and established an independent sovereign new China, free from the historical burden of centuries of oppression. Deng successfully completed China's economic and social modernization and rejuvenated a nation disillusioned and traumatized by the Cultural Revolution. Now an international player too prominent to ignore, China has seen itself through the leadership philosophies and the distinct leadership styles of Mao Zedong and Deng Xiaoping. Mao's and Deng's approaches to leading China, and their successes and failures therein, deserve considerable interest in the field of leadership studies.

This chapter has aimed to encourage more research in leadership studies from the Chinese perspective via the introduction of the major leadership theories, philosophies, and practices of Mao Zedong and Deng Xiaoping, and via an explanation and comparison of their distinct leadership methodologies.

Is there a standard or criterion to judge who was better or more effective in his leadership endeavors, Mao or Deng? What can we learn from research on Mao's and Deng's leadership? Such questions are likely to arise in the study of Mao's and Deng's leadership philosophy and practice. Although there is no doubt about the indelible impact both Mao and Deng made on Chinese history, Mao's brilliant success during the Chinese revolutionary era seems to contrast as conspicuously with his own post-1949 failures as with Deng's success in reform. Such contrast invites us to reflect more carefully on the efficacy of their different leadership practices. In their fundamental leadership philosophies, Mao and Deng shared much, as explained previously. Mao's pre-1949 successes and Deng's reformist successes tend to lend credence to the validity of such leadership philosophies.

Mao and Deng's leadership philosophies may be rich in implications for contemporary leadership and management. Their leadership philosophy of "seeking truth from facts," if applied, for instance, to the job of a company CEO, would support what Gehani (1994) termed as the tortoise style of management. According to Gehani, there are two styles of leadership or management: the hare style and the tortoise style. A hare-like leader makes quick decisions in a top-down manner; however, implementation of such decisions may be rather slow as these hastily made decisions, not derived from organizational reality and frontline employees, may encounter resistance from the frontline employees, who are the actual implementers of company decisions. In the tortoise style, careful investigation of the company reality is conducted with the frontline employees before a decision is made. Decision-making in the tortoise style may be slow, but implementation of "tortoise decisions" may be rather precipitous as the making of the decision has incorporated the input, and thus the support, of the implementers (i.e. frontline employees) of the decision.

An analytical comparison of Mao's and Deng's successes and failures suggests the important synthesis of a revolutionary vision with a pragmatic and incremental methodology, a methodology based on societal or organizational reality. The combined lessons from the two also suggest effective matching between leadership philosophy and leadership practice, between the knowing and the doing, between the intention and the method, between the visionary and the pragmatic, and between the revolutionary and the incremental. Some may even contend that Mao and Deng represent the two weights on the "leadership scale," and that the "perfect leadership pivot" should be positioned between the two weights, the precise position of which to be determined by organizational and societal conditions.

The leadership philosophies and practices of Mao Zedong and Deng Xiaoping, and the successes and failures arising from them, represent a rich collage of historical, social, cultural, and political forces. Further studies will certainly shed light on the everlasting and important issue of effective leadership from a global perspective.

*Notes*

1 Mao issued the "Three-Anti Campaign" (1951) and "Five-Anti Campaign" (1952) in an effort to rid China of corruption and enemies of the state. The Three-Anti Campaign targeted waste, inefficiency, and corruption within governmental agencies, and the "Five-Anti Campaign" was against bribery, fraud, theft from the government, tax evasion, and industrial sabotage within business.

2 Chinese philosopher and author, Ai Siqi (1910–1966) was born in Yunnan province and later traveled to Hong Kong, where he studied English at a Protestant school and was exposed to Sun Yat-sen's *Three principles of the people* and Marxism. His copious reading of Marxism in Japanese translation formed the root of Ai's most important works such as *Historical materialism and dialectical materialism* and *Philosophy for the masses.*

3 Born in Changzhou, Jiangsu province, China, and spending much of his early life in Moscow, Qu Qiubai (1899–1935) was a leader of the CCP in the late 1920s and an important Chinese Marxist writer and thinker. He organized revolutions and uprisings (such as the Guangzhou Uprising of December 11, 1927) and was arrested and executed by the Kuomintang in 1935. Heavily criticized as a "renegade" during the Cultural Revolution, Qu was absolved by the CCP Central Committee in 1980. From its Russian translation, Qu created the official Chinese translation of the Internationale, used as the national anthem of China.

4 Born in Hunan, China, Li Da (1890–1966) was an educator and Marxist philosopher. Elected as the director of propaganda by the First Congress of the CCP in 1921, he left the party in 1923 over disputes regarding the issue of a CCP–Kuomintang coalition. After 1927, he was mainly a professor at different universities. He was reintroduced into the CCP in 1949 and served as the leader of various academic institutions. Challenging some of Mao's leftist thoughts in the late 1950s and early 1960s, he died in the course of persecution in 1966 during the Cultural Revolution.

5 For a comprehensive list of intertextual links between Mao's major philosophical works and the sources he used, see the table in *Mao Zedong on dialectical materialism* (Knight, 1990: 80–82).

6 For a more detailed exposition of the controversy, see Knight (2005: 149–150).

7 Readers may find Mao's "mass line" reminiscent of the Shewhart Cycle for learning and improvement (i.e. plan; do; study; act) as explained by Deming (1993: 131–133).

8 Although the well-known version of Deng's quote was "black cat or white cat," the analogy was first used by Deng's colleague, Liu Bocheng, who used the phrase "yellow cat or black cat," quoted here by Deng.

## References

Andrew, A. M., and Rapp, J. A. 2000. *Autocracy and China's rebel founding emperors: comparing Chairman Mao and Ming Taizu*. New York: Rowman & Littlefield.

Barnett, A. D. 1986. "Ten years after Mao," *Foreign Affairs* 65(1): 37–65.

Bergmann, T. 1993. "Changes in agrarian structure and paradigms in the agricultural policies of the PR China," *Quarterly Journal of International Agriculture* 32(1): 36–44.

Bisson, T. A. 1973. *Yenan in June 1937: talks with the Communist leaders.* Berkeley: Center for Chinese Studies, University of California.

Chai, W., and Chai, M. L. 2001. "Confucianism," in S. M. Lipset (ed.), *Political man*, Cambridge: Cambridge University Press, pp. 35–36.

Chen, K., Jefferson, G. H., and Singh, I. 1992. "Lessons from China's economic reform," *Journal of Comparative Economics* 16(2): 201–225.

Chen, Z., and Yang, G. 1992. *Deng Xiaoping zhexue sixiang yanjiu* (Studies of Deng Xiaoping's philosophical thoughts). Shenyang: Liaoning Renmin Chubanshe.

Deming, W. E. 1993. *The new economics.* London: MIT Press.

Deng, Xiaoping 1984. *Selected works of Deng Xiaoping (1975–1982).* Beijing: Foreign Languages Press.

  1992. *Selected works of Deng Xiaoping (1938–1965).* Beijing: Foreign Languages Press.

  1994. *Selected works of Deng Xiaoping*, vol. III. Beijing: Foreign Languages Press.

Dernberger, R. F. 1999. "The People's Republic of China at 50: the economy," *China Quarterly* 15: 606–615.

Dittmer, L. 1974. "Power and personality in China," *Studies in Comparative Communism* 7(1/2): 21–49.

Dow, T. I. 1977. *Confucianism vs. Marxism: an analytical comparison of the Confucian and Marxian theories of knowledge-dialectical materialism.* Washington, DC: University Press of America.

Evans, R. 1997. *Deng Xiaoping and the making of modern China.* London: Penguin.

Gehani, R. 1994. "The tortoise vs. the hare," *Quality Progress* 27: 99–103.

Gorman, R. A. 1982. *Neo-Marxism: the meanings of modern radicalism.* London: Greenwood Press.

Han, Z. 1987. *Mao Zedong.* Taipei: Tianyuan Chubanshe.

Harding, H. 1997. "China after Deng Xiaoping: minimal immediate impact," *Asian Affairs: An American Review* 24(2): 78–84.

Knight, N. 1990 (ed.). *Mao Zedong on dialectical materialism: writings on philosophy, 1937.* Armonk, NY: M.E. Sharpe.

Knight, N. 2005. *Marxist philosophy in China: From Qu Qiubai to Mao Zedong, 1923–1945.* New York: Springer.

Li, Z. 1994. *The private life of Chairman Mao: the memoirs of Mao's personal physician*, trans. Tai Hung-chao. New York: Random House.

Liou, K. T. 1999. "Strategies and lessons of China's post-Mao economic development," *Policy Studies Review* 16(1): 183–208.

Liu, C. 2001. *Deng Xiaoping's san qi san luo* (Deng Xiaoping's three rises and falls). Shenyang: Liaoning Renmin Chubanshe.

Luo, J. 2005a (ed.). *China today: an encyclopedia of life in the People's Republic.* Westport, CT: Greenwood.

　　2005b. "Reforms of Deng Xiaoping (1904–1997)," in Luo (ed.), pp. 118–121.

Mao, Tse-Tung. 1954a. *Selected works of Mao Tse-Tung*, vol. I. Beijing: Foreign Languages Press.

　　1954b. *Selected works of Mao Tse-Tung*, vol. II. Beijing: Foreign Languages Press.

Mao, Zedong. 1957. *Jianguo yilai Mao Zedong wengao* (Mao Zedong's manuscripts since 1949), vol. VI. Beijing: Zhongyang Wenxian Chubanshe.

　　January 30, 1962. "7000 cadres speech," cited in Schram (1974, pp. 163–164).

　　July 8, 1966. "Private letter to Jiang Qing," cited in Oksenberg (1977, p. 90).

　　1975. *Selected works of Mao Zedong*, vol. III. Beijing: Foreign Languages Press.

　　1988. *Mao Zedong zhexue pizhuji* (The philosophical annotations of Mao Zedong). Beijing: Zhongyang Wenxian Chubanshe.

Metzger, T. A. 1977. *Escape from predicament: Neo-Confucianism and China's evolving political culture.* New York: Columbia University Press.

Mitin, M. B. 1936. *Bianzhengfaweiwulun yu lishiweiwulun* (Dialectical and historical materialism), trans. Shen Zhiyuan. n.p.: Shangwu Yinshuguan.

Naím, N. 2005. "Three wise men," *Foreign Policy* 146: 96–97.

Oksenberg, M. 1977. "The political leader," in Wilson (ed.), pp. 70–116.

Ostrov, B. C. 2005. "Something of value: the religious response to de-Maoization in China," *Social Science Journal* 42(1): 55–70.

Pye, L. W. 1976. *Mao Tse-tung: the man in the leader.* New York: Basic Books.

　　1986. "On Chinese pragmatism in the 1980s," *China Quarterly* 106 (January): 207–234.

Rost, J. C. 1993. *Leadership for the twenty-first century.* Westport, CT: Praeger.

Salisbury, H. E. 1992. *The new emperors: China in the era of Mao and Deng.* Boston: Little, Brown.

Schram, S. R. 1974. *Mao Tse-tung unrehearsed.* London: Penguin.

Schwartz, B. I. 1977. "The philosopher," in Wilson (ed.), pp. 9–34.

Shan, P. F. 2005. "Mao Zedong (1893–1976)," in Luo (ed.), pp. 376–381.

Shirokov, M., and Aizenberg, A. *et al.* 1932. *Bianzhengfa weiwulun jiaocheng* (A course on dialectical materialism); trans. Li Da and Lei Zhongnian. Shanghai: Bigengtang.

Snow, E. 1944. *Red star over China.* New York: Random House.

1972. *Red star over China.* Harmondsworth: Penguin.

Solinger, D. J. 1981. "Economic reform via reformulation in China: where do rightist ideas come from?" *Asian Survey* 21(9): 947–960.

Stewart, W. 2001. *Deng Xiaoping.* Minneapolis, MN: Lerner.

Tang, Y. J. 1991. *Confucianism, Buddhism, Daoism, Christianity and Chinese culture.* Beijing: University of Peking, Council for Research in Values and Philosophy.

Wagner, R. G. 2003. *A Chinese reading of the Daodejing: Wang Bi's commentary on the Laozi with critical text and translation.* Albany, NY: State University of New York Press.

Wilson, D. 1977. "Introduction," in Wilson (ed.), pp. 1–8.

1977 (ed.). *Mao Tse-tung in the scales of history.* London: Cambridge University Press.

Wu, T. W. 1983. *Lin Biao and the Gang of Four: Contra-Confucianism in historical and intellectual perspective.* Carbondale, IL: Southern Illinois University Press.

Yang, X. 2005. "Politics of Deng Xiaoping (1904–1997)," in Luo (ed.), pp. 114–117.

Yu, S. 1995. *Deng Xiaoping and Mao Zedong.* Beijing: Central Party School Press (in Chinese).

Zheng, Y. 1999. "Political incrementalism: political lessons from China's 20 years of reform," *Third World Quarterly* 20(6): 1157–1177.

# 8 | Chinese traditions and Western theories: influences on business leaders in China

ZHI-XUE ZHANG, CHAO-CHUAN CHEN, LEIGH
ANNE LIU, AND XUE-FENG LIU

THIS chapter concerns contemporary Chinese business leaders'
management philosophies and the sources of these philosophies. Semi-structured interviews were conducted with
thirty-five successful business leaders from enterprises in China.
Content-analyzing the interviews, we identified seven management
philosophies held by these business leaders: sincerity is essential;
pursuit of excellence; social responsibility; harmony is precious;
the Golden Mean (acting in the middle way); specialization; and
scientific management. We found that both Chinese cultural traditions and Western management theories influence Chinese business
leaders' management philosophies and practices. While the Western
management theories have great impact on their task-related operations, Chinese culture has a significant influence on their people
management practices. These findings suggest that modern business administration education should balance Western theories and
Chinese philosophies and integrate the wisdoms from the two streams.

## Introduction

The term "management philosophy" has appeared frequently in
Chinese popular mass media and Chinese business leaders' speeches.
In a database named Chinainfobank, we searched for articles contain-
ing "guan li zhe xue [management philosophy]" in newspapers in
China. We found 44 articles published in the period 1990–1999, 198
in 2000–2002, and 165 in 2003–2005. Then we searched for "guan

li li nian [management ideas]" in the same database and found a huge number of articles: 164 published in 1990–1999, 2595 in 2000–2002, and 4904 in 2003–2005. Given that the majority of articles in this database are news reports of management practices, we had a glimpse of how Chinese business leaders are concerned with management philosophies in their business operations. However, despite the huge number of media reports about business leaders' management philosophies, there is a need to delve into the content of the management philosophies and their sources. We tried to meet this need in our research.

In the academic community, business leadership research has focused on business leaders' competencies and styles with little attention to leadership philosophies. While there are monographs providing cultural and philosophical analyses of Chinese management practices (Cheng, 1999; Zeng, 2004), which prescribe management principles that business leaders "should" or "should not" adopt, little is known of the extent to which business leaders indeed subscribe to those principles and put them into practice. Some books that claim to cover management philosophies only provide basic knowledge of general management such as business strategy or effective human resource management (e.g. Chen, 2004), without discussing philosophical notions of management.

It therefore befits the theme of this book that we initiated a research project to explore Chinese leaders' management philosophies. We conducted semi-structured interviews with business leaders in China to identify their management philosophies and to examine the sources of these philosophies and their impact on management practices. Through this research we seek to draw attention to this important area, to provide insights into the fundamentals of Chinese management practices, and to provide the groundwork for cross-cultural comparative research on leadership and management.

The term "business leader" in this chapter refers to the top-level manager of a firm who is equivalent to a chief executive officer. The official title could be Chairman of the Board, Chief Executive Officer, General Manager, or President. We define management philosophies as general, overarching notions or principles that business leaders use to guide their business operations and management practices. These philosophies capture business leaders' fundamental values and beliefs: values regarding organizational missions and priorities, and beliefs regarding causes and effects among various business and management forces such as relationships among various stakeholders.

## Research method

### *Participants*

We selected participants using two criteria: they must be leaders of firms with at least a hundred employees, and they must have been in an executive position for at least three years. We recruited thirty-five business leaders, and, with one exception, they were all male. Their mean age was 42.84 years, with a range from 31 to 52 years. They had an average length of education of 16.7 years (equivalent to a college education), and an average tenure in their current position of 6.73 years. Nine were from state-owned enterprises in various industries such as telecommunications, pharmaceuticals, transportation and textiles, and the remaining twenty-six were from private enterprises in information and communication technology, logistics, manufacturing, chemistry, real estate, business and trading, education, finance or consulting. These thirty-five business leaders were from different regions of China. At the time of the interviews, their companies had 1380 employees on average, with a range from 110–5000 employees; the average assets of these enterprises were 853.12 million Chinese yuan (about $105.32 million), and the average sales were 1,105.93 million yuan (about $136.53 million).

### *Procedure*

We identified possible participants from three sources. First, with approval from the administration, the first author contacted business leaders in Beijing and Shenzhen who attended executive business programs offered by a management school. Second, we relied on some CEOs' personal references. The third source was a management consulting firm with a wide network of business executives, which nominated potential participants. The executives who met our criteria were formally invited to participate in the study by a letter stating the research purpose and method. They were told that a face-to-face interview of about one hour would be conducted and were assured of anonymity in any publications of this project. They were also promised a summary report upon the completion of the project. We contacted forty-five executives and thirty-five of them agreed to participate. Of the latter, seventeen were the executives who attended the executive programs at the management school and the remaining eighteen were recommended by other CEOs and the consulting firm.

The first author conducted the interviews, mostly at the interviewees' business offices, according to the interview guideline (see the appendix to this chapter). The interviews lasted from 60 to 150 minutes, with an average length of about 80 minutes. All except one participant agreed to be tape-recorded. Detailed notes were taken during the interview for the one that was not tape-recorded.

A typical interview started with the participant briefly describing his/her personal experience as well as the history of the firm, including major business areas, total sales, the profit, and the number of employees. Following this "warming-up" introduction, interviewees were asked whether they had a management philosophy and, if so, to describe it. If they gave a "no" answer or could not say exactly what their philosophy was, the interviewer would ask them to list some general principles that they had followed in running their business or managing their company. All but four participants stated that they had a personal management philosophy and went on to provide examples of the philosophy. After that, they were asked to reflect on the sources of their management philosophy. Finally, the interviewer summarized the whole interview, and asked the participants for any additional comments or complementary information.

## Content analysis

The first author and an assistant listened to the taped interviews and took detailed written notes. The final notes of all interviews contained more than 100,000 words. The contents of the interview notes were summarized in three tables: company backgrounds, interviewee backgrounds, and key interview topics including philosophical notions of management. Content analysis for participants' management philosophies was performed by the first author and a research assistant. It had two steps. The first involved identifying and recording distinct philosophical sayings by the business executives and the second involved sorting those sayings into theme categories.

The first step, recording philosophical sayings, turned out to be quite straightforward because most of the interviewees made explicit philosophical statements either before or after describing their management practices. Those statements typically used well-known Chinese maxims such as "Harmony begets wealth" (*he qi sheng cai*), "Harmony is precious" (*he wei gui*) and "the Golden Mean" (*zhong yong zhi dao*). In the four cases where the executives described their management practices without making explicit philosophical statements, philosophical notions of management were inferred from descriptions of management practices. The first author and his research assistant conducted the first step of the content analysis separately for twenty-five interviews, with an inter-rater agreement of nearly 90 percent. They discussed their differences and achieved agreement. Afterwards, the research assistant analyzed the remaining ten interviews.

A total of 152 distinct sayings was recorded and the average number of sayings per participant was 4.34 (s.d. = 1.85). Those sayings were sorted into distinct philosophical notions according to their thematic similarity through discussion and consensus among three of the authors of this chapter. For example, all sayings about the importance of harmony such as "Harmony begets riches" and "Harmony is precious" formed the philosophic notion of "Harmony is precious". This method created seven general categories of management philosophy that are mutually exclusive.

## Results

### Philosophical notions of management held by business leaders

Table 8.1 lists the seven philosophical notions of management and the frequency with which each was nominated by the business executives.

**Sincerity is essential (*yi cheng wei ben*)**
*Sincerity is essential* was the philosophical notion most frequently cited (66 percent) by the participants. It means being honest and honoring promises in dealing with people and business. This notion was expressed in terms such as "honesty and no deception," "earnestness," "be tolerant of others," "self-discipline," "set an example with one's own conduct," "trustworthy," and "being honest to others."

Table 8.1. *Frequencies of management philosophical notions mentioned by the thirty-five interviewed business leaders.*

| Philosophical notions | Frequency |
|---|---|
| Sincerity is essential | 23 |
| Pursuit of excellence | 21 |
| Social responsibility | 16 |
| Harmony is precious | 13 |
| The Golden Mean (Acting in the middle way) | 11 |
| Specialization | 11 |
| Scientific management | 11 |

From the executives' perspective, being sincere means keeping promises, not telling lies, being tolerant of others, taking care of employees' welfare, keeping speaking and behavior consistent, and being self-disciplined. The target of sincerity includes dealings with both employees (internal) and business partners (external).

According to the interviewed executives, *sincerity is essential* is extremely important and beneficial to the company. It creates trust in the management by employees and it builds a good reputation for both the executives and their firms. It also helps the firm establish cooperative relations with other enterprises. An interviewed executive from a state-owned company reported that he had been highly trusted by others because he had always kept his promises in dealing with them. For example, in China, it is common that state-owned companies borrow money from state-owned banks and do not repay the loans on time because both the company and the bank are state-owned and such a delay incurs no serious penalty. But this CEO said that despite tremendous difficulties, he always made sure that the loans were repaid on time. Similarly, in dealing with customers, his company always compensated for any losses without making excuses.

Being honest and sincere in China can often be costly because of the lack of effective regulations. As the market economy is relatively new in China, business norms and rules are not well established. On many occasions, business people can act wrongfully without suffering any legal penalty. In such circumstances, if one person is honest while others are not, the honest one will be put at a disadvantage. Despite the potential risk of being exploited for being honest, more than half of the interviewed business leaders reported that they tried to be sincere. In fact, honesty pays in the long run, according to those who endorse it. For example, an executive from a private company said that he always paid his debts on time and being honest allowed him to be credible and to get support from others who trusted him, which had helped him and his company overcome many difficulties. On one occasion, he could not repay a debt to a bank because of a shortage of cash, but one of his suppliers lent him the money without his asking.

### Pursuit of excellence (*zhui qiu zhuo yue*)

*Pursuit of excellence* means that a company should provide its customers with the best products and services, and make an effort to achieve the best performance and sustain continuous development. The interviewed leaders illustrated this notion in the following terms: "building a hundred-year-old shop [a long-lasting company]"; "insistence on making every effort to be the No.1 in the industry"; "developing the firm bigger and more fine-grained"; "making the enterprise larger and stronger"; "solving problems for customers." Twenty-one of the interviewed participants (60 percent) reported this philosophy.

Several leaders from private enterprises said that they had dedicated their resources to develop their companies into "centennial enterprises." The CEO of one mobile phone manufacturer said, "the last generation of entrepreneurs successfully sold Chinese products in international markets. Our generation should attempt to develop some renowned product brand with a global reputation. Enterprises should spare no effort to improve the image of their brands, to improve the quality of their products, to minimize the cost and thus be able to sell high-class products to foreigners. My goal is to build up internationally renowned Chinese brands, changing people's perception that there is no excellent brand in China." It is worth noting that excellence here is conceived in terms of business scope (large corporations) and longevity (enduring if not immortal) both of which are in the vision of being a global business organization.

*Pursuit of excellence* is also interpreted as searching for better products and services which can better meet the market and create more value for customers. The CEO from a company that had developed software products for financial services said the management philosophy he had cherished was "trying to be perfect and developing high-quality products." Under the guidance of this philosophy, his company had always taken back its old products by offering new products for clients.

### Social responsibility (*she hui ze ren*)

The notion of *social responsibility* means that what a firm does should be beneficial for both its stakeholders and the whole of society. The interviewed executives interpreted this notion as follows: "not considering a firm as a money-making machine but as a carrier which can push the society forward"; "to deem it one's own responsibility to develop one's nation and to bring stability to the country"; "attempting to build up a long-lived enterprise to strengthen the nation"; "enterprises need to reciprocate contributions by employees and society"; and "sharing can bring more happiness than keeping all for oneself." Sixteen business leaders (46 percent) said they had held this philosophy in their managerial career.

While talking about the notion of *social responsibility*, the interviewed executives mentioned two aspects. First, a company should reward its employees, shareholders, and other stakeholders for their contributions. The company must take care of the employees' well-being and their development, and the company needs to share profits honestly with the shareholders; moreover, the company must work to ensure that customers or clients get the high-quality products or services that fully satisfy their needs. Second, a company should create value for society and behave as a good citizen of society.

The CEO from a garment factory in Shenzhen offered his practices as an example. In the Pearl River delta region near Hong Kong, there are thousands of clothing factories located in Guangzhou, Shenzhen, Dongguan and other cities. The clothing manufacturing industry is labor-intensive, and the majority of the employees in this industry are from the poor, rural areas in central or western parts of China. Employees are paid at piece rates and employers did not offer any other benefits before 2005. Nevertheless, the CEO reported that his company not only made payment to the local government authority to get a provisional residential certificate for every employee but also purchased safety insurance for each employee. To protect employees better, the company bought an additional amount of accident insurance for every employee. This is rarely seen in the industry because most employees move frequently from one factory to another. Although providing these benefits to employees increased the management cost, the CEO believed that it was his responsibility to do so.

A few executives believed that the success of a firm is not only reflected in the amount of profit it earns but also indicated by whether it reciprocates the contributions of its employees and society by returning part of the profit to them. The notion of social responsibility is not only targeted at employees in companies but can be extended to the local community. An entrepreneur from a private company said, "I do not consider my firm as a money-making machine but as a carrier which can push the society forward." His enterprise made profits of 60,000 Chinese yuan (about $7500) in the first year, and he donated 20,000 yuan (about $2500) to his village for building a public road. In the second year, he again donated 100,000 yuan (about $12,500) to support the village's infrastructure construction. He believed that an enterprise should be responsible for its people and the society who have supported and bred the enterprise directly or indirectly.

Another interviewed leader cited an example to illustrate his emphasis on social responsibility. He acquired a state-owned hotel. According to the contract signed by both parties, he could dismiss 30 percent of the employees and managers in the hotel. By doing so, he could not only make more profits, but also greatly improve the service quality by recruiting some qualified employees and managers. However, without dismissing a single employee, he instead provided them training to improve their skills and knowledge and allocated all employees to proper posts. He believed it was his responsibility not to increase the burden on society when conducting business: "one or two million may not be a big deal for me and the company, but it makes a great difference for a family."

### Harmony is precious (*he wei gui*)

*Harmony is precious* means that top management must keep harmony internally or externally in order to keep the company running smoothly and making profits. This notion was expressed by the interviewed leaders as follows: "keeping harmonious interpersonal relationships"; "being kind to others"; "harmony brings wealth"; and "smooth cooperation with others," etc. Thirteen participants (37 percent) reported that they held this philosophy in their management practices.

In the interviewees' understanding, *harmony is precious* is functional for both internal management and external relations. Internally, this notion helps firms avoid conflict and reduce the management cost. Externally, it helps firms establish harmonious environments that are advantageous to the firms.

For several interviewed executives, harmony took precedence over the firms' profit goals in some circumstances. This phenomenon occurs particularly when firms are making a transition and change. Having been developed in the planned economy, many firms must change to fit the new market economy. To achieve this goal, firms had to lay off some employees who did not meet the new requirements. However, it is difficult for the dismissed employees to accept the firms' decision and they usually are strongly against the management and the firms, which in turn may harm the firms. Holding the notion of *harmony is precious*, some business leaders did not just dismiss employees according to the depersonalized downsizing policy. On the contrary, they did all they could to minimize the negative impact of layoffs. For example, they communicated with these employees and made great efforts, beyond their duties, to solve the employees' problems. Some executives offered the dismissed employees extra financial support, helped them find new jobs, or created some temporary positions such as "assistants" for those managers who had to leave their original positions.

Several leaders reported that harmony is especially precious for the cohesion of the senior management team. They believed that managing employees at lower levels should be based on rules; however, for middle and senior managers, reliance on rule-based management alone is not enough. In dealing with these people, the head of the company should consider their feelings and respect them. The CEO of a telecom company affiliated to China Network Communications Corporation provided an excellent example. To maintain the cohesion of the middle managers in the company, the CEO kept personal communication with all subordinates so as to be aware of problems they were facing, and he always took action to solve those problems.

Some leaders stuck to the "harmony" principle in developing relationships with the external environment. They even developed harmonious relationships with their competitors. They believed that competition between companies could allow them to improve their services and products, which could be beneficial for all of them. The

CEO of the above-mentioned affiliated telecom company of China Network Communications Corporation had adopted a unique way to handle his competitors. The Chinese government broke the monopoly of the original China Telecom[1] when it allowed more companies such as China Unicom, China Railway Communication Corporation, and China Network Communications Corporation to provide telecommunications services. China Telecom tried to maintain its market share by preventing these new companies from growing in the telecommunications service market. These companies considered their competitors as enemies and fought viciously with each other. The consequence of such commercial battles was that all companies lost profits.

The CEO of the affiliated telecom company is a strong believer of "harmony bringing wealth" and put this notion into his management practices. During traditional Chinese holidays, he visited the head of the biggest competitor to his company, the affiliated company of China Unicom. His actions led to positive competition in the local telecommunications market and his company got a much greater local market share than the average market share of other branch companies of China Netcom. The harmony principle also guided the action of this general manager in his dealings with local government when his company aided the government by sponsoring welfare activities and helped solve other problems.

### The Golden Mean (Acting in the middle way)
### (*zhong yong zhi dao*)

During the interviews, eleven people emphasized the philosophy of doing things in the middle way, which is *the Golden Mean* principle. The words they used included "keeping balance in management" and "going beyond is as wrong as falling short."

Three meanings can be noted in the way the interviewees talked about the Golden Mean. First, it means that a leader should do all things in an appropriate manner. These interviewees believed that there was a boundary for everything and going to extremes was strongly opposed. Second, one should weigh the consequences of the extreme positions in an argument and identify the right solution from competing or conflicting perspectives. Third, one should be flexible in managerial activities. Leaders need to take the opportunity at the right time and make necessary adjustments according to the situation. Keeping flexibility is the essence of acting in the middle way.

Most interviewees mentioned that the Golden Mean suggested that one should maintain stability in running a business. If an enterprise develops too quickly, troubles are inevitable. Steady development is the best way to avoid risks and keep an enterprise vigorous in the long run. A general manager from a branch company affiliated to China Telecom in a southern city successfully carried out an ERP (enterprise resource planning) reform using this philosophy. In 2002, China Telecom was making preparations for ERP reconstruction. In order to implement the reform successfully, the company decided to launch a pilot project in a single branch company before generalizing the reform. Three branch companies were chosen to do experiments, one of which was the above-mentioned branch. The general manager realized that the new ERP system would create dramatic changes for his company, and he decided that such "shock therapy" would put his company at risk. After thoughtful consideration, he adopted a gradual reform rather than the radical change required by the general company. Specifically, he started the reform in the marketing department, achieved success and then extended the reform successfully to other departments. Other branch companies that pursued rapid reform were not successful. The general manager said he was greatly influenced by the Confucian idea that "going beyond is as bad as falling short" and he believed that reform should be implemented gradually to avoid "more haste, less speed."

Some interviewees believed that the head of a company is always facing contradictions; therefore, keeping balance and coordination are of supreme importance. In order to maximize overall benefits, the head must be willing to make necessary compromises without going against principles in order to gain future concessions from the other party. As one interviewee said, the head figure could not stick to his/her own position all the time and should distinguish major issues from trivial ones so as to know when concessions could be made.

One problem faced by any enterprise is how to establish a good relationship with employees. A general manager from a state-owned enterprise deemed that management means balance. He thought that no employee was immoral in nature, but employees differed in abilities. In his company, when a manager and subordinates were in conflict, he transferred the manager to another position and the newly appointed manager would in general treat the subordinates well in order to prove that he/she could do better than the ex-manager. At the same time, the transferred manager in the new position generally works very hard to prove that he/she is a competent manager.

### Specialization

Another managerial philosophy/principle mentioned by our interviewees is *specialization*, which was described by eleven interviewees in terms of "professional people working on specialized tasks," "fully devoting oneself to the task one is doing," and "never do business that one is not familiar with."

Interviewees generally held that a company should do what it is good at and make the best use of its advantages but avoid its disadvantages. They believed that in today's intensely competitive market, each firm should develop its unique competence and find its niche. A general manager from a mold-manufacturing factory held a master's degree in mold manufacturing. The majority of graduates in this major would rather find a job in a popular industry like finance than stay in their major. Unlike most members of his cohort, this interviewee developed a mold-manufacturing business in which he could make full use of his special skills. His company became the leading organization in that specialty area. Another general manager was from an electronic product manufacturing enterprise, which concentrated solely on the research and development of laser products, and had become very competitive in both local and international markets. Its products had taken 70 percent of the market share in the Chinese market.

The following case illustrates that the philosophy of specialization is in part one of business professionalization. It is a team of husband and wife providing consulting services for real estate developers including project planning, promoting sales of apartments and flats, and evaluating property value. The husband is the chairman of the board and his wife is the CEO. The husband had worked in Hong Kong for several years and accumulated rich experience of real estate service. When his wife, who used to work in the government's Land Bureau, set up the real estate consulting company, he resigned from his job in Hong Kong and joined his wife. Both were graduates of economics from top universities in China and had professional expertise in property valuation. The couple's original objective was to earn some money for a living. After their company made substantial profits that were enough for their whole life's expenditure, they started to think about what they should do next. After discussions among their management teams, they believe that the Chinese term for "business," *sheng yi*, means the significance of life (*sheng ming de yi yi*), which they would consider as their management philosophy.

From then on, they aimed to accomplish their values through providing professional services for their clients. To adhere to their philosophy, the company does not make money from projects that do not need its professional input. In the 1990s, real estate developers were in an advantageous position in the trade market because many people needed to buy their own apartments. Once a project was completed, real estate developers moved to the next one and they requested a real estate agency to sell the apartments for them. Many real estate agencies competed to get the opportunity to sell the established apartments. However, the couple often rejected such opportunities. They set three principles for their consulting services: the first is to save transactional costs for their clients; the second is to increase the value of the property; and the third is to reduce the professional risk for clients. With these principles in mind, the couple refused to make easy money by just selling apartments.

### Scientific management

During the interviews, eleven respondents expressed the philosophy of *scientific management*, which often translated into standardization, institutionalization, and transparency of managerial practices.

A company needs to standardize internal management first. The CEO of a software company believed that companies in software engineering in China do not have a standardized system for software development, which prevented these companies from becoming as competitive as the software companies in India. The CEO said that his company failed to adopt the CMM III (company maturity model) at first because software engineers did not like to follow the procedure and standards in CMM. After that, he decided to establish a standardized management system in his company. He developed rules such as major task recording and reporting rules which are popular in foreign companies in the same industry. He believed that a company must establish standardized management along with business development.

Management standardization of companies can lead to the development of the whole industry. The chairman of the board of the real estate consulting firm mentioned above cited a good example. In the late 1990s, there was no order in the developing market of real estate assessment. Developing relationships and giving kickbacks were the effective ways of getting projects. The highest kickback was up to 60 percent and the average was 40 percent. In order to reduce the risk faced by the company and society, he considered that it was important for the industry to take actions to self-regulate. He formulated "200 questions" to guide employees in making operational service decisions. Under the guidance of the "200 questions," employee performance greatly improved even after they left the company to join other companies. Gradually, the "200 questions" became the universal standards for everyone who wanted to get employment in the industry. These practices facilitate fair competition in the industry.

## Influences on the formation of management philosophy

We asked our interviewees what influenced the formation of their leadership/management philosophies. Based on the sources mentioned by them, we classified their answers into four categories: life experiences, books and literature, role models, and business administration education and training.

## Life experiences

Life experiences include those inside China and those in Western societies. Life experiences in China include childhood experiences, influences of parents, family, and teachers (from primary school to university), experiences during the Cultural Revolution or experiences in labor camps, and even recreational activities such as learning how to play golf, and the like. Life experiences in the West are primarily study and work experiences. The accumulation of life experiences, and reflections on them, led to the formation of management philosophies.

Twenty-one interviewees indicated that the formation of their management philosophy was based on their life experiences, and eight of them mentioned the impact of their parents or family. Several interviewees mentioned that their parents, who had a good reputation in their community, taught them how to act properly as a member of the society, particularly to be honest and not to bully others. One executive from a private company said that his father's influence on him had extended beyond personal style to business philosophy. His father, being a leader of a state-owned company for thirty years, related to the executive how the state-owned business failed because of (a) poor management of returns on investment/assets (or financial control) and (b) failure to establish brand names. The father's experience taught the son a lesson about scientific management – systematic accounting and diligent marketing are critical in running a business, which made his electrical engineering company very successful in the market.

Some interviewees who were about fifty years old reported that they were deeply influenced by their experiences during the Chinese Cultural Revolution in the 1960s and 1970s. One of the interviewees related his experience in the countryside during the 1960s and up to 1972. He was one of a large number of young people from cities who were sent to the poor areas in remote rural China and settled there as peasants. The executive witnessed many youths losing their personal integrity and dignity in order to get better treatment or to have the opportunity to return to the cities from which they came. This experience led him to the realization of the importance of sincerity and respect for human dignity, which he strongly emphasized in his company.

Some business leaders attributed their philosophical insights to the influence of some seemingly small and insignificant things. An interviewee liked to play golf, and discovered an analogy between managing a company and playing golf. First, to play golf well, one must have good body balance and strength and a calm mind. Second, it is more important to hit the golf ball to exactly the right place than just to hit it a long distance. From this insight, he realized the importance of having an organization that is in harmony and balance, as well as the importance of achieving "fit" for each employee in the organizational processes and systems. From playing golf, he also claimed to have recognized the need to have stable growth and development. These insights have allowed him to respond to market needs and opportunities in a steady manner and to think carefully before taking actions.

Two interviewees were educated abroad and two other interviewees had worked in Hong Kong for several years. This direct exposure to Western societies greatly influenced them. One of them had studied in

Europe and then returned to China in the late 1980s. By 2002, he had more than twenty chain restaurants serving food in both Chinese and Western styles. The restaurant business in China differs from that in the West in two major ways. First, the process of cooking traditional Chinese food is not standardized, which makes the quality of the food dependent on the culinary skills of the chef. To ensure food quality, owners of Chinese restaurants usually have to pay their chefs high salaries in order to retain them. Second, in China, the government places restrictions on restaurants regarding the ratio of the size of the serving area to that of the kitchen area. A restaurant that uses a lot of space for the kitchen must limit space for customers, which will reduce the restaurant's profit. High salaries and the regulations on space increase the cost of business and make it difficult to have chain restaurants. However, borrowing from the business practices of Western restaurants such as McDonald's that offer Western fast food, this general manager set up a central kitchen in a suburban area providing semi-finished food to each chain restaurant in the down-town of the city. The chef in the restaurant cooks the already prepared food very quickly and does not need a large kitchen. At the same time, the manager developed a standardized process of cooking Chinese food which made the cooking consistent across different chain res-taurants and chefs, thereby ensuring high food quality. These practices enabled the executive to have a booming restaurant business in China. He believes that his life experiences in Europe allowed him to learn how to manage his company in a more scientific and standardized manner.

Another interviewee, who is the general manager of a state-owned company, said that he was impressed by Hong Kong employees' remarkable commitment to work. He recalled an episode when he was asked to close down a branch company in Hong Kong. Upon hearing the closing-down news, employees from mainland China did not work as hard as before. However, Hong Kong employees continued to work as usual even though they knew that they would lose their jobs very soon. In another instance, he was surprised to find that a female Hong Kong employee did not show any signs of idleness during the month before she quit her job. When the interviewee returned to China to take the position of general manager, he became very committed to his job and pursued the goal of inculcating a sense of work commitment among his employees.

*Books and literature*

Books that interviewees mentioned had influenced them included those on Chinese history and on Western history, culture, philosophy, and management. The Chinese literature mentioned included the Four Books (*The great learning, The doctrine of the mean, The analects of Confucius,* and *The Mencius*), the Five Classics (the *Book of songs,* the *Book of history,* the *Book of changes/I-ching,* the *Book of rites,* and the *Spring and Autumn annals*), *The classics of Taoism, The classics of opposition, The romance of the three kingdoms,* Sunzi's *Art of war, Zi zhi tong jian, Cai gen tan,* and other books on Chinese philosophy. The Western literature mentioned included *The Protestant ethic and the spirit of capitalism, A letter to Garcia,* the *Biography of Napoleon,* and *Jean-Christophe.* Economics and management books and magazines included *Built to last: successful habits of visionary companies, In search of excellence: lessons from America's best run companies,* and reports on Fortune 500 companies.

Books from the West were cited by twenty-five of the thirty-five interviewees as a source of knowledge about management theories and were influential in the development of the interviewed executives' management philosophy. The interviewees believed that thoughts reflected in Western literature, history, and philosophy books emphasize efficiency and equality, and management theories developed in the West are more scientific and analytical in their reasoning and enabled executives to understand the importance of specialization and standardization.

Among the Western books, *Built to last* was mentioned most. Most of the interviewees believed that this book inspired them to develop a "hundred-year-old shop." In *Built to last,* Jim Collins and Jerry I. Porras examined eighteen successful and enduring companies in comparisons with each company's top competitor. The authors identified key traits or habits that distinguished the visionary companies from their rivals. The visions included preserving the core ideology, having ambitious goals, using home-grown and internally promoted management, having a cult-like culture, and never being complacent. Collins and Porras believed that the most important success factor of these visionary companies is that they had a core ideology that surpassed purely economic reasoning by including people and company culture values. It appears that the central message – that business longevity if not immortality calls for looking beyond profit – resonates with many Chinese business leaders.

Twenty-one interviewees indicated that they like reading books on Chinese history and Chinese culture. The interviews revealed that they have a strong identification with traditional Chinese culture and are deeply influenced by it, especially the teachings of Confucianism, Taoism, and Buddhism. These executives repeatedly cited some popular sayings that are embedded in Chinese culture, including "harmony is precious," "the Golden Mean (acting in the middle way)," "seeking changes within stability," "sticking together and cooperating," "seeking things that enrich the country and benefit the people," and "striving for continuous improvement." Traditional Chinese culture seemed also to add a strong moral dimension to the management philosophies. Interviewees emphasized the ability to command respect and win support through one's virtues such as kindness or generosity, as well as having high self-expectations and self-discipline, embodying the best of both Western and Chinese cultures.

## Role models

Almost all interviewees believed that their management philosophies and practices have been largely influenced by historical figures or contemporary role models in or outside China.

In Chinese history, there have been people who built their success by relying on a combination of traditional Chinese culture and self-cultivation according to traditional Chinese values. Many contemporary Chinese executives consider them as role models; those most mentioned by our interviewees included Zeng Guo Fan, Hu Xue Yan, and the Qing dynasty emperor Kang Xi, who have long been famous in Chinese history for their achievement and wisdom, notwithstanding they happened to be featured in recent popular books or TV series in China.

Zeng Guo Fan is the most frequently mentioned historical figure (1811–1872, a high-ranking official in the Qing dynasty). Highly respected for his virtues, he is considered as a hero in preserving order and stability. He was the first government official to realize that there was an invasion of Western thoughts and called for China to adapt to the changes taking place in the world. He exemplified the strength of Confucian thoughts in his leadership behavior by practicing a lifelong self-reflection (*fan si*). The idea of self-reflection was to seek continual improvement of one's character through constant reflection on one's actions and thoughts. Zeng Guo Fan firmly believed in the Confucian ideal of leading by moral example. He knew when to delegate authority, and his successes were in large part due to his trust in his able associates. His emphasis on cultivating and using an individual's talents helped the Qing dynasty in the last years of its reign to cultivate more than eighty exceptional persons such as Li Hong Zhang and Zuo Zong Tang.

Hu Xue Yan, a successful businessman during the late Qing dynasty, was also frequently mentioned. He had businesses in banking, silk, and Chinese herbal medicine. Since he guaranteed the support of military supplies in times when the government was fighting its enemy, he was promoted to a ministerial position, and thus became a powerful and influential "official merchant" in his later years. In 1874, he opened a Chinese herbal medicine shop in Hangzhou named Hu Qing Yu Tang Pharmacy, and he personally made a plaque that said "Quit cheating." In running this business, he kept to his principle of honesty. He was well known both at home and overseas as "The Medicine King of Southern China."

Kang Xi was the second emperor of the Qing dynasty. He was not extravagant but practical and hardworking. During the sixty-one years of his reign, China attained unprecedented prosperity. He conducted private investigations to expose and punish corrupted officials. Kang Xi went through tough situations during his reign. Some government officers raised their own troops in their controlled places and wanted to rebel against the Qing government, and there were forces that sought the separation of Taiwan from China. Kang Xi firmly and successfully fought against these forces and kept China united.

The contemporary figures mentioned most by the interviewees were primarily successful entrepreneurs: Hong Kong businessman Li Ka Shing, Legend Group's chairman Liu Chuan Zhi, the CEO of Huawei Technologies Ren Zheng Fei, Haier Group's CEO Zhang Ruimin, and others. The lessons learned from these role models were seizing all business opportunities, conscientiously managing both internal company affairs and external business relations, developing and choosing successors, implementing professional business management policies and practices, and building global brands.

These interviewed business leaders also learned a valuable lesson from the experiences of infamous contemporary Chinese entrepreneurs such as Mu Qi Zhong, Zhou Zheng Yi, and Yang Bin. All of them were once successful and became infamous due to their aggressive, unethical, or even illegal business practices. With these negative examples, the business executives emphasized the importance of following laws as well as principles of economics. To the interviewees, illegal and unethical profiteers disrupted the economic and market order, and learning the lessons of the notorious entrepreneurs helped avoid "management traps" and "paying high tuition fees."

Foreign figures that our interviewees mentioned most included successful executives such as Konosuke Matsushita, the founder of Matsushita Electric Corporation in Japan and Jack Welch, the legendary past CEO of General Electric. The participants said they learned the latest management practices from the Western business leaders by reading their biographies.

## Business administration education and training

The executives also cited business education, management training and consulting as their source of learning and understanding of Western management thoughts and practices. Twenty-one of the interviewees participated in business administration education or management training, and they believed that contemporary business education allows them to understand what management is about, to be more keenly aware of the need to acquire knowledge of scientific management, such as the importance of planning, having a systematic way of doing things, and formal decision-making processes.

Beyond classroom learning, foreign management consulting firms gave these business leaders a refreshing look at business by providing them with "continuing education" in using tools of Western management.

The majority of business cases taught in Chinese business schools are on Western companies. These interviewees thought that it is useful to learn through these case studies what the best practices are. In addition, these cases helped them understand what made the companies fall into crisis, how crises spread, and how to find ways to deal with such problems. However, all interviewees highlighted that, in implementing the management theory learned in schools, they had to take into consideration the specific situation in China. These executives stated that using management tools from the West without adapting them to the Chinese business environment would only result in failure.

## Summary and discussion

### *A conceptual framework for Chinese business leaders' management philosophies*

We have developed a conceptual framework for Chinese business leaders' management philosophies on the basis of the main findings of this research (see Figure 8.1). In this framework, we have categorized the influences on Chinese management philosophies into four sources including life experiences, books and literature, role models, and business administration education and training. The first three sources are from both China and the West, while the last source is mainly from the West.

Seven philosophical notions for management were identified in our study: *sincerity is essential, pursuit of excellence, social responsibility, harmony is precious, the Golden Mean, specialization,* and *scientific management.* These philosophical ideas are manifested in management practices in two broad areas, namely, dealing with social relationships and dealing with business operations.

Philosophical notions governing social relationships are primarily *sincerity is essential, social responsibility, harmony is precious,* and *the Golden Mean.* Those that govern business operations are primarily *pursuit of excellence, specialization,* and *scientific management.* These latter notions guide the technical aspects of business operations such

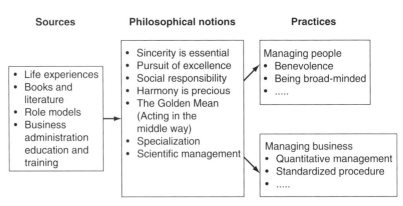

**Figure 8.1.** A summary model of Chinese business leaders' management philosophies.

as plant operations, finance, and quality control, although *pursuit of excellence* goes beyond the technical and all of the operational principles inevitably also affect the social relational principles and vice versa.

We further speculate that some philosophical notions represent terminal values of the business leaders whereas others represent instrumental values for the purpose of achieving the terminal values. Social harmony has been the ultimate goal of the Chinese people in social life (Yang, 1995) and arguably *sincerity* and *the Golden Mean,* or even *social responsibility* are in part means toward the end of greater overall social harmony among individuals, social groups, and organizational stakeholders. However, if one pushes the distinction between the instrumental and the terminal values, pursuit of excellence seems to be emerging as a new terminal value in addition to, if not in place of, social harmony. Interestingly, it had the second highest frequency of being mentioned and the terminology is new, modern, ambitious, and inspiring, reflecting the aspirations of Chinese business leaders to grow bigger and better global businesses, ones that last for centuries if not eternally. That pursuit of excellence is held as a terminal value may not be as explicit or as conscious as social harmony or social responsibility, but it seems to be as potent as, if not more than, social harmony. The following is an example of how in the mind of the business executive social harmony is a path toward business success.

One case from the telecom company affiliated to China Network Communications Corporation, mentioned earlier, provides strong evidence for the importance of maintaining harmony. The CEO had kept harmony among top and middle managers, who in turn fully supported the CEO, which led to the successes of this company during the dramatic organizational changes from 2002 to 2005. This company had maintained a harmonious relationship with local government, which enabled the company to launch the Personal Handy-phone System business in this location much earlier than in other regions. Among all the affiliated companies of China Network Communications Corporation, this company has been a role model (Zhang and Wang, 2006). In our interview with the CEO, he attributed his success significantly to his painstaking effort to build harmonious relationships.

## Impacts of traditional Chinese culture and Western management theories and practices

A closer look at sources as well as practical manifestations of the philosophical notions revealed that the Chinese executives drew insights from Chinese traditional culture for philosophical thinking about managing interpersonal relationships but turned to Western sources to articulate their philosophies regarding business operations.

### The influence of Chinese culture and experiences

Five of the thirteen holders of the notion *harmony is precious* explicitly stated that Chinese philosophical thoughts shaped the formation of this notion. Five of the holders of notion of the *Golden Mean* reported that it resulted from their exposure to Confucian thoughts. Seven executives clearly linked their notion of *social responsibility* to their life experience in China, their parents' teaching, their belief that China is relatively poor and needs more support from enterprises, and their being touched by the hardworking employees who deserve better care from the companies. From these results, we can conclude that the formation of three notions – *harmony is precious, the Golden Mean*, and *social responsibility* – is influenced by Chinese culture and experience. That these philosophical notions are rooted in Chinese culture was seen in previous chapters of this book, especially Chapter 1 on Confucian statesmanship.

Although there is a tradition of emphasizing social conscience in Chinese culture, the understanding and the terminology of social responsibility of modern organizations in a market economy may be influenced to some extent by more recent Western management theories, especially the stakeholder perspective (Crane, Dirk, and Jeremy 2004; Ruf *et al.*, 2001).

The traditional Confucian social conscience gave primacy to the welfare of the state, the community, and the clients instead of the profit and wealth of the merchants, and the pre-reform Communist Party gave primacy to social and political goals rather than economic ones. The market-oriented economic reform (starting in the late 1970s and early 1980s) set free the entrepreneurial spirit of money-making and wealth creation of the Chinese that had long been suppressed by a state-controlled economy and a leftist political ideology. The Chinese business executives faced competing pressures from the traditional social conscience, the Communist political ideology, and the new-found freedom to get rich big and fast. The concept of social responsibility with a stakeholder perspective therefore allowed the Chinese business leaders to reconcile and balance their feelings of social conscience with their desire to legitimate the making of profit.

## The influence of Western theories and practices

Of the twenty-one executives who held the notion of pursuit of excellence, twelve said they had learnt from role models like companies in Japan or the United States. Of the eleven executives who held the notion of specialization, seven talked about the influence of the practices of contemporary companies. Moreover, all of the seven are in industry sectors such as telecommunications services, software development, electronic engineering, etc. Their companies had been in fierce competition with local or foreign competitors. Of the eleven executives who had adopted the notion of scientific management, nine mentioned the influences of modern management practices in famous companies or management theories.

Modern business management has benefited from the Western pioneers' thoughts. Starting from the late 1890s and the early 1900s, Western managers expected their organizations to function like well-oiled machines, putting emphasis on scientific management and pursuing effectiveness and standardization. Max Weber emphasized the importance of establishing standard operating procedures in organizations, impersonality, specialized division of labor, authority hierarchy, lifetime employment and rationalization (see Wren, 1994). In order to increase production efficiency, Taylor (1947: 66–71) emphasized specialized division of labor where managers at every hierarchical level are in charge of their own work, and workers only need to engage in routine work with standard operating procedures. Fayol (1949) developed a framework for studying management and clearly indicated the role of managers. His fourteen principles of management are still used as guidelines for contemporary management practices (see Wren, 1994).

Our executives acknowledged that they had been influenced by these Western management thoughts and practices. They realized that they had to do their best in reducing costs, increasing their quality of customer service, and strengthening their R&D, in order to gain a competitive advantage, especially over their international competitors.

In recent years, with increasing competition, these executives realized that they should concentrate on the business in which they have specialized and with which they are familiar, like those world-famous international companies. Several interviewees said that they would like to emulate overseas' enterprises such as GE and Panasonic to strengthen and expand their businesses.

In sum, the present research shows that Western management theories have been an important influence on the management philosophies of Chinese business leaders, especially in achieving business excellence, specialization, and scientific management.

### Joint influence of Chinese and Western thoughts

Sincerity was the most frequently mentioned notion among the interviewed executives. At the interviews, fourteen of the executives reported sources of influence on this philosophy. Interestingly, half of them said they learned it from Chinese thoughts and the other half said they recognized the importance of sincerity from studying the practices adopted by Japanese and Western companies.

Although honesty is a central value in Chinese philosophy as shown in earlier chapters on Confucius and Xunzi, it is not unique to the Chinese. Honesty and trustworthiness are central values in Western or perhaps any other civilization. For example, the ancient Roman law delineated honesty as the first of three basic ethical principles. According to Ross (2002), honesty is one of the six basic duties in Western societies. Indeed a few of our executives commented that they understand why honesty is important in business and management by reading Western books such as *The Protestant ethic and the spirit of capitalism, A letter to Garcia, Built to last,* and *In search of excellence.* Nevertheless, we wonder why some Chinese executives had to turn to Western literature to realize the importance of honesty in doing business? Could it be that honesty in Chinese philosophy is conceived as a moral virtue on its own, and is often opposed to motives of making profit or wealth? Discussions in the West on honesty as instrumental to doing business and making profit may therefore appeal to the sensitivity of some Chinese business executives as they are confronted with the issues of morality and business which we alluded to with regard to the notion of social responsibility.

We asked twenty-five executives whether traditional Chinese thinking or Western management theory had a more important influence on them. Thirteen of them (52 percent) said that traditional Chinese thoughts inspired them in terms of strategy while Western management theory influenced them in terms of tactics. Many interviewees also pointed out the differences between Chinese and Western cultures: the Chinese emphasize relationships, while Westerners emphasize rationality; the Chinese emphasize quality, while Westerners emphasize quantity, etc. The interviewees pointed out that it is impossible to rely only on relationships to run a company, and standard operating procedures are also necessary. However, it was also not possible to run Chinese companies solely on the basis of a Western management theory that focused on efficiency and standard operating procedures, because Chinese employees and subordinates expect that their managers will take their personal situations into consideration. Several interviewees believed that in Chinese management, relationship considerations, together with moral persuasion, should supersede rules and regulations.

The interviewees categorized corporate problems into two types: managing people and managing tasks. They believed that the strong emphasis on operations and quotas in Western management theory had been very helpful in the management of their companies' production and distribution. On the other hand, traditional Chinese culture had helped them to manage their employees and subordinates effectively and reasonably. A case in point can be found in the division of labor between the husband and wife executives that we reported earlier. We were told that the husband used Western economics and management theories to design the corporation's structure and standard operating procedures whereas the wife used what she learnt from the philosophies of Confucius and Xunzi to build relationships with employees and subordinates.

The interviewed executives generally believed that they learnt the production and operation techniques from modern business administration training which is mostly imported from the West, and they depended on Chinese history, society, and culture for inspiration to manage people effectively.

These interviewees said that both traditional Chinese culture and Western management practices had merits. The combination of the two streams allowed one to manage a company effectively and efficiently. Some interviewees who had received business administration education said that a successful business leader not only had to understand traditional Chinese culture but also had to know Western management theory. A business executive needed to use Western management theories flexibly and creatively with the specific Chinese situation.

One CEO of a company talked about his change of management philosophy in recent years. His business is in manufacturing central air-conditioning machines, non-electric chillers, and energy-saving control systems. He embraced Western management practices for their rationality, depersonalization, and efficiency. He instituted strict management procedures and work discipline in his company, which he believed had ensured the quality of the company's products, and enhanced the company's reputation both in China and abroad. However, the strict operating procedures alienated the company's employees, especially its managers. Middle managers regarded the management system as harsh and most left after working for the company for only two years. The high turnover prompted the executive to realize that relying solely on Western scientific management is not workable. He said, "I have a better understanding of Western culture and values compared to Chinese culture. Now, I am rectifying some inadequacies." He changed his management philosophy to give more consideration to human needs. He is currently revising his company's operating systems. "In the past, I emphasized having a strict operating system. Now, I emphasize workability. We need to have a system that works."

### The ability to learn and to reflect contributes to the formation of management philosophies

Executives form their management philosophy through their observations of and reflections on their and others' management practices.

We were impressed that as a group, the Chinese business executives that we interviewed put emphasis on learning, whether through observation, reflection, reading, or conversing. One of the executives said that he persisted in keeping a diary on what he learnt. After every business trip, he would reflect and write down the outstanding practices of companies from the same industry. This helped his company to come up with new products. He reported that his notebook contained more than 500 million words. Through reflecting, these executives abstracted patterns from problems and solutions and became more aware of their own thoughts and feelings, hence their greater willingness and ability to articulate their management philosophies.

## Future research directions and implications

This research is our first step in examining the management philosophy and practices of contemporary business leaders in China. The research has implications for both academics and managers.

### Future research directions

This study has several limitations. First, our interviewees were highly educated and running successful companies in emerging or high-growth industries, and all except one were male. These special sample characteristics limit the generalizability of our findings. Future research should increase the diversity of the executives, for example in terms of gender and educational background. Second, since the participating executives were all leading successful businesses in China, we do not know if their philosophies were different from those leading less successful companies. Future research should compare management philosophies of successful and non-successful companies. Third, although we took steps to reduce self-serving biases of the interviewees by, for example, asking for specific examples of practices to support philosophical ideas, we could not rule out the possibility of *post hoc* embellishment of ideas and behaviors. To help overcome this problem, future research should seek input from peers and subordinates of the executives to cross-validate the findings.

Despite the limitations, our study is a first important step toward identifying the content, sources, and implications of contemporary Chinese management philosophies. It opens further research avenues. For example, systematic surveys could be conducted with large samples to identify and validate these and other Chinese philosophical notions from the perspective not only of managers but also of employees. A second interesting question is the extent to which these philosophical notions are associated with each other. We speculate that some notions such as harmony and the Golden Mean may be more closely related than others and that there may be a hierarchy among the notions in terms of instrumentality. In addition to further qualitative studies, measurements of the philosophical notions could be developed and quantitative research conducted to test these relationships empirically. Third, the linkage between management philosophies, practices, and organizational outcomes could be investigated. Last but not least, cross-cultural research could be conducted on

Chinese and non-Chinese companies to uncover differences and similarities in the content and the effects of philosophical notions of management.

## Practical implications

China has a rich cultural history and Chinese companies have accumulated rich management practices since the 1980s. However, neither management scholars nor practitioners have noticed this. Some scholars (e.g. Hsu, 1994) analyzed the rise and fall of Chinese dynasties from the perspective of modern management thinking. Western management theories that are based on a scientific and standardized approach emphasize specialized knowledge and techniques, division of labor and work flow, with the aim of increasing productivity. However, Western practices usually place high levels of stress on workers and make them feel estranged from the organization (Frew and Bruning, 1987). In contrast, Chinese leaders who are influenced by Chinese culture, especially Confucian thinking, emphasize that managers should set good personal examples and be role models, and that managers and subordinates should have close interpersonal relationships (Farh and Cheng, 2000). The type of management practice that values people is more aligned with the expectations of Chinese workers, and enables workers to identify more with the leader and the organization. Hence, management scholars should learn Chinese history and culture. Many of the interviewed executives in this study were able to integrate the best of both the Western theories and Chinese philosophies and to derive some management philosophies and principles.

Many Western management theories were introduced into China in the early 1990s, mainly through MBA education. Many Chinese business leaders consider management education and training as a vital means of developing their leadership and management skills. The current curriculum of MBA education in China is primarily imported from the West. The business schools in China have used original or translated teaching materials from abroad, and the business cases used are mostly from North America. Most of the teaching materials developed by local scholars are based on Western theories and practices. With regard to the newly introduced Executive MBA education, there is a high proportion of foreign professors teaching the courses. Some foreign professors have simply transplanted the teaching methods and materials from their home countries to the classrooms in China. The bestselling management books and magazines in China are about Western management theories and practices, such as *In search of excellence*, the *Biography of Jack Welch*, and *Built to last*. The willingness of a large number of Chinese executives to pay high fees to attend Jack Welch's talk in China in June 2004 is an indication that Chinese executives embrace Western management theories and practice.

However, many of the interviewed executives in this study said that they have obtained only very limited insights from many Western management theories and business cases. They said that there is a gap between what foreign professors teach and the reality of management practices in Chinese companies. In business administration education, many senior executives prefer professors who are able to understand both Chinese companies and culture and Western management theories. These findings suggest that MBA programs in China should integrate Chinese practices and the Western theories.

## Note

1 In 2002, the central government of China reorganized the two large telecommunications service companies: China Telecom Group Corporation and China Network Communications Corporation. In the ten northern provinces (autonomous regions and municipalities), all the affiliated companies of the China Telecom Group Corporation were merged with the China Network Communications Corporation.

## References

Chen, S. F. 2004. *Qi ye jia de guan li zhe xue* (The management philosophy for entrepreneurs). Guangzhou: Guangdong Economics Press.
Cheng, Z. Y. 1999. *C li lun: zhong guo guan li zhe xue* (Theory C: Chinese management philosophy). Shanghai: Xuelin Publishing House.
Crane, A., Dirk, M., and Jeremy, M. 2004. "Stakeholders as citizens? Rethinking rights, participation, and democracy," *Journal of Business Ethics* 53: 107–122.
Farh, J.-L., and Cheng, B.-S. 2000. "A cultural analysis of paternalistic leadership in Chinese organizations," in J. T. Li, A. S. Tsui, and E. Weldon (eds.), *Management and organizations in the Chinese context*. London: Macmillan.
Fayol, H. 1949. *General and industrial management*. London: Pitman.

Frew, D. R., and Bruning, N. S. 1987. "Perceived organizational characteristics and personality measures as predictors of stress/strain in the work place," *Journal of Management* 13: 633–646.

Hsu, C.-Y. 1994. *Cong li shi kan ling dao* (Looking at leadership from Chinese history). Beijing: San Lian Shu Dian.

Nisbett, R. 2003. *The geography of thought: how Asians and Westerners think differently . . . and why.* New York: Free Press.

Ross, W. D. 2002. *The right and the good.* Oxford: Clarendon Press.

Ruf, B. M., Krishnamurty, M., Robert, M. B., Jay, J. J., and Karen, P. 2001. "An empirical investigation of the relationship between change in corporate social performance and financial performance: a stakeholder theory perspective," *Journal of Business Ethics* 32: 143–156.

Sternberg, R. J. 1996. *Successful intelligence: how practical and creative intelligence determine success in life.* New York: Simon & Schuster.

Taylor, F. W. 1947. *Scientific management.* New York: Harper & Row.

Wren, D. A. 1994. *The evolution of management thought,* 4th edn. New York: Wiley.

Yang, K. S. 1995. "Chinese social orientation: an integrative analysis," in T. Y. Lin, W. S. Tseng, and E. K. Yeh (eds.), *Chinese societies and mental health.* Hong Kong: Oxford University Press.

Zeng, S. Q. 2004. *Guan li da dao: zhong guo guan li zhe xue de xian dai hua ying yong.* (The road of management: the application of Chinese management philosophy in the contemporary era). Beijing: Peking University Press.

Zhang, D. N., and Cheng, Z. Y. 1991. *Zhong guo si wei pian xiang.* (Chinese thinking preferences). Beijing: China Social Sciences Press.

Zhang, Z. X., and Wang, H. 2006. "Initiating the organizational learning through reshaping the organizational culture: a case study of Qingdao Netcom," in CESS (ed.), *Organizational learning and innovation: the 2006 report on the growth and evolution of Chinese entrepreneurs.* Beijing: China Machine Press.

*Appendix: Interview guideline*

1. Please briefly describe your company's history.

2. Please describe your career history.

3. In your experience as a CEO, do you have leadership and management philosophies?
   A. If so, what are they?
   B. If not, do you have some general principles in running your company?

4. How have these leadership philosophies/principles guided you in leading and managing your company? Can also ask: How have these philosophies/principles helped you meet leadership and management challenges or overcome leadership and management difficulties? (Ask probing questions when and where appropriate in the conversation. For example: How did you do that? Can you give me an example? Let the person tell stories; pay attention to what issues are involved, under what circumstances, and what philosophy/principle is called upon, and how the philosophy is used to guide practices.)

5. How have the practices been received by the employees? Are some more difficult/challenging than others to practice? Why?

6. How have your leadership philosophies been shaped? (More specific questions include: did you have these philosophies from the very beginning of your career as a manager? Where did you learn them? Did they become stronger or did they change as you gained more experience?)

7. In your experience as an enterprise leader, from where do you draw inspiration, wisdom, and guidance? (*linggan, zhihui, qifa*)

8. Which schools of thought and which philosophers, thinkers, statesmen, enterpreneurs have influenced your leadership and management thoughts and practices? (Look for examples.)

9. Looking back, of the various schools of thought and people that have influenced you, which ones have you relied on more than others? Which ones seemed to be more successful?

10. Looking toward the future, which schools of thought and which people may gain importance or lose importance for enterprise leadership and management?

11. Where do you think enterprise leaders should go for further learning and education to enrich their leadership thoughts or prepare them for future challenges of leadership?

# 9 | Linking Chinese leadership theory and practice to the world: leadership secrets of the Middle Kingdom

GEORGE BEAR GRAEN

T HIS book focuses on Chinese history lessons on leading Chinese people and is a testament to the need for Americans to understand our long-separated brothers at a deep level and also a plea to reject the tempting alternative of surface-level, national stereotypes and caricatures portrayed in the popular press. Americans have discovered the hard way that Japanese lessons on how to lead American people must be interpreted in terms of their culture and history, as signaled by the failure of Theory Z. Just as the Japanese Toyota system for manufacturing cannot be arbitrarily applied piecemeal to American manufacturing (Graen and Hui, 1995), American manufacturing cannot do so to the Chinese system. Post-modern Chinese managers working under Western manufacturing systems in China do not respond the same as Western managers (Graen, Hui and Gu, 2005). What is needed is a deep understanding of the critical disconnects between effective Chinese and American leadership in Sino-American organizations in China. We begin with a deep-level discussion of the significance of Chinese leadership theories, from the various historical theories of Confucianism to Farh's post-modern version called "paternalistic" leadership.

## Introduction

Confucianism and its several modifications guided past generations of Han Chinese more or less adequately until it was turned upside down on the mainland during the Cultural Revolution of 1966 to 1976. Although Confucianism had been weakened progressively since the 1950s by Chairman Mao, the severity of the Cultural Revolution forced a generation of Chinese to miss their socialization and education into Confucianism. Today, many scholars of mainland China think that China must find a new and inspiring ideology such as the one that Singapore developed to inspire her people.

Leadership theories based on almost five thousand years of Chinese recorded civilization have a way of making humble even the more knowledgeable senior scholars of modern leadership. China had a civilization when most of the rest of the world was populated by tribes of hunter-gatherers. China has reason to be proud of her many contributions to human advancement. She has been the mother of Asian culture from the early years and has taught her children to think, read, write, count and live together peacefully in spite of being one of the most diverse nations on earth. Of course, Chinese history included many wars to maintain political unity; however, it appears somewhat more peaceful when I compare its history to that of Europe.

Although I am neither Asian nor European but American, I was educated cross-culturally in Japan during my formative years as a scholar. The dramatic experiences of being allowed "deep inside" the hermit culture of Japan drove home to me the many fundamental differences in national strategies, operations and tactics between "Nippon" and "America".

Similar differences make extremely difficult, and often impossible, the task of adequately translating Western leadership concepts into Chinese thoughts and vice versa. What Buddha, Jesus, Mohammed, or your favorite moral leader would do in a given situation does not help because each leader's thoughts have been filtered by these cultural differences. The words may be translated the same, but the connotative meanings are different in East and West. Before this East–West transfer of connotative isomorphic meaning can take place cross-culturally, experts on both sides must be trained for this task (Graen *et al.*, 1997). Most of the contributors to the present volume are at the level of expertise in leadership that is called "Sino-American transculturalist" which indicates that they understand their Chinese and American culture and history well enough to validly offer their understanding of Chinese leadership to the West. As the deep-level reader can see, they did wonderful work.

My role in this presentation of Chinese leadership thoughts offered to the world is to comment as a Western leadership scholar on the contributions of Chinese leadership philosophies covered in this book and point out new directions for cross-cultural leadership research and practice. I plan to accomplish this by commenting on the Chinese contributions to leadership understanding contained herein and by viewing the totality as a student of modern Sino-American leadership in China. However, I must admit that my firsthand understanding of Chinese culture in general and Chinese leadership in particular is limited to Han Chinese in coastal China during the recent open-door era. My first visit to China was in 1985 although I have been an eager student of Chinese history and thought since reading, as a child, my first adult novel: Pearl Buck's *The good earth*. Finally, I gladly leave judgments on the adequacy of my colleague's translations to others.

My study of leadership in China has benefited enormously from my cross-cultural studies with my Japanese mentors, Professors Katsuo Sano and Mitsuru Wakabayashi at Keio and Nagoya Universities during the 1970s and 1980s. From them I learned the difference between surface-level behavior and deep-level behavior. Surface-level behavior is the stuff of cultural stereotypes and caricatures such as those found in popular culture-based books. Although some people believe that these surface-level, cultural stereotypes contain some introductory useful information, I believe that they are on balance dysfunctional for any meaningful cross-cultural relationship. For example, I have never owned a cow or horse, yet I am stereotyped in Japan and China as an American "cowboy." I reject that image and object to anyone treating me as a John Wayne clone.

## Historical outcropping

Chinese leadership history differs from that of the West in many respects, but a few of the more noteworthy are the absence of a Magna Carta in 1215 in which the King of England agreed to be under the laws (the rule of law), the early decline of the Western feudal system, and the rise of the scientific and industrial revolution with its steam engine and machine technology. These events fostered colonialism and the rise of corporations in the West. Instead, China became a giant country early in its history and was ruled by emperors without the rule of law. It continues to survive under these conditions and only the emperors have changed through forces of various kinds upto the present day.

I was told by my Chinese mentors early in my studies that "the Chinese are pragmatic and the emperor is far away." This meant that because the emperor and his representatives have always been above the law, Chinese business must use the "backdoor." Many Chinese told me that "it is better to go to hell than go to a Chinese court." The English Star Chamber was the same before the Magna Carta. Fortunately, the Chinese legal system has recently made advances toward the rule of law for everyone.

Leadership in China is to be found at all levels of society and profits enormously from past Chinese scholars' works on the theories and practices of convincing people to follow righteous opportunities, while maintaining the overall cost-benefit ratios and keeping faith with those who would sacrifice all for the good of the many.

The impact of Chinese theories of leadership can be found wherever Han Chinese people live, and these theories are adapted to their local situation. Strains of Chinese leadership theories can be found on every continent and many islands, around the globe. "Confucianism" (today a mixture of Confucianism, Taoism, and Legalism with a Buddhist flavor) can be found in its stronger forms in Taiwan and to a lesser degree in Hong Kong. It was turned upside-down in mainland China during the ten years of the Cultural Revolution by Chairman Mao, but it recovered somewhat under Deng's "open-door revolution." However, under Deng's revolution, the old values of the ancestral village home have been replaced, for many young Chinese entrepreneurs, by personal self-interest, wealth, and power, all free of family responsibility. For many of these business people, Confucianism is an old superstition held by their ancestors, with little relevance to them. In sum, mainland China is searching for a moral philosophy to bring order and unity to a turbulent nation.

Chinese business is in search of leadership theories for the twenty-first century that will be useful in developing leadership networks that include people from other Eastern and Western countries. These theories must help find the "true middle ground" between people from vastly different cultures, so that they can truly bond cross-culturally. Thousands of years of Chinese isolation with the objective of remaining unstained by the "unclean outsiders" have not prepared China's children to deal with offers from many strange foreigners. Hunkering down in one's small Chinese family business may serve the Confucian family, but it is not the answer needed in competing with large multinational corporations, because large fish eat small fish that cannot hide. The traditional Chinese family business, with some notable exceptions, has been severely restricted in terms of growth by its inherent risk aversion. No head of a Chinese family business wants to be the one that bankrupts the family. Chinese business must learn to blend the effective business technology of the West with the cultural forces of China to find a workable leadership theory. In addition, China is growing at such a rate that she will soon be the largest economy on the globe and she will need effective theories of international leadership to avoid becoming the world's greatest factory and largest polluter without attendant leadership on the global stage. It can be hoped that ingredients in the Chinese philosophies will contribute to developing such international leadership theories.

China and America must find the "third way" (Graen and Wakabayashi, 1994) and leap-frog the process of becoming sophisticated in international business partnership networks. The first step is to be knowledgeable regarding the lessons of Chinese leadership from the ancients to the present. This book is directed toward that goal. The next step is to integrate this understanding with that of foreign leadership to be capable of true cultural bonding with foreigners. This book's contributors are preparing for this next step.

## Competing social structures and political ideologies

A brief outline of the major social structures used by mainland China from its early development as a feudal system to the present is presented in Table 9.1. As shown, the stages of development begin with the Confucian (about 600 BCE) dual system (A1 and A2) under which the people served the hierarchy up to and including the emperor and the nine classes of nobles served both the emperor and the people. In addition, the value systems of A1 and A2 differed in that the A1 values were directed at harmony in interpersonal hierarchical relationships and A2 values were directed at scholarly pursuits. Equity struggles between people and nobles were frequently based on the two-class system of privilege. Leaders emerged under the two classes differently, with seniority, birth order, and gender for families, and testing and seniority for nobles. The dark side of the heavenly system of Confucius and Mencius was proposed as a missing component of the complete social system by Xunzi (about 285 BCE) and his Legalist student Hanfei (B). The system of Legalism moved the favored nobles back under a common law and introduced the struggle with A2.

**Table 9.1.** *Chronology of competing social structures in China.*

| Characteristic | Confucian-I | Confucian-II | Legalism | Maoism | Dengism | US legalism |
|---|---|---|---|---|---|---|
| Final say | Emperor | Emperor | Court | Chairman | Chairman | Court |
| Some say | People | Nobles | People | Party | Party | People |
| System | A1 | A2 | B | C | D | E |
| Values | Workers | Elite | Social contracts | Peasant values | International business values | Due Process |
| Prime Mover | Serve family | Serve society via nine classes | Protect society | Punish enemies of Revolution | Open door and suspend Legalism | Constitution World Court |
| Leader | Seniority | Testing and seniority | Appointment | Long March with Mao | Party bureaucrats | Master networks |
| Struggles | A1 vs. A2 | A2 vs. B | C vs. A1, A2, B | D vs. C | E vs. D |  |
| Time Line | 600 BCE | 600 BCE | 285 BCE | 1950 CE | 1976 CE | 2000 CE |

*Source:* Modified from Hwang (1995).

The emperor was still above the law. The value system was based on social contracts, and violations of these were punished according to judgments handed down by legal courts. Legal positions of leaders were filled by the emperor's authority.

This three-part system was the framework in China until the last emperor. Even the many invasions of China failed to change the Chinese way. However, the fall of the emperor and his replacement by Chairman Mao and his party spelled the tragic end of the Chinese system. As outlined in Chapter 7, Maoism (1950) replaced the emperor with the Chairman of the Communist Party, replaced intellectual merit by party loyalty during the Long March, elevated "peasant values" to the highest level, and sought to punish all enemies of the Revolution. Leaders were appointed by the Chairman and those who made the Long March were favored. Mao's ten-year Cultural Revolution was successful in tearing apart much of the Confucian system for a generation of Chinese, but the Confucian system still remains strong in Taiwan and other places outside China.

After Mao's death, Deng became Chairman and opened the door for trade with the world (D). The final say was by the Party although a weak legal system remained. The Party was above the law and used selective enforcement to attract foreign funds and modern manufacturing technology. China was open for international business and privatization was encouraged for all state-owned enterprises. All of the necessary conditions for capitalism were put in place except the transparent economic and legal due process required by the American legal system. Dengism struggles to find a Chinese way to achieve these two missing components, but China prospers without them.

Today Taiwan's system is a mixture of Confucianism and American legalism that makes it very different from mainland China. What may work well in Taiwan, such as the paternalistic model (this Volume, Chap. 6), may not work so well in mainland China. Entrepreneurs in China must deal with resource systems that are controlled by the state. Clearly Taiwan has developed a system that works in international trade based on a post-modern mix of Confucian values and Western legalism. Progress on this in China is encouraging as portrayed in a recent incident involving human rights.

On November 29, 2006, in China, people were outraged by the local police parading in the street citizens accused of being or visiting prostitutes. They saw this as a violation of their legal rights. Moreover, they complained that prostitution was a violation of the social order and is punishable by administrative detention rather than a criminal conviction and a prison sentence. A Party leader promoted the parade as a way to discourage prostitution. The struggle between Party and legal authority continues (*Business Week*, 2006).

## Leadership in feudal China

China, with its high-density population, discovered very early in her history the value of networks of human relationships for ordering family affairs, village commerce, and interactions with the state. As described in Chapter 1, these networks were transformed into systems of obligations to superiors and parental responsibility for the welfare of subordinates by the Confucian system. On the surface, this system was based on ancestry of family and virtue of all including government. As discussed in Chapter 2, it was later revised to recognize the dual nature of man. Confucius and Mencius saw only the god-man side of humans and designed a structure for their society. However, they overlooked the animal-man side of humans that needed to be socialized by education, beginning in the family and extending throughout the networks. They also recognized individual differences in people. These things were documented through research in psychology in the West during the nineteenth and twentieth centuries. Later, Hanfei made his contributions to refining bureaucracy, by which large populations could be governed.

Daoistic leadership, described in Chapter 3, turns to the concept of "like water" and reminds us that leaders often appeal to values to attract dedicated followers. Humans need their values to give them something beyond their short and otherwise animal existence. We need a higher calling to become a sage leader. To many Chinese, Daoism is the path to be followed.

Hwang, a social psychologist, outlined in Chapter 4 the history of leadership thought from a modern Taiwanese perspective focusing on Hanfei's theory of leadership. Hwang contends that Hanfei's theory of Legalism can be reorganized to be applicable to both a feudal state and a modern organization in Taiwan. He outlines how Legalism rationalized the Confucian order to become akin to Weber's bureaucracy and replaced the old aristocracy with bureaucrats. Unfortunately, the competitive knowledge economy has made the classic bureaucratic organization obsolete and replaced it with overlapping team organization (Orton and Dhillon, 2006; Seers, 2004).

As discussed in Chapter 5, Sunzi's *Art of war*, a handbook for leaders in competition, counsels leaders to think twice before they act. Strategy is all-important and the battle not fought and the prize achieved is the best. Know your enemy better than you know yourself and use his strengths against him. These thoughts have been commercialized in the West in the usual piecemeal fashion.

In Chapter 6, Farh and his colleagues present a progress report on their 2000 proposed model of paternalistic leadership (PL) in overseas Chinese family businesses. They outline the historical background, empirical research, and revised model of PL. Their PL model proposes three independent leadership facets: moral leadership, authoritarian leadership, and benevolent leadership. These three facets are used to define eight leadership types à la Fiedler (1967) by dichotomizing each and crossing them as high morality, high authority, and high benevolence (HM HA HB). Finally, a revised contingency model is proposed involving the eight cells. This is an average leadership style (ALS) model of leader behavior in which authoritarian leadership leads to compliance by subordinates, benevolent leadership to obligation, and moral leadership leads to respect and identification. As expected, a set of high ratings on all three facets is the best and a set of low ratings on all facets is the worst, but different combinations of high and low predict different responses by followers.

Modifying Farh and Cheng (2000) to include modern corporate and true cultural bonding (TCB) systems results in Table 9.2. As shown in this table, the three facets produce different results for the three systems. The moral leadership facet yields family values, health of corporation, and health of Sino-Western ventures. In terms of authority leadership, the prescriptions are clear lines of authority and trust according to family ties, bureaucratic structures supported by the legal system, and network organization with sharing network leadership at all levels and functions. Finally, servant-leader facet prescriptions are treating all employees as extended family, individual consideration of employee needs by bureau, and bi-cultural servant leader of employees. I prefer these three leadership facets, because they acknowledge the human needs for moral leadership, authority leadership, and servant leadership. Chinese and American people

Table 9.2. *Leadership in mainland China.*

| Leadership facet | Traditional Chinese paternalistic | Modern corporate economic | True cultural bonding |
|---|---|---|---|
| Moral | Obligation to enhance and preserve reputation of family as demanding respect and esteem (*Face-enhancing*) | Obligation to enhance and preserve health of company for all stakeholders, equitably (*Create wealth*) | Achieve profit, be a good citizen and ensure welfare for all by managing efficiency, risk, and adaptation (*Fairness*) |
| Authority | Clear lines of authority and trust according to family ties (*Confucian values*) | Bureaucratic structures supported by legal system (*Legitimate*) | Network organization characterized by sharing network leadership at all levels and in all functions (*Functional*) |
| Servant | Treat all employees as extended family or family by patriarch or his representatives (*Father's duty*) | Standardized and group consideration of all employees' needs by bureau (*Personnel department*) | Bi-cultural servant and mentor of employees as needed for both inside- and outside-work issues (*Brother's duty*) |

*Source:* Modified from Farh and Cheng (2000).

cannot commit to organizations whose leaders are not described by them as excelling on all three facets.

Networks of lasting relationships have characterized the Han people throughout their history and any leadership theory that denies this feature will suffer thereby. Leadership theory for the Han people must include sharing with followers networks of relationships. To get anything out of the ordinary accomplished that a Chinese leader cannot do alone requires some trusted relationships. This is one way pragmatism emerges in Chinese society.

The implications of this for leadership in Sino-American dyads should be clear. In contrast to the Chinese history of reliance on networks of relationships, American history describes rugged individuals and self-reliance. Both of these myths contain a grain of truth, but clearly both the Chinese and American relied on both individual and network activities to survive and prosper. It has been a mistake for scholars to call Americans "individualistic" and young Chinese in coastal China "collectivistic" in the twenty-first century when even the family networks are breaking down, not to mention the village networks and the state networks. The pendulum of network to individual has swung from one pole to the other for both peoples from one generation to the next, but both require leadership theory that speaks to both individualism and collective networking. Such a theory is available and has been tested empirically in both China and America (Graen and Graen, 2006).

Leaders must be the best in the network and dependent on the network over time. The network must grant leadership and can reclaim it (Graen, 2007b). American organizations have recently accepted the power of teams and are beginning to discover that leadership cannot be contained by them but requires networks (which may include numerous teams).

## Dramatic tidal change

As late as 1949 (the year the People's Republic of China was founded) China was a feudal society largely untouched by the scientific and industrial revolution in the West. Beginning in 1949, the new chairman Mao Zedong signaled the People's Revolution that would grant an iron rice bowl of universally shared prosperity to all Chinese and a philosophy of "never forget class struggle." His plan called for the nationalization of all property and organizations and strict adherence to Mao's way. For over a quarter-century Chinese Communist Party (CCP) state-owned organizations were maintained despite huge annual losses. Finally, Deng opened the door to the world in 1978 with CCP's official rejection of Mao and Maoism and gradually allowed the steady privatization of property and organizations until today only a third of the GDP has yet to be privatized.

One clear consequence of this change to private and Sino-foreign ventures was that Chinese workers who were socialized into the roles

**Table 9.3. *Ten limiting characteristics of a traditional SOE.***

1. When you hire a Chinese employee you have to accept his or her family's interest. One employee was fired for good cause after a lengthy procedure and his family appeared at the company gate until the individual was reinstated.
2. Appointed committee leaders are obeyed. Small groups of managers would not begin problem-solving on their own, but waited until their leader told them what and how to proceed.
3. All Chinese employees work for the Party and are contracted to the Sino-Western company to do as they are instructed. The Party provides them room and board, health care, education, and an income. They obey the Party first.
4. Chinese managers are not expected to innovate but to follow specific orders, forcing Western managers to micromanage or fail.
5. Western managers can only reward with praise, special assignments, and promotions. Punishments are only verbal.
6. Western managers are contract term limited, but Chinese employees are employed for life.
7. Western managers are paid much more than Chinese doing comparable work.
8. Chinese employees do not question their Western managers except to their countrymen.
9. Chinese employees will do nothing without instructions, no matter how long it takes.
10. Employees only get promoted when someone leaves.

of a state-owned enterprise (SOE) were not well suited for private ventures. In response to this many SOEs reduced their workforces to a minimum and preferred younger employees as replacements. Newly arrived Sino-foreign ventures and foreign ventures sought to hire Chinese without SOE experience. For example, in our MBA investigation we found a clear preference for younger managers without SOE experience. This preference in hiring was based solidly on the incompatibility between the roles of managers in SOEs and private enterprise. This can be seen in the results of our early three-year investigation of an SOE that was being privatized into a Sino-British venture. We were brought in to recommend procedures for transferring the informal systems from the SOE to the private company. Our findings regarding the SOE are shown in Table 9.3.

As shown, leadership was not needed in the SOE, but was needed in the Sino-British venture. The question became, how do you transform middle-aged employees from being SOE-friendly to being private-enterprise-friendly? The answer after three years of trying was that as long as the employees preferred the SOE way, no change was feasible. The venture continued to operate tolerably well as long as the British managers micromanaged tirelessly. When they were replaced by less motivated foreign managers, the expected happened.

## Intercultural sense-making

My remarks about the above Chinese leadership scholars' contributions to our understanding of leadership models in China call for a context. The reader needs to know that the era of Confucius and Mencius was one of transition from the slave system to the feudal system. The system of feudalism by which the society was structured and functioned included the emperor and his court at the top, followed in descending order by lords, vassals, peasants, and slaves. Members of the court discovered that the Confucian system could reinforce the feudal system and achieved its adoption throughout the empire. It worked tolerably well for each succeeding emperor until it was torn apart by the Cultural Revolution. It was planned to be replaced by the new leadership of peasants emerging from hard work and suffering. This plan failed and the value system of Deng was a return to pragmatism and the post-modern individuality of capitalism. Although traditional Confucian values are alive and well in Taiwan and Singapore, values in coastal China and Hong Kong have become more pragmatic.

Cultures should be understood by past history, current circumstance, and genetic endowment. Concepts and belief systems of different countries are understood by making sense of the developmental history of the countries as well as their present circumstances. We learn through our interactions with our local environment. Our feel of cultural concepts and belief systems depends on the community in which we engage in discourses.

For example, in China *guanxi* (social connections) are based on obligations owed to one's family by outsiders, whereas friendships are based on shared fellowship. Chinese seek friendships that are not necessarily instrumental or a means to a selfish end. Morris, Podolny, and Ariel (2000) showed that the Chinese *guanxi* ties are multiplex, that is, serve both instrumental and affective purposes, whereas American social ties tend to serve single purposes. In contrast, in the United States, while family connections are similar, work relationships can be mutually rewarding on the job or mutually satisfying off the job, or both. What we find in Sino-American ventures is that American employees seek to develop instrumental work relationships that may not be friendships. This creates problems for Chinese who see these American work relations in terms of Confucian values. Accordingly, supervisors should take care of their charges both professionally and socially (father–son relationship). Peer relationships also are seen in terms of Confucian values (sibling–sibling). In contrast, Americans view work relations in more limited terms, because they are relevant at work but do not extend outside of work to one's private life. This means that when we refer to leader–member exchange (LMX) or member–member exchange (MMX) we are talking about different phenotypic relationships between Chinese and Americans. Even though research shows that LMX predicts the same leadership outcomes for both China and America (Graen and Graen, 2007), the Chinese and American concepts of leadership ties involve different obligations. In the Chinese concept, Confucian values direct one's leader to play the role of surrogate father including private duties such as sponsoring suitors and attending weddings, funerals, and holidays. One's Chinese leader is a mentor, monitor, and motivator in both work and private life. Overall, leaders "take care" of their followers until the parent becomes the child and the child the parent.

Westerners, especially Americans, face apparently gross contradictions when attempting to understand Chinese rationality, because it is different from Western rationality. Similarly, Easterners, especially Japanese and Chinese cannot make much sense of Americans' apparently gross contradictions. Clearly, East and West employ different sense-making systems. For example, the present PRC government has enacted laws that outlaw capitalistic activities despite China's transformation from Chinese communism to a system more capitalistic than the American one in the last twenty-five years. As long as the enacted economic system benefits the country, the legal system can be held in abeyance. As long as the Party allows it, relevant laws do not apply. In contrast, the rule of law is supreme in the United States. Westerners should remember the two keys to Chinese sense-making: the Emperor is far away; and the Chinese are pragmatic but also judge the government according to Confucian standards of correct practice.

Another example is that the presently unMaoist nationalism based on a "harmonious society" is a multipolarized world between the "haves" and the "have nots," the "connected" and the "not connected," the "coastal" and the "inland," and the "employed" and the "unemployed." Westerners sense polarization and disconnects, but the Chinese sense harmonious progress. It may help Westerners to recall that China has a long history of obsolete authoritarianism. The central government has been above the law, and the Chinese people, to survive, learned to do whatever works regardless of legality and government oversight. Westerners for hundreds of years have grown up under a more or less transparent, comprehensively enforced legal system that included everyone. We cannot understand a society that historically had one set of laws for common people and another set for the imperial family. We would do well to reflect on growing up under a system where most of the necessary economic and political activities could land us in jail or worse.

One mechanism for dealing with such a social system is to act one way in public and another way in private. In China the extended family is the private domain. Only family members are trusted with inside information, family authority, and the "backdoor" connections in Sino-Western ventures. In China, Chinese workers look for familiar family-like relations, but they are pragmatic and adjust. Chinese college graduates seek advancement in such companies through progressively more valuable contributions. They are prepared to act appropriately to succeed, but judge their treatment according to Confucian values. Western managers in these companies need to be trained appropriately in the development of Chinese managerial talent and encouraged to follow this training. Multinational corporations should understand that East is not West and the relevant differences need to be identified and dealt with in a cooperative manner. As described in Chapter 8, Eastern people do not care to be treated as second-class citizens in their own country. On the contrary, they expect to be treated as appropriately different but equal. Organizations that ignore these conditions will suffer the economic and social consequences. At present, the companies are not paying much attention to this wound that bleeds profits, but they shall reap what they sow in terms of becoming an accepted joint venture in the East.

## Cost of ethnocentric leadership in China

Although the cost of ethnocentric leadership in Sino-Western enterprises in China is not captured by the accounting process, it is a drag on Sino-Western and Sino-Japanese enterprise profits. This is the cost of failed true cultural bonding (Graen and Graen, 2007). Those companies which can match the successes in combining traditional Chinese values with Japanese and Western ways of doing business will likely be the survivors in the China market in the coming shake-outs.

Let's consider, for example, postgraduate young Chinese in Sino-Western enterprises in China. What do young MBA students seek in their Sino-Western or Sino-Japanese enterprise positions? They seek opportunities to develop professionally and to be promoted for their performance above expectations by a competent and personally interested leader. They seek to be understood at some deeper-than-surface level and be listened to when making important suggestions. Although they are heavily recruited by search agents for more attractive positions with other companies, they would prefer not to leave. But they do leave when they lose hope of improvement. Based on our five years of research on 150 Chinese MBAs in Sino-Western corporations doing business in Shanghai's economic areas, the companies are wasting valuable Chinese managerial resources by failing consistently to train and control their middle-level Western managers so that they lead by combining traditional Chinese values with Japanese and Western ways of doing business. This book should be required reading for all Western and Japanese managers posted in Sino-Western or Sino-Japanese enterprises in China. The simple act of discussing this book with their Chinese subordinate managers should open the doors to better communication. To convince young Chinese managers that they are interested in understanding traditional Chinese values, Western superior and peer managers should avoid many superficial cultural stereotypes and caricatures of Chinese values. Young Chinese managers reject such surface-level descriptions. Remember that the turnover cost is larger than the cost of replacement by a warm body. It also includes the loss of production during the learning-curve interval and during the network-rebuilding interval. This can become a significant figure after it is multiplied by the number of talented young managers lost per year. In our five-year study, among those most valued by the company, 48 percent of those with poor leaders quit their companies and only 24 percent of those with good leaders did so (Graen, Hui, and Gu, 2005).

My colleagues at Procter and Gamble (P&G) are amazed at these percentages, because they were training Chinese managers very early in Deng's open-door period and claimed to have lost not one young Chinese manager who they really wanted to keep. It can be done. Western college-educated leaders can be trained to do true cultural bonding with their Chinese managers. Wal*Mart with the assistance of P&G trainers is currently in the process of learning true cultural bonding in China (M. R. Graen, 2007).

Research in China (Aryce and Chen, 2006; Chen, 2006; Chen, 1996; Chen, Lam, and Zhong, 2007; Cheng and Rosett, 1991; Cheng and Farh, 2001) has generated findings compatible with those in America regarding the usefulness of the genotypic model of leader–member exchange (LMX) with sharing network leadership (LMX SNL).

## What is sharing network leadership?

Leading private business ventures in both China and the United States employ different organizational structures for different environmental conditions. For relatively routine and stable conditions of production or service, the well-known bureaucratic structure is used for a variety of sound reasons; however, for relatively complex and dynamic conditions, the more complex leadership sharing model is employed. For most business conditions, the bureaucratic structures of scientific management are protected from environmental turbulence as much as possible. Only when the turbulence becomes disruptive to routine and stable operations is the backstop system called the complex sharing network leadership model used to change the bureaucratic system, or to change some aspect of the environment, or both, so that routine and stable operations may continue unabated.

Procedures for building and running bureaucratic structures are well known and are adaptable to accepting new technologies with a minimum of help from the leadership system. Unfortunately, organizational executives cannot predict when their routine and stable process may be disrupted by environmental events and must be prepared for them as much as possible in order to fulfill their due diligence to their owners. Thus, leadership structures are built as solvers of large, complex, and dynamic problems.

Within these organizations, managers' jobs are to make the routine and stable production and service systems function efficiently and improve continuously. In contrast, leaders' positions are to go outside of the bureaucracy and deal with environmental issues that can and do disrupt the bureaucratic process. Both managers and leaders are required for the economic, social or political process to continue. It must be managed continuously, but it must be saved periodically from a multiplicity of perils. While managerial structures are common knowledge, leadership structures have changed for the twenty-first century. Early in the twentieth century, leadership structures were designed for autocratic heroic individuals who saved our routine and stable existence. Later in that century, they became leaders of "special project teams"; now they have become "leaders of networks of leaders." This is sometimes called the "network-centric" approach to leadership (Graen and Graen, 2006, 2007). An example of a leadership network composed of many positions is shown in Figure 9.1. The leaders are in the central positions of the figure whereas their supporters are in the peripheral positions. The lines between the positions indicate the presence of the necessary preconditions for taking discretionary interdependent action (shared leadership). Directions of the arrowheads represent the directions of the judgments. Finally, the absence of a line means that the necessary conditions have not been met. Only those dyads with double arrowheads may share leadership (Graen and Graen, 2006, 2007).

The necessary conditions for sharing leadership within a leadership network are the big three of (1) mutual respect for competence, (2) mutual trust in motivation, and (3) mutual commitment to partner's welfare, and training for sharing leadership within a leadership network (Graen and Graen, 2006, 2007). This SNL model of leadership has been validated by a number of studies in both China and the United States and was introduced to the US Army at West Point Military Academy recently by Graen (2007b).

Based on all of the research on this LMX model of sharing network leadership, we boldly state our rules for multinational LMX sharing network leadership. These rules are not exhaustive, but they are a beginning.

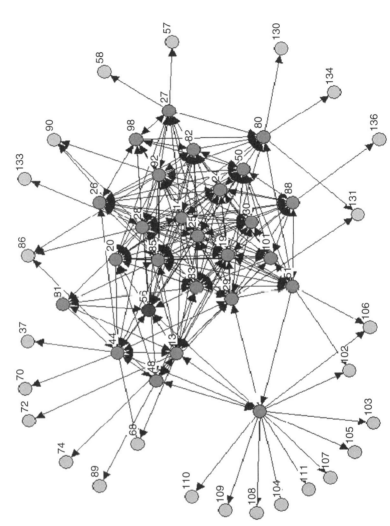

Figure 9.1. A leadership network.

## Rules for Sino-Western or Sino-Japanese leaders of leaders

1. Develop a serious interest in understanding the background of the post-modern Chinese people you work with and around. Read about their history and current circumstance. Ask questions and ask for help in understanding.
2. Show an authentic interest in the values of your Chinese associates.
3. Learn to communicate at a deep level by sharing your understanding of values and explaining that for you surface-level stereotypes get in the way and tourist-level conclusions are displeasing.
4. Build the required level of cross-cultural trust by showing that you can be an "outsider" who can be treated as an "insider." Treat your Chinese associates as unique individuals who have their own families.
5. Attempt to share network leadership with your Chinese colleagues using the shared network leadership (SNL) practices.
6. Learn the difference in leadership expectations between you and your associates.
7. When in China try to do things that are compatible with the modern Chinese way and be a cordial guest.

Clearly, four research-based leadership models dominate the post-modern scientific literature in China and America: paternalistic leadership (modern father–son Confucianism), transactional leadership (reward and punish), transformational leadership (ministering to subordinates) and sharing network leadership (developing trust with many networks of colleagues). All have been researched in both Chinese and American organizations as well as in many organizations in other countries. For summaries of research, see Chen and Lam (2007), Fahr and Cheng (2000), Graen and Graen (2006), Northhouse (2001), and Yukl (1998).

In Chinese organizations, research has shown that the American transformational leadership style does not work in China without first achieving the conditions for sharing network leadership (Wang *et al.*, 2005) and that Graen's theory of leadership predicts organizational citizen behavior (OCB) in both China and the United States (Hackett *et al.*, 2003).

The well-known career-long, longitudinal investigation of the careers of Japanese managers (Graen *et al.*, 2006) demonstrated the power of the SNL model in Japanese corporate society. It documented that career-long progress in a Japanese corporation is predictable using the model. Recent studies in China suggest that this SNL model works well to predict job performance and job satisfaction of Chinese employees in both Sino-Western ventures and Chinese corporations in coastal China (Graen and Graen, 2007). This model also was shown to be helpful in highlighting cross-cultural leader and member communications problems in Sino-Western ventures and suggested remedies (Graen, Hui, and Gu, 2005). Paternalistic leadership is discussed in detail in the preceding chapter by Farh and his associates. Its success in describing certain large family companies in Taiwan suggests that it can be integrated successfully with Western and Japanese technology.

## Recommendations

Modern leadership theory in the West is beginning to appreciate the ideals, stated long ago, of being a Daoist leader (Johnson, 2000). Although Western scholars prefer to struggle against nature, Daoist and Buddhist thinkers cooperate with nature. Confucianism early on prescribed the social hierarchy of lasting relationships that specified humanity, righteousness, knowledge, trust and filial piety, with all moral authority flowing down from the Sun God through the Middle Kingdom emperor. This impractical system of Confucianism was alerted to its shortcomings by the pragmatism of early Legalism. The fundamental question of the necessity of war between states was a *yin* (Mohism) versus a *yang* (Art of War School). In sum, the Chinese models of leadership are filled with a multitude of *yin* and *yang* tensions that allow leaders to choose their personal calling from among Chinese traditions.

Western leaders are offered similar *yin* and *yang* tensions. For example, a leader who shares network leadership strives to be seen as "wateristic" by followers and endeavors to instill these values in followers through sharing leadership (Kramer, 2006). In this theory, followers choose to share network leadership after it is offered. Leaders who refuse to share network leadership choose to be seen as authoritarian and "rock hard." In this information age, the merging of admired leadership values, such as those of being a wateristic leader employing modern and scientific production and service technology through day-to-day struggles between *yin* and *yang*, continues. For the purposes of the American manager in China the *yins* are Chinese values and the *yangs* are American values. Until we accept that the struggles must be acknowledged, understood, and joined, little progress can be expected in the mission of incorporating the two more less equally within a single organization that respects both nations and leads to the sharing of network leadership between Chinese and Americans. Let us proceed with this Sino-American mission.

In Graen, Hui, and Gu's (2005) five-year study of college-degree Chinese managers in Sino-Western companies in the Shanghai–Pudung economic zone, several particular *yin* and *yang* conflicts were identified by our Chinese managers between their Chinese way and the modern Western bureaucratic organization way. These are shown in Table 9.4. As shown, the US way was seen by our Chinese managers as giving unfair advantages to the Western managers at the expense of the Chinese managers. These conflicts must be struggled with by teams of both American and Chinese managers across the corporation. The mission of these teams should be to invent new procedures that will be fair to those who grew up in either China or the West.

Although our mission to find a Chinese *Dao* for corporations to follow in Sino-Western ventures in China has only begun, it has identified the above fundamental *yin* and *yang* struggles that must be addressed as continuing tensions that define leadership. Our hope is that this in-depth struggle to integrate the East and West, without either dominating, will yield a functional marriage, with the strengths of one complementing those of the other and sharing network leadership to prosper and live long. Finally, true cross-national managers must remember their credo: *People who were socialized in another country are not better or worse than you — only the same or different, and you should understand the difference before judging.*

Table 9.4. *Third-culture management issues in Sino-Western ventures.*

**Performance appraisal**

| | |
|---|---|
| American way: | Prepare your case with paper documents and sell it hard by pushing the envelope with accomplishment. |
| PRC way: | Prepare your Zen to be judged by your father/superior by emphasizing process not achievements. |

**Leadership/followership**

| | |
|---|---|
| American way: | Be a team player and seek to grow out of your job by excelling at special assignments from your boss (self-actualize). |
| PRC way: | Be a super team player and maintain group harmony (selflessness) and expect to be "looked after" by leader. |

**Participation in decision-making**

| | |
|---|---|
| American way: | Seek to contribute to your boss's decisions through suggestions, background work, consultations, and playing devil's advocate (all when appropriate). |
| PRC way: | Seek to do your own job and not involve yourself in your boss's job; only do what is specifically requested by your boss. |

**Teamwork**

| | |
|---|---|
| American way: | Be a team player but push the team to excel by going beyond your assigned tasks and helping your teammates when appropriate. |
| PRC way: | Be a team player and maintain harmony by not becoming too visible (the nail that sticks up gets hammered). |

**Documentation and proposal-writing**

| | |
|---|---|
| American way: | Prepare documentation and proposals with great care and precision because these documents may become part of your permanent file. |
| PRC way: | Prepare documentation and proposals in a terse outline form so as to minimize loss of face through Chinese-English awkwardness and weak English vocabulary. |

**Presentations**

| | |
|---|---|
| American way: | Prepare with great care, precision and for optimal data impact using PowerPoint slide shows with sound and clips because these are opportunities to be discovered by people upstairs. |
| PRC way: | Prepare with technical accuracy, but above all avoid loss of face due to language and cultural disadvantage. |

Table 9.4. (*cont.*)

| | |
|---|---|
| **Organizational citizenship** | |
| American way: | Try to be a decent citizen, but both individual competition and team cooperation must be emphasized to advance your career. |
| PRC way: | Commit to being a good citizen and emphasize cooperation over competition to maintain harmony with your peers; avoid conflict through silence. |
| **Cross-national conflict** | |
| American way: | Rationalize as particular human weaknesses that must be overcome to do the job properly and if these cannot be overcome, replace individual. |
| PRC way: | Accept differences and work cooperatively to overcome their consequences where feasible. |

## *References*

Aryce, S., and Chen, Z. X. 2006. "Leader–member exchange in a Chinese context: antecedents, the mediating role of psychological empowerment and outcomes," *Journal of Business Research* 59: 793–801.

*Business Week* 2006. "Chinese police parade prostitute's customers," December.

Chen, T. Y. 2006. "Review on antecedents and outcomes of leader–member exchange quality," *Management Consulting* 4: 49–50.

Chen, Z. 1996. "Managerial skill formulation in Chinese state-owned corporations: focusing on the leader–member exchange relation as a facilitator for skill learning," *Forum of International Development* 6: 217–236.

Chen, Z., and Lam, W. 2007. "Making LMX leadership work in China: is generalizability a problem for the Western concept of LMX in China?" in Graen and Graen (eds.), pp. 65–77.

Chen, Z., Lam, W., and Zhong, J. A. 2007. "Leader–member exchange and member performance: a new look at individual-level negative feedback-seeking behavior and team-level empowerment climate," *Journal of Applied Psychology* 92: 202–212.

Cheng, B. S., and Farh, J. L. 2001. "Social orientation in Chinese societies: a comparison of employees from Taiwan and Chinese mainland," *Chinese Journal of Psychology* 43: 207–221.

Cheng, L. Y., and Rosett, A. 1991. "Contract with a Chinese face: socially embedded factors in the transformation from hierarchy to market, 1979–1989," *Journal of Chinese Law* 5: 143–244.

Farh, J. L., and Cheng, B. S. 2000. "A cultural analysis of paternalistic leadership in Chinese organizations," in J. T. Li, A. S. Tsu, and E. Weldon (eds.), *Management and organizations in the Chinese context*, London: Macmillan, pp. 94–127.

Fiedler, F. 1967. *A theory of leadership effectiveness*. New York: McGraw-Hill.

Gibbons, D. E., and Grover, S. L. 2006. "Network factors in leader–member relationships," in Graen and Graen (2006), pp. 63–93.

Graen, G. B. 2007a. "Growing power using cherry picking strategies," in D. Tjosvold and B. Van Knippenberg (eds.), *Power and interdependence in organizations*, Cambridge: Cambridge University Press, in press.

2007b. "Shared network leadership for coping with dangerous 21st century contexts," invited address at the Global Leadership Conference, West Point Military Academy, New York, April 14.

Graen, G. B., Dharwadkar, R., Grewal, R., and Wakabayashi, M. 2006. "Japanese career progress over the long haul: an empirical examination," *Journal of International Business Studies* 37: 148–161.

Graen, G. B., and Graen, J. A. 2006 (eds.), *Sharing network leadership, LMX leadership: the series*. Greenwich, CT: Information Age Publishing.

2007 (eds.), *New multinational network sharing, LMX leadership: the series*. Charlotte, NC: Information Age Publishing.

Graen, G. B., and Hui, C. 1995. "Finally a production system that works and allows everyone to be an insider," *International Journal of Applied Psychology* 45(2): 130–135.

Graen, G. B., Hui, C., and Gu, Q. L. 2005. "A new approach to intercultural cooperation," in G. B. Graen and J. A. Graen (eds.), *New frontiers of leadership, LMX leadership: the series*, Greenwich, CT: Information Age Publishing, pp. 225–246.

Graen, G. B., Hui, C., Wakabayashi, M., and Wang, Z. M. 1997. "Cross-cultural research alliances in organizational research: cross-cultural partnership-making in action," in C. Earley and M. Erez (eds.), *Cross-cultural research in industrial organizational psychology*, San Francisco: Jossey Bass, pp. 160–189.

Graen, G. B., and Wakabayashi, M. 1994. "Cross-cultural leadership making: bridging American and Japanese diversity for team advantage," in H. C. Triandis, M. D. Dunnette, and L. M. Hough (eds.), *Handbook of industrial and organizational psychology*, Chicago: Rand-McNally, pp. 415–446.

Graen, M. R. 2007. "Creation of the Wal*Mart team of Procter & Gamble," in G. B. Graen and J. A. Graen (eds.), pp. 93–104.

Hackett, R. D., Farh, J. L., Song, L. J., and Lapierre, L. M. 2003. "LMX and organizational citizenship behavior: examining the links within and across Western and Chinese samples," in G. B. Graen (ed.), *Dealing with diversity, LMX Leadership: The Series*, Greenwich, CT: Information Age Publishing.

Hwang, K. K. 1995. "The struggle between Confucianism and legalism in Chinese society and productivity," in K. K. Hwang (ed.), *Easternization: socio-cultural impact on productivity*, Tokyo: Asian Productivity Organization, pp. 15–46.

Johnson, C. E. 2000. "Taoist leadership ethics," *Journal of Leadership Studies* 7: 82–91.

Kramer, M. W. 2006. "Communication strategies for sharing leadership within a creative team: LMX in theater groups," in G. B. Graen and J. A. Graen (eds.), pp. 1–24.

Morris, M. W., Podolny, J., and Ariel, S. (2000), "Missing relations: incorporating relational constructs into models of culture," in P. C. Earley and H. Singh (eds.), *Innovations in international and cross-cultural management*, Thousand Oaks, CA: Sage, pp. 52–90.

Northhouse, R. G. 2001. *Leadership: theory and practice*, 2nd edn. Thousand Oaks, CA: Sage.

Orton, J. D., and Dhillon, G. 2006. "Macrostrategic, mesostrategic, and microstrategic leadership processes in loosely coupled networks," in G. B. Graen and J. A. Graen (eds.), pp. 137–167.

Seers, A. 2004. "Leadership and flexible organization structures: the future is now," in G. B. Graen (ed.), *New frontiers of leadership, LMX leadership: the series*, Greenwich, CT: Information Age Publishing, pp. 1–31.

Wang, H., Law, K. S., Hackett, R. D., Wang, D., and Chen, Z. X. 2005. "Leader–member exchange as a mediator of the relationship between transformational leadership and followers' performance and organizational citizenship behavior," *Academy of Management Journal* 48: 420–432.

Yukl, G. A. 1998. *Leadership in organizations*, 4th edn. Englewood Cliffs, NJ: Prentice Hall.

# Index

6/4 pro-democracy movement (1989),
229
100 Schools of Thought, 1, 2, 33, 145
375 Rent Reduction Program, 131

Absolute (Daoism), 88
active leadership, 13
active non-action (*wei wu-wei*), 2, 10,
11, 13, 21, 24, 93
adaptations, 148, 150, 164
administration, 68–69, 76
agriculture reform, 225, 228
Ai Siqi, 215, 235
altruism, 89, 90, 91
*Analects* (Confucius), 32, 33, 256
Anti-Japan War (1937–1945), 208, 210
appointment by talents/abilities,
120–121
armies
organization of, 162–163
in Warring States, 144–145
art of manipulation (*shu*), 111, 112,
120–123
*Art of war* (Sunzi), 10, 89, 143, 144, 256
contents of, 146–151
French translation, 162
frequency of keywords, 152
leadership perspective, *see* strategic
leadership
versions of, 145–146
assembling ability, 62–64, 71
authentic paternalistic leaders, 185,
187, 189, 190, 191
authoritarianism, 11, 173, 176
construct domain, 193, 194, 195–196
effects on subordinate, 176–177,
178–179
subordinate responses, 182, 183,
189, 192
autocratic leadership, 19

balance, 40; *see also* harmony
benevolence, 3–4, 33–36, 52–53, 59
in Maoism, 216
in strategic leadership, 154–155, 163
benevolent government, *Dao* of,
36–37
benevolent leadership, 4, 11–12,
17–18, 173–174, 176
building community, 44–45
character-shaping followers, 43–44
construct domain, 194, 195, 196
*Dao* of benevolent government,
36–37
effects on subordinate, 177–178,
179, 183
foundation of, 34
goals and tasks of, 41–43
historical background, 47–48, 52
models of, 38
rule of virtue, 45–47
self-cultivation, 5, 11–12, 38–41
significance in modern world, 48–49
*Bible of virtue, The* (Laozi), *see Dao
de jing* (Laozi)
*Biography of Jack Welch, The*, 269
*Biography of Napoleon*, 256
*Book of changes, The*, 89, 256
*Book of history*, 45, 256
*Book of Lord Shang* (Shang), 111
*Book of rites, The*, 256
*Book of songs, The*, 256
Buddhism, 275
building community, 44–45
*Built to last: successful habits of
visionary companies* (Collins
and Porras), 256–257, 264
bureaucracy, Weber's theory of, 76
Burton's case, 99–100
business organizations, challenges
to, 22

cadres, 223–224
*Cai gen tan*, 256
calmness (*jin*), 111
Cao Can, 98
capability, 115
capitalism, 14–15
    and socialism, 226, 227
capitalist management, 226, 227;
    *see also* scientific management
CEOs
    Confucian view on, 49
    Daoist influence on, 99, 103
    management philosophy of,
    *see* management philosophy
Chang Si-de (Zhang Side), 214
character-shaping followers, 43–44
Chen Duxiu, 207
Chen Yun, 225
Cheng, Borshiuan, 171, 172–173
Chiang Chingkuo, 132, 135, 136
Chiang Kaishek, 207, 210
Chin state, *see* Qin state
China Telecom, 249, 250, 269
Chinainfobank, 239
Chinese civilization, 273
Chinese consciousness, 136
Chinese culture
    characterizations of, 6
    lack of understanding by Western
    scholars, 1, 3
    stereotypes, 274
Chinese leadership, lack of
    understanding by Western
    scholars, 1, 3
Chinese spirit of capitalism, 15
Civil War (1945–1949), 208, 210
*Classics of opposition, The*, 256
*Classics of Taoism, The* (Laozi),
    *see Dao de jing* (Laozi)
Clausewitz, C. von, 161
collectivism, 7–9, 165, 208
command, unity of, 162
communism, 215
Communist Party, 129, 207, 210
    leadership theories, 23; *see also*
    Deng Xiaoping, theory
    of; Maoism
community-building, 18
compliance, 177, 178, 183
comprehensiveness, 156

conduct propriety, *see* ritual/conduct
    propriety
*Confucian analects*, 32, 33, 256
Confucianism, 182, 272, 275, 278
    and capitalism, 15
    culture-building, 18, 21, 46, 71, 76–77
    education, 32
    ethics for ordinary people, 123–126
    historical background, 47–48, 52
    human nature, 3–5, 33–36, 52–53,
    55–58, 62
    human society, 62–64
    impact on Sunzi, 145
    influence on Maoism, 216
    influence on paternalistic leadership,
    173–174
    laws and regulations, 67–68
    leadership theories, *see* benevolent
    leadership; sage-kingship
    and Legalism, 108–109, 126–128,
    129–130, 272, 275; *see also*
    Taiwan
    and Marxism, 217
    moral character, 18–19, 65–66, 67
    origin of, 1
    self-conception, 7
    social hierarchy/distinction, 9, 44,
    64–67, 276, 278, 279
    and socialism, 13–14
    values and virtues, 35–36, 39–41,
    59–62; *see also* ritual/conduct
    propriety
    in Warring States, 144
    *see also* Confucius; Mencius; Xunzi
Confucius, 3, 31–32, 33
    and Laozi, 85
consideration (*lü*), 58–59
contingency approach, 24
contradiction, 230, 250–251
    law of, 211–214
control mechanisms, 20
"cooking a small fish," 94–97
courage, 159, 160
*Course on dialectical materialism, A*
    (Shirokov), 215
cross-national conflict, 293
Cultural Revolution, 14, 109, 208,
    210, 211, 213
    Confucianism and Legalism, 129,
    272, 275

Cultural Revolution (cont.)
   Deng's review of, 221
   influence on management
      philosophy, 254
   Mao's charisma in, 220
   motivation of, 215, 230
culture-building, 18, 21, 46, 71, 76–77

Dao, 5, 8, 10
   defined, 86
Dao de jing (Laozi), 85, 256
   versions of, 84
Dao jia, see Daoism
Dao jiao (religion), 85
Dao of benevolent government, 36–37
Dao of war, 10
Daoism, 5–6, 24, 100, 156, 275, 279
   application of, 98–100
   change between opposites, 89
   creation of world, 87–88, 156
   on hierarchy, 9–10
   humans and nature, 86–87
   impact on Sunzi, 145
   implication of, 102–104
   influence on Maoism, 216–217
   influence on Western theories,
      101–102
   leadership personality, 90–93, 94,
      279
   leadership strategies, 13, 94–98
   origin of, 1
   self-conception, 8–9
   two meanings of, 86
   way of living, 89–90
   see also Laozi; yin and yang;
      Zhuangzi
Dazhai, Shanxi, 230
de, defined, 86
deception tactics, 167; see also
   intelligence
decision-making, 294
deep-level behavior, 274
democratic centralism, 217, 218
Democratic Progressive Party, 136
Deng Xiaoping, biography of, 220–221
Deng Xiaoping, theory of, 233–234,
   275, 278
   and Confucianism, 13–14
   historical background, 11
   implications of, 233–234

leadership style, 23, 226–229
   and Maoism, 221–222, 225,
      226–227, 229–233
   pragmatism, 224–226
   reformism, 221–224
deploying troops, 148–149, 150
Dialectical and historical materialism
   (Mitin), 215
dialectical materialism, 211,
   215–216, 217
dialecticism, 19–20, 100
   in strategic leadership, 156–157
dictatorial paternalistic leaders,
   186, 187
disciplinarian paternalistic leaders,
   185, 187, 191
disposition, 147–148, 150
dispositionalists, 165
distributed responsibility system, 231
diversity of thoughts, 21–22, 24
Doctrine of the mean, The, 40, 256
documentation/proposal writing, 294
Dong Zhongshu (Tung Jongshu), 74, 108
dualism, 156–157
dyadic leadership, 11–13, 44, 45

Earley, P. C., 181–182
economic development, in Asian states,
   129–130, 131–133
economic rationality, 14–15
economic recovery, 223
education, 4, 41, 42, 259; see also MBA
   education; moral education
egalitarianism, 208
eclecticism, 22–23
Eleventh CCP Central Committee
   Sixth Plenum, 221
   Third Plenum, 221, 223
emotions, 160
emptiness (xu), 111
En Wei Corporation, 99
enforceability, of laws, 118–119
equality, in socialism, 13–14
ethnocentric leadership, 287–288
Eupsychian management (Maslow),
   101–102
evaluation, 122
evilness of human nature, 4–5, 53,
   55–58
excellence, pursuit of, 245–246

experimentalism, 227
external contradiction, 211

facts, defined by Mao, 208
families, 253–254, 280, 286
family-based relationalism, 7, 44–45,
   125, 129; *see also* father–son
   relationship
family businesses, 133–135, 275–276
Farh, J. L., 171, 173, 181–182
*Farther reaches of human nature,*
   *The* (Maslow), 101
father–son relationship, 173, 174
Fayol, H., 12, 162, 263
fear, of leaders, 177, 183
feasibility, of laws, 118
filial piety, 35
fire attacks, 149, 151
firmness, 159
Five-Anti campaign, 213, 234
Five Classics, 256
flaws, in leadership personalities,
   159–160
flexibility, 92, 249
Fortune 500 companies, 256
Four Books, 256

Gehani, R., 234
gender equality, 14
General Electric, 259
gentleness, 92
Godfather paternalistic leaders, 185, 187
Golden Mean, 249–251
gradualism, 227–229, 250
gratitude, 177
Great Leap Forward, 129, 207–208,
   210, 211, 230
*Great learning, The*, 43, 256
Great Proletarian Cultural Revolution,
   *see* Cultural Revolution
Guan Zhong, 111
*guanxi* network, 125, 129, 133,
   134, 135, 137
   intercultural implications, 280–282,
      284–286
*Guan Zi*, 111
Guo Mo-ruo, 52

Haier Group, 258
Han dynasty, 98, 108

Han state, 109, 110
Hanfei, 5, 51, 53
   art of manipulation, 111, 112,
      120–123
   biography of, 109–110
   human self-interest, 112–113
   influenced by other Legalists,
      111–112
   laws/regulations, 116–120
   power (*shi*), 5, 112, 113–115
hare-style leadership, 234
harmony, 23, 40, 247–249, 261, 286;
   *see also* balance
hedonistic motives, *see* self-interest
Hegel, G., 73
heroic spirit, 41
holism, 19, 22, 23–24, 165–166
   in strategic leadership, 156
honesty/sincerity, 243–245, 261, 264
Hong Kong, 171, 221, 226, 227,
   255, 275
Hu Jintao, theory of, 23
Hu Xueyan, 257, 258
Huawei Technologies, 258
Hui, Prince, 32
human badness, 4–5, 53, 55–58
human goodness, *see* benevolence
human nature, Daoist conception
   of, 5–6; *see also* benevolence;
   human badness
human society, 62–64
humanism/humaneness, *see*
   benevolence
humanistic/hierarchical need theory,
   101–102
humans and nature, 86–87

ideological paternalistic leaders, 186,
   187, 189, 191
*In search of excellence: lessons from*
   *America's best run companies*
   (Waterman *et al.*), 256, 269
incrementalism, 227–229, 250
independent thinking, 39
India, 200
individual level of leadership, 11–13
individual self, 20–21
individual solitude, 8
individualism, 6–9
Indonesia, 171

indulgent paternalistic leaders, 186, 187
information, *see* intelligence
institutional leadership, 11–13
intelligence, 149, 151, 161, 166–167; *see also* deception tactics
intercultural sense-making
  ethnocentric leadership, 287–288
  *guanxi* network, 284–286
  leadership structure/rules, 288–291, 292
  third-culture management issues, 293
  *yin* and *yang* implications, 292–293
internal contradiction, 211
investigation, 208, 209, 210
Investment Encouragement Law, 132

Japan, 132, 200, 207
*Jean-Christophe* (Rolland), 256
Jia Yi, 74
Jie, king of Xia, 113, 114, 115
Jixia, town, 51, 52
Johnson, C., 83

Kang Xi, Emperor, 257, 258
knowledge, 40, 209, 216, 217
Korea, 200
Kuomintang (Nationalist Party), 207

*laissez-faire* paternalistic leaders, 186, 187
Land-to-the-Tiller Program, 131
Lanling County, 52
Laozi, 32
  biography of, 84–85
laws/regulations, 4, 20, 162, 174, 274–275, 276–279
  Confucian view on, 46, 67–68
  Deng's view on, 228
  interpretation of, 133, 137, 285–286
  Legalist belief in, 5, 111, 112, 116–120
leader–member exchange (LMX), 200, 285, 288–290
  rules for, 289, 291
leadership agency, 20–21
leadership personality, flaws in, 159–160
learned virtues, 5

learning, 39–40
Lee Tenghui (Li Denghui), 136
Legalism (*Fa jia*), 4, 275, 279
  and Confucianism, 108–109, 126–128, 129–130, 272, 275; *see also* Taiwan
  on hierarchy, 10, 276, 278
  historical background, 110–111
  impact on Sunzi, 145
  influence on paternalistic leadership, 173
  on leadership, 12–13
  literature review, 111–112
  self-conception, 7–8
  *see also* Hanfei; Xunzi
*Letter to Garcia, A* (Hubbard), 256, 264
leveraging, 164
Li Da, 215, 235
Li Dazhao, 207
Li Denghui (Lee Tenghui), 136
Li Hongzhang, 258
Li Kashing, 258
Li Shimin, Emperor, 98–99
Li Si (Li Ssu), 51, 109–110
Liang Qichao, 72
Liezi, 84
life experience, 253–255
Lin Biao, 207
Lin, Shuchi, 181–182
Lincoln, A., 218
Liu Bocheng, 225, 235
Liu Chuanzhi, 258
Liu Shaoqi, 207, 225
Lo Yang, 32, 110
Lu Jia, 74
Lu Jinchuan, 92

Macao, 226, 227
Malaysia, 171
management philosophy
  books and literature's influence on, 256–257
  defined, 240–241
  education and training influence on, 259
  future research directions, 267–268
  Golden Mean, 249–251, 261
  harmony, 247–249, 261
  learning, 266
  life experience influence on, 253–255

practical implications, 268–269
pursuit of excellence, 245–246, 261
research background, 239–240
research limitations, 267
research method, 241–243
role models' influence on, 257–259
scientific management, 252–253
sincerity, 243–245, 261, 264
social responsibility, 246–247, 261
specialization, 251–252
traditional culture's influence on,
    262–263, 264, 265, 266
Western theories' influence on,
    263–264, 265, 266
maneuvering, 148, 150
manipulation, 5
Mao Zedong, 129
    biography of, 206–208
    charisma and personality, 218–220
Maoism, 11, 23, 206, 230, 233–234
    analytical dialectics of contradiction,
        211–214, 230
    and Confucianism, 13–14, 278
    and Deng Xiaoping's theory/practice,
        221–222, 225, 226–227,
        229–233
    implications of, 233–234
    leadership style, 217–218
    origin of, 215–217
    "Seek truth from facts," 208–211
    "Serve the people," 214–215
market economy, 226
market-oriented enterprises, 133, 137
market-oriented socialism, 14
martial law, Taiwan, 131, 136
Marx, K., 138
Marxism, 14, 129, 164
    and Confucianism, 217
    Mao's adoption of, 208, 210, 214,
        215, 216, 218
Maslow, A., 101–102
mass line, 217, 218
masters (*zi*), 1
Matsushita, K., 259
Matsushita Electric Corporation, 259
May Fourth Movement, 207
MBA education, 268–269
    managers with, 287–288
McGregor, D., 101
member–member exchange (MMX), 285

Mencius, 3, 32–33
    and Xunzi, 73–74
*Mencius* (Mencius), 32–33, 256
military strategy, *see* strategic
    leadership
modern Chinese leadership, influenced
    by Western philosophies, 15–16
modernization, 182
modesty/humbleness, 91–92
Mohists, 53
momentum, 148, 150, 163
moral character, 18–19, 65–66, 67,
    174, 176, 191
    effects on subordinate, 178, 179, 183
    revision of construct domain, 195,
        196–197
moral education, 46
morality/righteousness, 4, 9, 35, 60, 163
    in strategic leadership, 154, 155
*Motivation and personality* (Maslow),
    101
Movement of Ideological Liberation,
    222
Mu Qizhong, 259
Muslims, 219–220
Mutual Security Act (1951), 132
mutuality, 173–174

*Nan Hua Jing (Zhuangzi)*, 84
Nationalist Party (Kuomintang), 207
Nationalist government, 131–133, 136
nature, *see* universe
nature and humans, 86–87
neo-Confucianists, 48
neo-traditionalism, 11
network, *see guanxi* network
networkcentric leadership, *see* sharing
    network leadership (SNL)
New Philosophy, 215, 216
Nineteen-Point Reform Program, 132
non-action (*wu wei*), 10, 13, 21, 24
noninterference, 94–96, 97, 162–163
nurturant–task-oriented leadership, 200

objectivity, of laws, 117–118
"one country, two systems," 226, 227
one mind (*yi*), 111
opening to outside world, 223
optimism, 41
organizational citizenship, 295

organizations
    Confucian view of, 49
    family businesses, 133–135
    Xunzi's principles on, 69–70, 76–77
    orthodox socialism, 14
    Ouchi, W., 101

parents, 253–254
particularity, of contradiction,
    211–212
paternalistic leadership, 11, 17, 18,
    134, 135
    distribution in organizations,
        187–189
    effects on subordinate, 176–179
    eight types of, 185–186
    employee preferences for, 186–187,
        192
    limitations on research, 180–181,
        192–193
    models of, 174–175, 197–200,
        280, 281
    moral character, 191
    origin of, 13, 171–174
    and other theories, 200–201
    research instruments on, 175–176
    revision of construct domain,
        193–197
    satisfaction with, 189–191
    situational moderators of, 181–184
    and transformational/transactional
        leadership, 180
    see also authentic paternalist leaders,
        Godfather paternalist leaders,
        ideological paternalist leaders,
        indulgent paternalist leaders,
        laissez-faire paternalist leaders,
        selfless benefactor paternalist
        leaders
Paternalistic Leadership Scale, 176
perception, 209
performance appraisal, 294
perseverance, 41, 92
Philippines, 171
philosophical diversity, 21–22, 24
philosophy, major schools of, 2
political structure, reform of, 223, 224
popular opinion, 218
population, 41, 42
position power, 113–114

power (shi), 5, 112, 113–115
practicability, of laws, 120
practice, 209
pragmatism, 224–226
presentations, 294
principal contradiction, 212
pro-democracy movement (1989), 229
project management, 121–122
proletarian dictatorship, 14
promotion, 122–123, 223–224
propriety, 4, 5, 12, 19, 31, 35–36, 39,
    46, 48, 51, 55, 56, 59–62, 64–70,
    71, 73, 75, 76–78, 123–124, 145
    norms of, 46, 71
    rules of, 35, 37, 39, 48
Protestant ethic and the spirit of
    capitalism, The (Weber), 256, 264
Protestant religion, 15
publicity, of laws, 117
punishment, 4, 114, 115, 122, 162
pursuit of excellence, 245–246

Qin dynasty, 48
Qin state, 111, 144
    king of, 109–110
Qing dynasty, 258
Qu Qiubai, 215, 235
qualitative change, 212, 213
quantitative change, 212

realism, 231–232
reason, 209
reciprocity, 174, 177, 178
Records of the Historian (Sima),
    see Shih ji
Red star over China (Snow), 219–220
Redding, S. G., 15, 172
reductionism, 184
reformism, 221–224
relation-oriented enterprises, 133
relationalism, 6–9
relationship, see guanxi network
Ren Zhengfei, 258
repayment, 174, 177, 178
resource dependence, 182–183
revolutionaries, 16
Revolutionary Committees, 14
Revolutionary War (1921–1937), 208,
    210, 213
reward, 114, 115, 122, 162

righteousness, *see* morality/
  righteousness
ritual/conduct propriety, 4, 35, 46,
  60, 61, 64
  administrative and organizational
    principles, 68–70, 77
  laws and regulations, 46, 67–68
  symbolic and cultural rituals, 67
Roman law, 264
*Romance of the three kingdoms,*
  *The* (Luo), 256
rule of law, 5
rule of virtue, 45–47
rules/regulations, *see* laws/regulations

sage-kingship, 54–55, 59, 70–72
  assembling ability, 63–64, 71
  and transformational leadership,
    75–76
sages, in Daoism, 6, 94, 98; *see also*
  "superior-minded" (*jun zi*);
  sage-kingship
Sano, K., 274
scholars, ethics for, 126, 127–128, 129
Scholars' Palace, 51, 52
scientific management, 252–253
"Seek truth from facts," 208–211, 222,
  227, 230
*Selected works of Deng Xiaoping,* 221
*Selected works of Mao Zedong,* 208
self-criticism, 41
self-cultivation, 5, 11–12, 38–41, 56,
  61–62, 126
  foundation of, 58–59
  Xunzi's model of, 70–71
self-examination, 41
self-interest, 4, 5
  Daoist conception of, 6
  Legalist conception of, 8, 112–113,
    138
self-transformation, 18–19
selfless benefactor paternalistic leaders,
  186, 187, 189, 190, 191
"Serve the people," 214–215, 222
shamanism, 1, 87
Shang dynasty, 37, 48, 98
Shang Yang (Shang Ian), 74, 111
sharing network leadership (SNL),
  288–290
  rules for, 291–292

Shen Buhai, 74, 111, 112
Shen Dao, 111, 112
*Shih ji* (Records of the Historian)
  (Sima), 109
Shun, king of Xia, 45
Silin, R. H., 172
Sima Qian, 32, 45, 84–85, 214
simplicity, 89, 90
sincerity/honesty, 243–245, 261, 264
Singapore, 171
singlemindedness, 160
Sino-American transculturalist, 273
Sinologists, 48
situationalism, 158–159, 160–161
  leveraging and adaptation, 164
  moral advantage, 163
  organizational advantage, 162–163
  positional advantage, 161
  theoretical/practical implications,
    165–167
Snow, E., 219
social development, 212–213
social equality, 11
social hierarchy/distinction, 9–11, 44,
  64–67, 182, 276–279
social responsibility, 246–247, 261
social structure, *see* social hierarchy/
  distinction
socialism, 13–14
  and capitalism, 226, 227
  *see also* Maoism
solitude, 8
sovereign, 162–163
Soviet Union, 207, 231
special economic zones, 227
specialization, 251–252
*Spring and Autumn annals, The*
  (Confucius), 108, 138, 256
Spring and Autumn Period (722–480
  BCE), 33, 47
  debate on social order, 52–55
stability, 250
Stalin, J., 231
standardization, 252–253
state-owned enterprises (SOEs),
  282–284
strategic leadership, 10, 12, 21,
  89, 281
  defined, 152–153
  historical background, 143–145

strategic leadership (cont.)
    holistic/dialectic foundations of,
        156–157
    humanist foundation of, 153–155
    individual attributes, 159–160
    influenced by other schools of
        thought, 145
    strategic situationalism, *see*
        situationalism
    theoretical/practical implications,
        164–167
    strengths/weaknesses, 157
    strategic use of, 148, 150
    subordinate responses, 174–175,
        176–179
    resource dependence, 182–183
    traditionality, 181–182
Sunzi
    biography of, 143–144
    leadership philosophy, *see* strategic
        leadership
    "superior-minded" (*jun zi*), 36
    characteristics, 39–41
    *see also* sage-kingship; sages
surface-level behavior, 274

Taiwan, 275, 278
    economic development (1945–1986),
        131–133
    empirical studies on paternalistic
        leadership, 171, 172, 173, 176,
        179, 186–187
    family businesses, 133–135
    political capitalism, 135–138
Taiwanese consciousness, 136
Tan Sitong, 74
Tang dynasty, 98
*Tao te ching* (Laozi), *see Dao de jing*
    (Laozi)
Taoism, *see* Daoism
Taylor, F. W., 263
teamwork, 294
Ten Big Construction Projects, 132, 135
terrains, 149, 150, 161
Thailand, 171
Theory X,Y,Z, 101, 272
third-culture management, issues,
    294–295
Thoughts of Mao Zedong,
    *see* Maoism

Three-Anti campaign, 213, 234
tortoise-style leadership, 234
traditionality, 181–182
transactional leadership, 180
transformational leadership, 18
    and paternalistic leadership, 180
    and sage-kingship, 75–76
transparency/honesty, 92
trustworthiness, 35, 159, 264
truth, 208
Tung Jongshu (Dong Zhongshu), 74, 108
Turkey, 200

United States, 131, 132, 135, 273;
    *see also* intercultural sense-making
universality, of laws, 119
universe, 5, 8, 87, 88, 156
urban development, 225

virtues, 5, 35–36, 39–41, 59–62

Wakabayashi, M., 274
war
    *Dao* of, 10
    mission and objectives of, 146–147
    Warring States Period (480–221 BCE),
        33, 47, 108, 109, 144–145
    debate of social order, 52–55
    water-like or "wateristic" personality,
        vii, 8, 10, 83, 90–93, 94, 98,
        102–105, 164, 279, 294
Way, *see Dao*
*Way of the sovereign, The* (Hanfei), 116
Weber, M., 14–15, 138, 263
Weber's bureaucracy, 76
*wei wu wei* (active non-action)
    noninterference/following nature,
        94–97
    symbolic leadership, 97–98
Welch, J., 259, 269
welfare, 41, 42, 43
Wen Jing, Emperor, 98
*Wen shi jing* (Liezi), 84
Western modern philosophies,
    influence on modern Chinese
    leadership, 15–16
Westwood, R. I., 172
wisdom, 35, 60, 159, 160, 166
*Works of Mencius, The, see Mencius*
Wu state, 144

Xia dynasty, 37
Xue Yongxin, 99
Xunzi, 14, 46
  biography of, 51–52
  bridging Confucianism and
    Legalism, 53–54, 74
  debate on, 72
  on deception tactics, 167
  enriching Confucianism, 72–74
*Xunzi: a translation and study of
    the complete works* (Knoblock), 52

Yan'an New Philosophy Association,
    216
Yang Bin, 259
Yang Kuoshu, 181
Yao, king of Xia, 45, 113, 114
*yin* and *yang*, 10, 19–20, 87, 88, 89, 156
  implications for modern leadership,
    292–293, 294–295

Yin Xi, 85
younger generations, 182, 287–288
Youzi, 45

Zeng Guofan, 257–258
Zhang Ruimin, 258
Zhang Side (Chang Si-de), 214
Zhou, king of Shang, 115
Zhou dynasty, 33, 37, 110, 144
Zhou Enlai, 225
Zhou Gongdan, 98
Zhou Zhenyi, 259
Zhu De, 207
Zhuangzi, 84, 96
*Zhuangzi (Nan Hua Jing)*, 84
Zi Si, 32
*Zi zhi tong jian*, 256
Zigong, 41
Zuo Zongtang, 258